PERESTROIKA

MIKHAIL GORBACHEV

PERESTROIKA

New Thinking for Our Country and the World

A Cornelia & Michael Bessie Book

HARPER & ROW, PUBLISHERS, New York
Cambridge, Philadelphia, San Francisco, Washington
London, Mexico City, São Paulo, Singapore, Sydney

FIRST EDITION

Library of Congress Cataloging-in-Publication Data

Gorbachev, Mikhail Sergeyevich, 1931–
    Perestroika : new thinking for our country and the world.

    "A Cornelia & Michael Bessie book."
    1. Soviet Union—Foreign relations—1975–
2. Soviet Union—Politics and government—1982–
3. World politics—1985–1995. I. Title.
DK289.G675   1987   327'.09'048   87-46197
ISBN 0-06-039085-9

87 88 89 90 91 HC 10 9 8 7 6 5 4 3 2 1

CONTENTS

To the Reader   9

PART ONE   PERESTROIKA

Chapter 1 *Perestroika: Origins, Essence, Revolutionary*
          Character   17
          Perestroika—An Urgent Necessity   17
          Turning to Lenin, an Ideological Source of
            Perestroika   25
          A Carefully Prepared Program, rather than a
            Pompous Declaration   27
          More Socialism and More Democracy   36
          Lessons of History   38
          What Inspired Us to Launch Perestroika   45
          Perestroika is a Revolution   49
          A "Revolution from Above"? The Party and
            Perestroika   55

Chapter 2 *Perestroika Gets Under Way: The First*
          Conclusions   60
     I Society is Put in Motion   60
          How It All Began   60
          Perestroika Gains Momentum   64
          We Have No Ready-Made Formulas   65
          More Light to Glasnost!   75
          Perestroika and the Intelligentsia   80

    II New Economic and Social Policy in Action   83
          Economic Reform: The June 1987 Plenary Meeting
            of the CPSU Central Committee   84
          On to Full Cost Accounting!   88

A New Concept of Centralism   89
Goal: World Technological Standards   92
Living Tissue of Perestroika   95
The Social Policy of Restructuring   98

III   Along the Road of Democratization   102

Our Main Reserve   102
Observance of Law—An Indispensable Element
   in Democratization   105
Perestroika and the Soviets   110
The New Role of Trade Unions   113
Young People and Perestroika   114
Women and the Family   116
The Union of Socialist Nations—A Unique
   Formation   118
Prestige and Trust   122

IV   The West and Restructuring   124

PART TWO   NEW THINKING AND THE WORLD

Chapter 3   *How We See the World of Today*   135
Where We Are   135
New Political Thinking   139
Our Road to a New Outlook   144
The "Hand of Moscow"   150
International Implications of New Thinking   151
For Honest and Open Foreign Policy   157

Chapter 4   *Restructuring in the USSR and the Socialist
World*   161
On Real Socialism   161
Toward New Relations   164

Chapter 5   *The Third World in the International
Community*   171
Regional Conflicts   173
Nations Have the Right to Choose their Own Way
   of Development   177
The Asia–Pacific Knot   180
On Nuclear Disarmament in Asia   183

Soviet–Indian Relations   185
At A Difficult Watershed   186
Latin America: A Time of Major Change   187
Cooperation, not Confrontation   188

Chapter 6 *Europe in Soviet Foreign Policy*   190
Heritage of History   191
Europe is Our Common Home   194
Necessity: Imperatives for Pan-European Policy   195
Europe's Opportunities   197
Two German States   199
Europe and Disarmament   201
European Cooperation   204
First Signs of the New Thinking in Europe   206
On Europe and the United States   207
Europe's Responsibility   209

Chapter 7 *Problems of Disarmament and USSR–USA*
            Relations   210
What Do We Expect from the United States of
    America?   212
The US: "Shining City Atop A Hill"   214
The "Enemy Image"   216
Who Needs the Arms Race and Why?   218
More About Realities: Removing the Ideological
    Edge from Interstate Relations   221
Alienation is Evil   222
On the Road to Geneva   225
Geneva   226
After Geneva   227
Moratorium   228
The Nuclear Disarmament Program   229
The US Since Geneva   232
The Lesson of Chernobyl   235
Reykjavik   236
After Reykjavik   241
The Moscow Forum and Medium-Range Missiles   244

Conclusion   253

To the Reader

In writing this book it has been my desire to address directly the peoples of the USSR, the United States, indeed every country.

I have met government and other leaders of many states and representatives of their public, but the purpose of this book is to talk without intermediaries to the citizens of the whole world about things that, without exception, concern us all.

I have written this book because I believe in their common sense. I am convinced that they, like me, worry about the future of our planet. This is the most important matter.

We must meet and discuss. We must tackle problems in a spirit of cooperation rather than animosity. I well realize that not everyone will agree with me. As a matter of fact, neither will I agree with everything others say on various issues. This makes dialogue all the more important. And this book is my contribution to it.

Perestroika is no scientific treatise or propaganda pamphlet though the views, conclusions and analytical approaches which the reader will find in it are naturally based on definite values and theoretical premises. It is rather a collection of thoughts and reflections on perestroika, the problems we face, the scale of the changes involved and the complexity, responsibility and uniqueness of our time. I purposefully avoid cramming the book with facts, figures and details. It is a book about our plans and about the ways we are going to carry them through, and—I repeat—an invitation to dialogue. A large part of it is devoted to new political thinking, to the philosophy of our foreign policy. And if this book helps strengthen international trust, I shall consider its role fulfilled.

What is perestroika, or restructuring? Why do we need it? What are its substance and objectives? What does it reject and what does it create? How is it proceeding and what might be its consequences for the Soviet Union and the world community?

These are all legitimate questions to which many seek answers: politicians and businessmen, scholars and journalists, teachers and

9

physicians, clergymen, writers and students, workers and farmers. Many want to understand what is actually taking place in the Soviet Union, especially since newspapers and television in the West continue to be swept by waves of ill-will toward my country.

Perestroika is the focus of the intellectual life of our society now. That is natural, because it concerns the future of this country. The changes it is bringing affect all Soviet people and deal with the most vital issues. Everyone is anxious to know the kind of society we ourselves, and our children and grandchildren, will live in.

Other socialist countries are showing a natural and lively interest in the Soviet restructuring. They, too, are living through a difficult but highly important period of quest in their development, devising and trying out ways of accelerating economic and social growth. Success here is largely linked with our interaction, with our joint undertakings and concerns.

So the current interest in our country is understandable, especially considering the influence it has in world affairs.

Considering all these things, I assented to the request of the American publishers to write this book. We want to be understood. The Soviet Union is truly living through a dramatic period. The Communist Party made a critical analysis of the situation that had developed by the mid-1980s and formulated this policy of perestroika, or restructuring, a policy of accelerating the country's social and economic progress and renewing all spheres of life. Soviet people have both understood and accepted this policy. Perestroika has animated the whole of society. True, our country is huge. Many problems have accumulated and it won't be easy to solve them. But change has begun and society cannot now turn back.

There are different interpretations of perestroika in the West, including the United States. There is the view that it has been necessitated by the disastrous state of the Soviet economy and that it signifies disenchantment with socialism and a crisis for its ideals and ultimate goals. Nothing could be further from the truth than such interpretations, whatever the motives behind them.

Of course, perestroika has been largely stimulated by our dissatisfaction with the way things have been going in our country in recent years. But it has to a far greater extent been prompted by an awareness that the potential of socialism had been underutilized. We realize

10

this particularly clearly now in the days of the seventieth anniversary of our Revolution. We have a sound material foundation, a wealth of experience and a broad world outlook with which to perfect our society purposefully and continuously, seeking to gain ever greater returns—in terms of quantity and quality—from all our activities.

I would say from the start that perestroika has proved more difficult than we at first imagined. We have had to reassess many things. Yet, with every step forward we are more and more convinced that we have taken the right track and are doing things properly.

Some people say that the ambitious goals set forth by the policy of perestroika in our country have prompted the peace proposals we have lately made in the international arena. This is an oversimplification. It is well known that the Soviet Union has long been working towards peace and cooperation and has advanced many proposals which, had they been accepted, would have normalized the international situation.

True, we need normal international conditions for our internal progress. But we want a world free of war, without arms races, nuclear-weapons and violence; not only because this is an optimal condition for our internal development. It is an objective global requirement that stems from the realities of the present day.

But our new thinking goes further. The world is living in an atmosphere not only of nuclear threat, but also of unresolved major social problems, of new stresses created by scientific and technological advancement and by the exacerbation of global problems. Mankind today faces unprecedented problems and the future will hang in the balance, if joint solutions are not found. All countries are now more interdependent than ever before, and the stockpiling of weapons, especially nuclear missiles, makes the outbreak of a world war, even if unsanctioned or accidental, increasingly more probable, due simply to a technical failure or human fallibility. Yet all living things on Earth would suffer.

Everyone seems to agree that there would be neither winners nor losers in such a war. There would be no survivors. It is a mortal threat for all.

Although the prospect of death in a nuclear war is undoubtedly the most appalling scenario possible, the issue is broader than that. The spiraling arms race, coupled with the military and political realities of the world and the persistent traditions of pre-nuclear political thinking,

11

impedes cooperation between countries and peoples, which—East and West agree—is indispensable if the world's nations want to preserve nature intact, to ensure the rational use and reproduction of her resources and, consequently, to survive as befits human beings.

True, the world is no longer the same as it was, and its new problems cannot be tackled on the basis of thinking carried over from previous centuries. Can we still cling to the view that war is a continuation of politics by other means?

In short, we in the Soviet leadership have come to the conclusion —and are reiterating it—that there is a need for new political thinking. Furthermore, Soviet leaders are vigorously seeking to translate this new thinking into action, primarily in the field of disarmament. This is what prompted the foreign policy initiatives we have honestly offered the world.

As regards the scope of new historical thinking, it really embraces all the basic problems of our time.

For all the contradictions of the present-day world, for all the diversity of social and political systems in it, and for all the different choices made by the nations in different times, this world is nevertheless one whole. We are all passengers aboard one ship, the Earth, and we must not allow it to be wrecked. There will be no second Noah's Ark.

Politics should be based on realities. And the most formidable reality of the world today is the vast military arsenals, both conventional and nuclear of the United States and the Soviet Union. This places on our two countries a special responsibility to the whole world. Concious of this fact, we genuinely seek to improve Soviet–American relations and attain at least that minimum of mutual understanding needed to resolve issues crucial to the world's future.

We openly say that we reject the hegemony-seeking aspirations and global claims of the United States. We do not like certain aspects of American politics and way of life. But we respect the right of the people of the United States, as well as that of any other people, to live according to their own rules and laws, customs and tastes. We know and take into account the great role played by the United States in the modern world, value the Americans' contribution to world civilization, reckon with the legitimate interests of the United States, and realize that, without that country, it is impossible to remove the

12

threat of nuclear catastrophe and secure a lasting peace. We have no ill intent toward the American people. We are willing and ready to cooperate in all areas.

But we want to cooperate on the basis of equality, mutual understanding and reciprocity. Sometimes we are not only disappointed but have serious misgivings when in the United States our country is treated as an aggressor, an "empire of evil." All manner of tall stories and falsehoods are spread about us, distrust and hostility are shown toward our people, all kinds of limitations imposed and, simply, uncivilized attitudes are assumed toward us. This is impermissible shortsightedness.

Time slips past and must not be wasted. We have to act. The situation does not allow us to wait for the ideal moment: constructive and wide-ranging dialogue is needed today. That is what we intend when we arrange television links between Soviet and American cities, between Soviet and American politicians and public figures, between ordinary Americans and Soviet citizens. We have our media present the full spectrum of Western positions, including the most conservative of them. We encourage contacts with exponents of different outlooks and political convictions. In this way we express our understanding that this practice helps us to move toward a mutually acceptable world.

We are far from regarding our approach as the only correct one. We have no universal solutions, but we are prepared to cooperate sincerely and honestly with the United States and other countries in seeking answers to all problems, even the most difficult ones.

PART ONE

Perestroika

Perestroika: Origins, Essence, Revolutionary Character

What is perestroika? What prompted the idea of restructuring? What does it mean in the history of socialism? What does it augur for the peoples of the Soviet Union? How might it influence the outside world? All these questions concern the world public and are being actively discussed. Let me begin with the first one.

Perestroika—An Urgent Necessity

I think one thing should be borne in mind when studying the origins and essence of perestroika in the USSR. Perestroika is no whim on the part of some ambitious individuals or a group of leaders. If it were, no exhortations, plenary meetings or even a party congress could have rallied the people to the work which we are now doing and which involves more and more Soviet people each day.

Perestroika is an urgent necessity arising from the profound processes of development in our socialist society. This society is ripe for change. It has long been yearning for it. Any delay in beginning perestroika could have led to an exacerbated internal situation in the near future, which, to put it bluntly, would have been fraught with serious social, economic and political crises.

We have drawn these conclusions from a broad and frank analysis of the situation that has developed in our society by the middle of the eighties. This situation and the problems arising from it presently confront the country's leadership, in which new people have gradually appeared in the last few years. I would like to discuss here the main results of this analysis, in the course of which we had to reassess many things and look back at our history, both recent and not so recent.

Russia, where a great Revolution[1] took place seventy years ago, is an ancient country with a unique history filled with searchings, accomplishments and tragic events. It has given the world many discoveries and outstanding personalities.

However, the Soviet Union is a young state without analogues in history or in the modern world. Over the past seven decades—a short span in the history of human civilization—our country has traveled a path equal to centuries. One of the mightiest powers in the world rose up to replace the backward semi-colonial and semi-feudal Russian Empire. Huge productive forces, a powerful intellectual potential, a highly advanced culture, a unique community of over one hundred nations and nationalities, and firm social protection for 280 million people on a territory forming one-sixth of the Earth—such are our great and indisputable achievements and Soviet people are justly proud of them.

I am not saying this to make my land appear better than it was or is. I do not want to sound like an apologist for whom "mine" means best and unquestionably superior. What I have just said is actual reality, authentic fact, the visible product of the work of several generations of our people. And it is equally clear that my country's progress became possible only thanks to the Revolution. It is the product of the Revolution. It is the fruit of socialism, the new social system, and the result of the historical choice made by our people. Behind them are the fears of our fathers and grandfathers and millions of working people—workers, farmers and intellectuals—who seventy years ago assumed direct responsibility for the future of their country.

I would like the reader to contemplate all this: otherwise it would be hard to see what has happened and is happening in our society. I shall return to the historical aspects of our development later. Let me first explain the far-from-simple situation which had developed in the country by the eighties and which made perestroika necessary and inevitable.

At some stage—this became particularly clear in the latter half of the seventies—something happened that was at first sight inexplicable. The country began to lose momentum. Economic failures became

[1] The Revolution began on 25 October 1917 according to the Julian Calendar which was used in Russia until February 1918. It was thirteen days behind the generally-accepted Gregorian Calendar. That is why we now celebrate the anniversary of the Revolution on 7 November.

more frequent. Difficulties began to accumulate and deteriorate, and unresolved problems to multiply. Elements of what we call stagnation and other phenomena alien to socialism began to appear in the life of society. A kind of "braking mechanism" affecting social and economic development formed. And all this happened at a time when scientific and technological revolution opened up new prospects for economic and social progress.

Something strange was taking place: the huge fly-wheel of a powerful machine was revolving, while either transmission from it to work places was skidding or drive belts were too loose.

Analyzing the situation, we first discovered a slowing economic growth. In the last fifteen years the national income growth rates had declined by more than a half and by the beginning of the eighties had fallen to a level close to economic stagnation. A country that was once quickly closing on the world's advanced nations began to lose one position after another. Moreover, the gap in the efficiency of production, quality of products, scientific and technological development, the production of advanced technology and the use of advanced techniques began to widen, and not to our advantage.

The gross output drive, particularly in heavy industry, turned out to be a "top-priority" task, just an end in itself. The same happened in capital construction, where a sizable portion of the national wealth became idle capital. There were costly projects that never lived up to the highest scientific and technological standards. The worker or the enterprise that had expended the greatest amount of labor, material and money was considered the best. It is natural for the producer to "please" the consumer, if I may put it that way. With us, however, the consumer found himself totally at the mercy of the producer and had to make do with what the latter chose to give him. This was again a result of the gross output drive.

It became typical of many of our economic executives to think not of how to build up the national asset, but of how to put more material, labor and working time into an item to sell it at a higher price. Consequently, for all "gross output," there was a shortage of goods. We spent, in fact we are still spending, far more on raw materials, energy and other resources per unit of output than other developed nations. Our country's wealth in terms of natural and manpower resources has spoilt, one may even say corrupted, us. That, in fact, is

19

chiefly the reason why it was possible for our economy to develop extensively for decades.

Accustomed to giving priority to quantitative growth in production, we tried to check the falling rates of growth, but did so mainly by continually increasing expenditures: we built up the fuel and energy industries and increased the use of natural resources in production.

As time went on, material resources became harder to get and more expensive. On the other hand, the extensive methods of fixed capital expansion resulted in an artificial shortage of manpower. In an attempt to rectify the situation somehow, large, unjustified, i.e. in fact unearned, bonuses began to be paid and all kinds of undeserved incentives introduced under the pressure of this shortage, and that led, at a later stage, to the practice of padding reports merely for gain. Parasitical attitudes were on the rise, the prestige of conscientious and high-quality labor began to diminish and a "wage-leveling" mentality was becoming widespread. The imbalance between the measure of work and the measure of consumption, which had become something like the linchpin of the braking mechanism, not only obstructed the growth of labor productivity, but led to the distortion of the principle of social justice.

So the inertia of extensive economic development was leading to an economic deadlock and stagnation.

The economy was increasingly squeezed financially. The sale of large quantities of oil and other fuel and energy resources and raw materials on the world market did not help. It only aggravated the situation. Currency earnings thus made were predominantly used for tackling problems of the moment rather than on economic modernization or on catching up technologically.

Declining rates of growth and economic stagnation were bound to affect other aspects of the life of Soviet society. Negative trends seriously affected the social sphere. This led to the appearance of the so-called "residual principle" in accordance with which social and cultural programs received what remained in the budget after allocations to production. A "deaf ear" sometimes seemed to be turned to social problems. The social sphere began to lag behind other spheres in terms of technological development, personnel, know-how and, most importantly, quality of work.

Here we have more paradoxes. Our society has ensured full employment and provided fundamental social guarantees. At the same time, we failed to use to the full the potential of socialism to meet the growing requirements in housing, in quality and sometimes quantity of foodstuffs, in the proper organization of the work of transport, in health services, in education and in tackling other problems which, naturally, arose in the course of society's development.

An absurd situation was developing. The Soviet Union, the world's biggest producer of steel, raw materials, fuel and energy, has shortfalls in them due to wasteful or inefficient use. One of the biggest producers of grain for food, it nevertheless has to buy millions of tons of grain a year for fodder. We have the largest number of doctors and hospital beds per thousand of the population and, at the same time, there are glaring shortcomings in our health services. Our rockets can find Halley's comet and fly to Venus with amazing accuracy, but side by side with these scientific and technological triumphs is an obvious lack of efficiency in using scientific achievements for economic needs, and many Soviet household appliances are of poor quality.

This, unfortunately, is not all. A gradual erosion of the ideological and moral values of our people began.

It was obvious to everyone that the growth rates were sharply dropping and that the entire mechanism of quality control was not working properly; there was a lack of receptivity to the advances in science and technology; the improvement in living standards was slowing down and there were difficulties in the supply of foodstuffs, housing, consumer goods and services.

On the ideological plane as well, the braking mechanism brought about ever greater resistance to the attempts to constructively scrutinize the problems that were emerging and to the new ideas. Propaganda of success—real or imagined—was gaining the upper hand. Eulogizing and servility were encouraged; the needs and opinions of ordinary working people, of the public at large, were ignored. In the social sciences scholastic theorization was encouraged and developed, but creative thinking was driven out from the social sciences, and superfluous and voluntarist assessments and judgments were declared indisputable truths. Scientific, theoretical and other discussions, which are indispensable for the development of thought and for creative

21

endeavor, were emasculated. Similar negative tendencies also affected culture, the arts and journalism, as well as the teaching process and medicine, where mediocrity, formalism and loud eulogizing surfaced, too.

The presentation of a "problem-free" reality backfired: a breach had formed between word and deed, which bred public passivity and disbelief in the slogans being proclaimed. It was only natural that this situation resulted in a credibility gap: everything that was proclaimed from the rostrums and printed in newspapers and textbooks was put in question. Decay began in public morals; the great feeling of solidarity with each other that was forged during the heroic times of the Revolution, the first five-year plans, the Great Patriotic War and postwar rehabilitation was weakening; alcoholism, drug addiction and crime were growing; and the penetration of the stereotypes of mass culture alien to us, which bred vulgarity and low tastes and brought about ideological barrenness increased.

Party guidance was relaxed, and initiative lost in some of the vital social processes. Everybody started noticing the stagnation among the leadership and the violation of the natural process of change there. At a certain stage this made for a poorer performance by the Politburo[1] and the Secretariat[2] of the CPSU Central Committee, by the government and throughout the entire Central Committee and the Party apparatus, for that matter.

Political flirtation and mass distribution of awards, titles and bonuses often replaced genuine concern for the people, for their living and working conditions, for a favorable social atmosphere. An atmosphere emerged of "everything goes," and fewer and fewer demands were made on discipline and responsibility. Attempts were made to cover it all up with pompous campaigns and undertakings and celebrations of numerous anniversaries centrally and locally. The world of day-to-day realities and the world of feigned prosperity were diverging more and more.

[1] *Politburo of the CPSU Central Committee*—the collective leadership body of the CPSU Central Committee, which is elected at a plenary meeting of the Central Committee to guide the Party work between the plenary meetings of the CPSU Central Committee.

[2] *Secretariat of the CPSU Central Committee*—a body of the CPSU Central Committee which is elected at a plenary meeting of the Central Committee to supervize the Party's day-to-day work, mainly in selecting the cadres and organizing the verification of the fulfilment of the decisions adopted.

22

Many Party organizations in the regions were unable to uphold principles or to attack with determination bad tendencies, slack attitudes, the practice of covering up for one another and lax discipline. More often than not, the principles of equality among Party members were violated. Many Party members in leading posts stood beyond control and criticism, which led to failures in work and to serious malpractices.

At some administrative levels there emerged a disrespect for the law and encouragement of eyewash and bribery, servility and glorification. Working people were justly indignant at the behavior of people who, enjoying trust and responsibility, abused power, suppressed criticism, made fortunes and, in some cases, even became accomplices in—if not organizers of—criminal acts.

In fairness, it must be said that over those years many vitally important issues were also resolved, one way or another. But, first, those were just a few of the problems which had long demanded attention, and, second, even where decisions were taken, they were only partially enacted, or not at all. And, most significantly, none of those measures were comprehensive; they affected only some aspects of the life of society, while leaving the existing braking mechanism intact.

Naturally, Party organizations worked and the overwhelming majority of communists did their duty to the people sincerely and selflessly. And still it has to be recognized that there was no effective effort to bar dishonest, pushy, self-seeking people. In general, practical steps which were taken by Party and state bodies lagged behind the requirements of the times and of life itself. Problems snowballed faster than they were resolved. On the whole, society was becoming increasingly unmanageable. We only thought that we were in the saddle, while the actual situation that was arising was one that Lenin warned against: the automobile was not going where the one at the steering wheel thought it was going.

Not that that period should be painted solely in dark colors. The overwhelming majority of Soviet people worked honestly. Science, the economy and culture continued to develop. All the more inadmissible and painful, then, were the negative phenomena.

I think I have said enough for you to realize how serious the situation was and how urgent a thorough change was. The Party has found the strength and the courage to soberly appraise the situation and recognize that fundamental changes and transformations are indispensable.

An unbiased and honest approach led us to the only logical conclusion that the country was verging on crisis. This conclusion was announced at the April 1985 Plenary Meeting of the Central Committee, which inaugurated the new strategy of perestroika and formulated its basic principles.

I would like to emphasize here that this analysis began a long time before the April Plenary Meeting[1] and that therefore its conclusions were well thought out. It was not something out of the blue, but a balanced judgment. It would be a mistake to think that a month after the Central Committee Plenary Meeting in March 1985, which elected me General Secretary, there suddenly appeared a group of people who understood everything and knew everything, and that these people gave clear-cut answers to all questions. Such miracles do not exist.

The need for change was brewing not only in the material sphere of life but also in public consciousness. People who had practical experience, a sense of justice and commitment to the ideals of Bolshevism criticized the established practice of doing things and noted with anxiety the symptoms of moral degradation and erosion of revolutionary ideals and socialist values.

Workers, farmers and intellectuals, Party functionaries centrally and locally, came to ponder the situation in the country. There was a growing awareness that things could not go on like this much longer. Perplexity and indignation welled up that the great values born of the October Revolution and the heroic struggle for socialism were being trampled underfoot.

All honest people saw with bitterness that people were losing interest in social affairs, that labor no longer had its respectable status, that people, especially the young, were after profit at all cost. Our people have always had an intrinsic ability to discern the gap between word and deed. No wonder Russian folk tales are full of mockery aimed

---

[1] *The April 1985 Plenary Meeting of the CPSU Central Committee* put forward and substantiated the concept of accelerated socio–economic development for the USSR, this formed the basis of the new edition of the Party Program, later endorsed by the 27th Party Congress as the Party's general policy line.

against people who like pomp and trappings; and literature, which has always played a great role in our country's spiritual life, is merciless to every manifestation of injustice and abuse of power. In their best works writers, film-makers, theater producers and actors tried to boost people's belief in the ideological achievements of socialism and hope for a spiritual revival of society and, despite bureaucratic bans and even persecution, prepared people morally for perestroika.

By saying all this I want to make the reader understand that the energy for revolutionary change has been accumulating amid our people and in the Party for some time. And the ideas of perestroika have been prompted not just by pragmatic interests and considerations but also by our troubled conscience, by the indomitable commitment to ideals which we inherited from the Revolution and as a result of a theoretical quest which gave us a better knowledge of society and reinforced our determination to go ahead.

Turning to Lenin, an Ideological Source of Perestroika

The life-giving impetus of our great Revolution was too powerful for the Party and people to reconcile themselves to phenomena that were threatening to squander its gains. The works of Lenin and his ideals of socialism remained for us an inexhaustible source of dialectical creative thought, theoretical wealth and political sagacity. His very image is an undying example of lofty moral strength, all-round spiritual culture and selfless devotion to the cause of the people and to socialism. Lenin lives on in the minds and hearts of millions of people. Breaking down all the barriers erected by scholastics and dogmatists, an interest in Lenin's legacy and a thirst to know him more extensively in the original grew as negative phenomena in society accumulated.

Turning to Lenin has greatly stimulated the Party and society in their search to find explanations and answers to the questions that have arisen. Lenin's works in the last years of his life have drawn particular attention. I shall adduce my own experience to corroborate this point. In my report of 22 April 1983, at a gala session dedicated to the 113th anniversary of Lenin's birth, I referred to Lenin's tenets on the need for taking into account the requirements of objective economic laws, on planning and cost accounting[1], and intelligent use of commodity–money relations and material and moral incentives. The audience enthusiastically supported this reference to Lenin's ideas. I felt, once again, that my reflections coincided with the sentiments of my fellow Party members and the many people who were seriously concerned about our problems and sincerely wanted to rectify matters. Indeed, many of my fellow Party members felt an urgent need for the renewal of society, for changes. However, I should say that I also sensed that not everybody liked the report, but felt that it was not as optimistic as the time required.

Today we have a better understanding of Lenin's last works, which were in essence his political bequest, and we more clearly understand why these works appeared. Gravely ill, Lenin was deeply concerned for the future of socialism. He perceived the lurking dangers for the new system. We, too, must understand this concern. He saw that socialism was encountering enormous problems and that it had to contend with a great deal of what the bourgeois revolution had failed to accomplish. Hence the utilization of methods which did not seem to be intrinsic to socialism itself or, at least, diverged in some respects from generally accepted classical notions of socialist development.

The Leninist period is indeed very important. It is instructive in that it proved the strength of Marxist–Leninist dialectics, the conclusions of which are based on an analysis of the actual historical situation. Many of us realized even long before the April Plenary Meeting that everything pertaining to the economy, culture, democracy, foreign policy—all spheres—had to be reappraised. The important thing was to translate it into the practical language of everyday life.

---

[1] *Cost accounting*—a method of work of an enterprise within framework of the national economic plan. It envisages an enterprise using publicly owned means of production and meeting all expenses and payments to the state budget with profits made through sales of products, scientific ideas and technologies, services and so on. However, the state finances the expansion and modernization programs of enterprises. With full cost accounting, introduced in 1987, an enterprise finances all its expenses itself, its payments to the state budget being reduced accordingly.

A Carefully Prepared Program, rather than a Pompous Declaration

The concept of restructuring with all the problems involved had been evolving gradually. Way back before the April Plenary Meeting a group of Party and state leaders had begun a comprehensive analysis of the state of the economy. Their analysis then became the basis for the documents of perestroika. Using the recommendations of scientists and experts, our entire potential, all the best that social thought had created, we elaborated the basic ideas and drafted a policy which we subsequently began to implement.

Thus, an arsenal of constructive ideas had been accumulated. Therefore, at the April 1985 Plenary Meeting we managed to propose a more or less well-considered, systematized program and to outline a concrete strategy for the country's further development and a plan of action. It was clear that cosmetic repairs and patching would not do; a major overhaul was required. Nor was it possible to wait, for much time had been lost as it was.

The first question to arise was one of improving the economic situation, stopping and reversing the unfavorable trends in that sphere.

The most immediate priority, which we naturally first looked to, was to put the economy into some kind of order, to tighten up discipline, to raise the level of organization and responsibility, and to catch up in areas where we were behind. A great deal of hard work was done and, for that matter, is continuing. As expected, it has produced its first results. The rates of economic growth have stopped declining and are even showing some signs of improvement.

To be sure, we saw that these means alone would not impart a great dynamism to the economy. The principal priorities are known to lie elsewhere—in a profound structural reorganization of the economy, in reconstruction of its material base, in new technologies, in investment policy changes, and in high standards in management. All that adds up to one thing—acceleration of scientific and technological progress.

And certainly it is not by chance that after the April Plenary Meeting the first move the new leadership of the Soviet Union made was to

27

discuss these matters at an important conference of the CPSU Central Committee in June 1985. It was not the sort of discussion we had been accustomed to for many years. A lot of criticism was made— bitter but passionate. But the main things discussed were specific and effective ways and means of going over to intensive economics, to a new quality of economic growth.

During that year, substantial comprehensive programs were worked out in major areas of science and technology. They are aimed at achieving a major breakthrough and reaching the world level by the end of this century.

In effect, we have here a new investment and structural policy. The emphasis has been shifted from new construction to the technical retooling of enterprises, to saving the resources, and sharply raising the quality of output. We will still pay much attention to the development of the mining industries, but in providing the economy with raw materials, fuel and power, the emphasis will now be on the adoption of resource-saving technologies, on the rational utilization of resources.

A special program has been developed for modernizing the engineering industry, which has been neglected. The program is aimed at a complete renewal of engineering products and at achieving the world level as early as the beginning of the 1990s. And, sure enough, the program includes a radical transformation of the economic mechanism, which, as we now know well, is essential for a breakthrough in technological progress and for increasing economic efficiency.

This question is so important that I will have to go back to it more than once, in many pages of this book.

The economy has, of course, been and remains our main concern. But at the same time we have set about changing the moral and psychological situation in society. Back in the 1970s many people realized that we could not do without drastic changes in thinking and psychology, in the organization, style and methods of work everywhere —in the Party, the state machinery, and upper echelons. And this has happened, in the Party's Central Committee, in the government, as well as elsewhere. Certain personnel changes at all levels were needed. New people took over leadership positions, people who understood the situation well and had ideas as to what should be done and how.

An uncompromising struggle was launched against violations of the principles of socialist justice with no account being taken of who committed these violations. A policy of openness was proclaimed. Those who spoke in favor of Party, government and economic bodies and public organizations conducting their activities openly were allowed to have their say and unwarranted restrictions and bans were removed.

We have come to the conclusion that unless we activate the human factor, that is, unless we take into consideration the diverse interests of people, work collectives, public bodies, and various social groups, unless we rely on them, and draw them into active, constructive endeavor, it will be impossible for us to accomplish any of the tasks set, or to change the situation in the country.

I have long appreciated a remarkable formula advanced by Lenin: socialism is the living creativity of the masses. Socialism is not an *a priori* theoretical scheme, in keeping with which society is divided into two groups: those who give instructions and those who follow them. I am very much against such a simplified and mechanical understanding of socialism.

People, human beings with all their creative diversity, are the makers of history. So the initial task of restructuring—an indispensable condition, necessary if it is to be successful—is to "wake up" those people who have "fallen asleep" and make them truly active and concerned, to ensure that everyone feels as if he is the master of the country, of his enterprise, office, or institute. This is the main thing.

To get the individual involved in all processes is the most important aspect of what we are doing. Perestroika is to provide a "melting-pot" for society and, above all, the individual himself. It will be a renovated society. This is how serious the job is that we have begun to tackle, and it is a very difficult task. But the goal is worth the effort.

Everything we are doing can be interpreted and assessed differently. There is an old story. A traveler approached some people erecting a structure and asked one by one: "What is it you're doing?" One replied with irritation: "Oh, look, from morning till night we carry these damned stones . . ." Another rose from his knees, straightened his shoulders and said proudly: "You see, it's a temple we're building!"

So if you see this lofty goal—a shining temple on a green hill— then the heaviest of stones are light, the most exhausting work a pleasure.

To do something better, you must work an extra bit harder. I like

29

this phrase: working an *extra bit harder*. For me it is not just a slogan, but a habitual state of mind, a disposition. Any job one takes on must be grasped and felt with one's soul, mind and heart; only then will one work an extra bit harder.

A weak-spirited person won't work an extra bit harder. On the contrary, he gives in before difficulties, they overwhelm him. But if a person is strong in his convictions and knowledge, is morally strong, he can't be broken, he can weather any storms. We know this from our history.

Today our main job is to lift the individual spiritually, respecting his inner world and giving him moral strength. We are seeking to make the whole intellectual potential of society and all the potentialities of culture work to mold a socially active person, spiritually rich, just and conscientious. An individual must know and feel that his contribution is needed, that his dignity is not being infringed upon, that he is being treated with trust and respect.When an individual sees all this, he is capable of accomplishing much.

Of course, perestroika somehow affects everybody; it jolts many out of their customary state of calm and satisfaction at the existing way of life. Here I think it is appropriate to draw your attention to one specific feature of socialism. I have in mind the high degree of social protection in our society. On the one hand, it is, doubtless, a benefit and a major achievement of ours. On the other, it makes some people spongers.

There is virtually no unemployment. The state has assumed concern for ensuring employment. Even a person dismissed for laziness or a breach of labor discipline must be given another job. Also, wage-leveling has become a regular feature of our everyday life: even if a person is a bad worker, he gets enough to live fairly comfortably. The children of an outright parasite will not be left to the mercy of fate. We have enormous sums of money concentrated in the social funds from which people receive financial assistance. The same funds provide subsidies for the upkeep of kindergartens, orphanages, Young Pioneer houses[1] and other institutions related to children's creativity and sport. Health care is free, and so is education. People are protected from the vicissitudes of life, and we are proud of this.

[1] *Houses and Palaces of Young Pioneers*—extra-mural establishments instiling in pupils a love for and interest in creative work and knowledge and promoting the creative abilities, vocational orientation, and social activity of the younger generation.

But we also see that dishonest people try to exploit these advantages of socialism; they know only their rights, but they do not want to know their duties: they work poorly, shirk and drink hard. There are quite a few people who have adapted the existing laws and practices to their own selfish interests. They give little to society, but nevertheless managed to get from it all that is possible and what even seems impossible; they have lived on unearned incomes.

The policy of restructuring puts everything in its place. We are fully restoring the principle of socialism: "From each according to his ability, to each according to his work," and we seek to affirm social justice for all, equal rights for all, one law for all, one kind of discipline for all, and high responsibilities for each. Perestroika raises the level of social responsibility and expectation. The only people to resent the changes are those who believe that they already have what they need, so why should they readjust? But if a person has conscience, if he does not forget about the good of his people, he cannot—and must not—reason in such a way. And then glasnost, or openness, reveals that someone enjoys illegal privileges. We can no longer tolerate stagnation.

We pose the question in the following way: worker and manager, farm machine operator and club director, journalist and politician—everyone has something to review in his style and methods of work, and needs to criticially assess their own position. We have posed the task of overcoming inertia and conservatism sharply—so as to prick everybody's pride. This struck a nerve with many people—they are the majority, although a few people reacted negatively, especially those who were aware of their adherence to the old. We must also look at ourselves in terms of whether we live and act according to our conscience. In some things we may have gone astray, adopting standards alien to us; for example, we have begun contracting a philistine consumerist mentality. If we learn to work better, be more honest, and more decent, then we shall create a truly socialist way of life.

It is essential to look ahead. We must have enough political experience, theoretical scope and civic courage to achieve success, to make sure that perestroika meets the high moral standards of socialism.

We need wholesome, full-blooded functioning by all public organizations, all production teams and creative unions, new forms of activity by citizens and the revival of those which have been forgotten. In

31

short, *we need broad democratization of all aspects of society.* That democratization is also the main guarantee that the current processes are
irreversible.

We know today that we would have been able to avoid many of
these difficulties if the democratic process had developed normally in
our country.

We have learned this lesson of our history well and will never forget
it. We will now firmly stick to the line that only through the consistent
development of the democratic forms inherent in socialism and
through the expansion of self-government can we make progress in
production, science and technology, culture and art, and in all social
spheres. This is the only way we can ensure conscious discipline.
Perestroika itself can only come through democracy. Since we see our
task as unfolding and utilizing the potential of socialism through the
intensification of the human factor, there can be no other way but
democratization, including reform of the economic mechanism and
management, a reform whose main element is promotion of the role
of work collectives.

It is exactly because we place emphasis on the development of
socialist democracy that we pay so much attention to the intellectual
sphere, public consciousness and an active social policy. Thereby we
want to invigorate the human factor.

In the West, Lenin is often portrayed as an advocate of authoritarian
methods of administration. This is a sign of total ignorance of Lenin's
ideas and, not infrequently, of their deliberate distortion. In effect,
according to Lenin, socialism and democracy are indivisible. By
gaining democratic freedoms the working masses come to power. It
is also only in conditions of expanding democracy that they can
consolidate and realize that power. There is another remarkably true
idea of Lenin's: the broader the scope of the work and the deeper the
reform, the greater the need to increase the interest in it and convince
millions and millions of people of its necessity. This means that if we
have set out for a radical and all-round restructuring, we must also
unfold the entire potential of democracy.

It is essential to learn to adjust policy in keeping with the way it is
received by the masses, and to ensure feedback, absorbing the ideas,
opinions and advice coming from the people. The masses suggest a
lot of useful and interesting things which are not always clearly

perceived "from the top." That is why we must prevent at all costs an arrogant attitude to what people are saying. In the final account the most important thing for the success of perestroika is the people's attitude to it.

Thus, not only theory but the reality of the processes under way made us embark on the program for all-round democratic changes in public life which we presented at the January 1987 Plenary Meeting of the CPSU Central Committee.

The Plenary Meeting encouraged extensive efforts to strengthen the democratic basis of Soviet society, to develop self-government and extend glasnost, that is openness, in the entire management network. We see now how stimulating that impulse was for the nation. Democratic changes have been taking place at every work collective, at every state and public organization, and within the Party. More glasnost, genuine control from "below," and greater initiative and enterprise at work are now part and parcel of our life.

The democratic process has promoted the entire perestroika, elevated its goals and has made our society understand its problems better. This process allowed us to take a wider view of economic issues, and put forward a program for radical economic reforms. The economic mechanism now well fits the overall system of social management which is based on renewed democratic principles.

We did this work at the June 1987 Plenary Meeting of the CPSU Central Committee, which adopted "Fundamentals of Radical Restructuring of Economic Management." Perhaps this is the most important and most radical program for economic reform our country has had since Lenin introduced his New Economic Policy in 1921. The present economic reform envisages that the emphasis will be shifted from primarily administrative to primarily economic management methods at every level, and calls for extensive democratization of management, and the overall activization of the human factor.

The reform is based on dramatically increased independence of enterprises and associations, their transition to full self-accounting and self-financing, and granting all appropriate rights to work collectives. They will now be fully responsible for efficient management and end results. A collective's profits will be directly proportionate to its efficiency.

In this connection, a radical reorganization of centralized economic

33

management is envisaged in the interests of enterprises. We will free the central management of operational functions in the running of enterprises and this will enable it to concentrate on key processes determining the strategy of economic growth. To make this a reality we launched a serious radical reform in planning, price formation, the financial and crediting mechanism, the network of material and technological production supplies, and management of scientific and technological progress, labor and the social sphere. The aim of this reform is to ensure—within the next two or three years—the transition from an excessively centralized management system relying on orders, to a democratic one, based on the combination of democratic centralism and self-management.

The adoption of fundamental principles for a radical change in economic management was a big step forward in the program of perestroika. Now perestroika concerns virtually every main aspect of public life. Of course, our notions about the contents, methods and forms of perestroika will be developed, clarified and corrected later on. This is inevitable and natural. This is a living process. No doubt, changes will pose new major problems which will require unorthodox solutions. But the overall concept, and the overall plan of perestroika, not only from the point of view of substance, but also of its component parts, are clear to us.

Perestroika means overcoming the stagnation process, breaking down the braking mechanism, creating a dependable and effective mechanism for the acceleration of social and economic progress and giving it greater dynamism.

Perestroika means mass initiative. It is the comprehensive development of democracy, socialist self-government, encouragement of initiative and creative endeavor, improved order and discipline, more glasnost, criticism and self-criticism in all spheres of our society. It is utmost respect for the individual and consideration for personal dignity.

Perestroika is the all-round intensification of the Soviet economy, the revival and development of the principles of democratic centralism in running the national economy, the universal introduction of economic methods, the renunciation of management by injunction and by administrative methods, and the overall encouragement of innovation and socialist enterprise.

34

Perestroika means a resolute shift to scientific methods, an ability to provide a solid scientific basis for every new initiative. It means the combination of the achievements of the scientific and technological revolution with a planned economy.

Perestroika means priority development of the social sphere aimed at ever better satisfaction of the Soviet people's requirements for good living and working conditions, for good rest and recreation, education and health care. It means unceasing concern for cultural and spiritual wealth, for the culture of every individual and society as a whole.

Perestroika means the elimination from society of the distortions of socialist ethics, the consistent implementation of the principles of social justice. It means the unity of words and deeds, rights and duties. It is the elevation of honest, highly-qualified labor, the overcoming of leveling tendencies in pay and consumerism.

This is how we see perestroika today. This is how we see our tasks, and the substance and content of our work for the forthcoming period. It is difficult now to say how long that period will take. Of course, it will be much more than two or three years. We are ready for serious, strenuous and tedious work to ensure that our country reaches new heights by the end of the twentieth century.

We are often asked what we want of perestroika. What are our final goals? We can hardly give a detailed, exact answer. It's not our way to engage in prophesying and trying to predestinate all the architectural elements of the public building we will erect in the process of perestroika.

But in principle I can say that the end result of perestroika is clear to us. It is a thorough renewal of every aspect of Soviet life; it is giving socialism the most progressive forms of social organization; it is the fullest exposure of the humanist nature of our social system in its crucial aspects—economic, social, political and moral.

I stress once again: perestroika is not some kind of illumination or revelation. To restructure our life means to understand the objective necessity for renovation and acceleration. And that necessity emerged in the heart of our society. The essence of perestroika lies in the fact that *it unites socialism with democracy* and revives the Leninist concept of socialist construction both in theory and in practice. Such is the essence of perestroika, which accounts for its genuine revolutionary spirit and its all-embracing scope.

35

The goal is worth the effort. And we are sure that our effort will be a worthy contribution to humanity's social progress.

More Socialism and More Democracy

Perestroika is closely connected with socialism as a system. That side of the matter is being widely discussed, especially abroad, and our talk about perestroika won't be entirely clear if we don't touch upon that aspect.

Does perestroika mean that we are giving up socialism or at least some of its foundations? Some ask this question with hope, others with misgiving.

There are people in the West who would like to tell us that socialism is in a deep crisis and has brought our society to a dead end. That's how they interpret our critical analysis of the situation at the end of the seventies and beginning of the eighties. We have only one way out, they say: to adopt capitalist methods of economic management and social patterns, to drift toward capitalism.

They tell us that nothing will come of perestroika within the framework of our system. They say we should change this system and borrow from the experience of another socio–political system. To this they add that, if the Soviet Union takes this path and gives up its socialist choice, close links with the West will supposedly become possible. They go so far as to claim that the October 1917 Revolution was a mistake which almost completely cut off our country from world social progress.

To put an end to all the rumors and speculations that abound in the West about this, I would like to point out once again that we are conducting all our reforms in accordance with the socialist choice. We are looking within socialism, rather than outside it, for the answers to all the questions that arise. We assess our successes and errors alike by socialist standards. Those who hope that we shall move away from the socialist path will be greatly disappointed. Every part of our program of perestroika—and the program as a whole, for that matter—is fully based on the principle of more socialism and more democracy.

More socialism means a more dynamic pace and creative endeavor,

36

more organization, law and order, more scientific methods and initiative in economic management, efficiency in administration, and a better and materially richer life for the people.

More socialism means more democracy, openness and collectivism in everyday life, more culture and humanism in production, social and personal relations among people, more dignity and self-respect for the individual.

More socialism means more patriotism and aspiration to noble ideals, more active civic concern about the country's internal affairs and about their positive influence on international affairs.

In other words, more of all those things which are inherent in socialism and in the theoretical precepts which characterize it as a distinct socio–economic formation.

We will proceed toward better socialism rather than away from it. We are saying this honestly, without trying to fool our own people or the world. Any hopes that we will begin to build a different, non-socialist society and go over to the other camp are unrealistic and futile. Those in the West who expect us to give up socialism will be disappointed. It is high time they understood this, and, even more importantly, proceeded from that understanding in practical relations with the Soviet Union.

Speaking so, I would like to be clearly understood that though we, the Soviet people, are for socialism (I have explained above why), we are not imposing our views on anyone. Let everyone make his own choice; history will put everything in its place. Today, as I told a group of American public figures (Cyrus Vance, Henry Kissinger and others), we feel clearly as never before that, due to the socialist system and the planned economy, changes in our structural policy come much easier for us than they would in conditions of private enterprise, although we do have difficulties of our own, too.

We want more socialism and, therefore, more democracy.

As we understand it, the difficulties and problems of the seventies and eighties did not signify some kind of crisis for socialism as a social and political system, but rather were the result of insufficient consistency in applying the principles of socialism, of departures from them and even distortions of them, and of continued adherence to the methods and forms of social management that arose under specific historical conditions in the early stages of socialist development.

37

On the contrary, socialism as a young social system, as a way of living, possesses vast possibilities for self-development and self-perfection that have yet to be revealed, and for the solution of the fundamental problems of contemporary society's scientific, techno-logical, economic, cultural and intellectual progress, and of the development of the human individual. This is indicated by the path our country has taken since October 1917, a path that has been full of innumerable difficulties, drama and strenuous work, and at the same time full of great triumphs and accomplishments.

Lessons of History

It is true to say that post-revolutionary development underwent diffi-cult stages, largely due to the rude meddling of imperialist forces in our internal affairs; policy mistakes and miscalculations also occurred. Nevertheless, the Soviet Union progressed, and a society has been created in which people have confidence in their future. And if truth is the guide, any objective observer must admit that Soviet history is in general a history of indisputable progress, despite all the losses, setbacks and failures. We advanced in the absence of roads, literally and figuratively: we would sometimes go astray and make mistakes, and more than enough blood was shed and sweat lost along our path. But we stubbornly marched on and never thought of retreating, of giving up the ground we had gained, or of questioning our socialist choice.

And it's hard to imagine that, as we marched into an unknown future, completing ambitious tasks within a short period of time, we could have avoided setbacks, that we could have had it all as smooth as the sidewalk of Nevsky Prospekt.[1] Take, for example, industrializ-ation. In what conditions did we accomplish it? The Civil War and intervention by fourteen foreign powers[2] had left the country

[1] *Nevsky Prospekt* (Avenue) in Leningrad is the city's main thoroughfare. It follows an absolutely straight path and is used in the Russian language as a metaphor to characterize those who think that social development can follow the same kind of path.
[2] *The Civil War and foreign intervention* (1918–22)—the Soviet Republic's struggle against the counter-revolution and the invasion of parts of its territory by British, French, US, German, Japanese, Polish and other foreign troops (in all, fourteen countries participated in the invasion).

38

completely devastated. There was an economic blockade and a "cordon sanitaire." No accumulations, no colonies; on the contrary, it was essential to use the money available for improving the national hinterlands that had been oppressed under tsarism. In order to save the revolutionary gains, we had to build—and quickly—a national industrial base with our internal resources, holding down consumption and reducing it to a minimum. The material burden of that new construction fell on the people, of whom the peasants formed the bulk.

In effect, we had to build up industry, especially heavy industry and the power and machine-building industries, from scratch. And we set out boldly to accomplish this task. The viability of the Party's plans, which the masses understood and accepted, and of the slogans and projects permeated with the ideological energy of our revolution manifested itself in the enthusiasm with which millions of Soviet people joined in the efforts to build up national industry. And that enthusiasm astounded the world. Under incredibly trying conditions, often far away from their homes, usually without any machinery, and half-fed, they worked wonders, so to say, out of nothing, from scratch. They drew inspiration from the fact that theirs was a great and historic cause. Although not very literate, they realized what a grand and unique job they were doing. That was truly a great feat in the name of their motherland's future and a demonstration of the people's loyalty to the free choice which they had made in 1917.

Our fathers and grandfathers overcome everything that befell them and made a crucial contribution to the development and consolidation of our society at a time when its entire future had to be decided.

Industrialization in the twenties and thirties really was a very hard trial. But let's now, with hindsight, try to answer the question: Was it necessary? Could such a vast country as ours have lived in the twentieth century without being an industrially developed state? There was another reason that also very soon made it clear that we had no option but to speed up industrialization. As early as 1933 the threat of fascism began to grow swiftly. And where would the world now be if the Soviet Union had not blocked the road for Hitler's war machine? Our people routed fascism with the might created by them in the twenties and thirties. Had there been no industrialization, we would have been unarmed before fascism.

But we did not find ourselves under the caterpillars of fascism. The whole of Europe had been unable to stop Hitler, but we smashed him. We defeated fascism not only due to the heroism and self-sacrifice of our soldiers, but also due to our better steel, better tanks and better planes. And all this was forged by our Soviet period.

Or take collectivization. I know how much fiction, speculation and malicious criticism of us go with this term, let alone the process itself. But even many of the objective students of this period of our history do not seem to be able to grasp the importance, need and inevitability of collectivization in our country.

If we are to take a really truthful and scientific look at the circumstances of the time and the special features of the development of our society, Soviet society; if we do not close our eyes to the extreme backwardness of agricultural production, which had no hope of overcoming this backwardness if it remained small scale and fragmented; if, finally, we try to make a correct assessment of the actual results of collectivization, one simple conclusion is inescapable: collectivization was a great historic act, the most important social change since 1917. Yes, it proceeded painfully, not without serious excesses and blunders in methods and pace. But further progress for our country would have been impossible without it. Collectivization provided a social basis for updating the agricultural sector of the economy and made it possible to introduce modern farming methods. It ensured productivity growth and an ultimate increase in output which we could not have obtained had the countryside been left untouched in its previous, virtually medieval, state. Furthermore, collectivization released considerable resources and many workers needed in other areas of development in our society, above all in industry.

Collectivization changed, perhaps not easily and not immediately, the entire way of life of the peasantry, making it possible for them to become a modern, civilized class of society. If it had not been for collectivization, we could not today even think of producing grain in the amount of 200 million tons, not to mention 250 million tons, as are our plans for the near future. Yet, we have already surpassed the total grain output of the Common Market countries taken together, despite the fact that our population is smaller.

However, it is true that we still face shortages of many foodstuffs, especially livestock products. But without collectivization we would not now be producing as much per capita as we do, satisfying for the most part our vital requirements. And, of particular importance, the possibility of hunger and undernourishment has been eliminated forever in our country. And this had been the scourge of Russia for centuries. In terms of a calorie-rich diet, the Soviet Union definitely ranks among the developed nations. And the main point is that thanks to collectivization and its over-fifty-year-old history, we have gained the potential to raise, in the course of the restructuring, the entire farming sector to a qualitatively new level.

Yes, industrialization and the collectivization of agriculture was indispensable. Otherwise the country would not have been rehabilitated. But the methods and forms of accomplishing these reforms did not always accord with socialist principles, with socialist ideology and philosophy. External conditions played a primary role—the country felt a continuous military threat against it. But apart from this there were excesses, administrative pressure prevailed, and people suffered. That was how it all was in fact. Such was the fate of the nation, with all its contradictions, including great achievements, dramatic mistakes and tragic events.

Yes, we also had a rough time, now and again very rough indeed, after victory in the war. I recall my railway trips from southern Russia to Moscow to study in the late forties. I saw with my own eyes the ruined Stalingrad, Rostov, Kharkov, Orel, Kursk and Voronezh. And how many such ruined cities there were: Leningrad, Kiev, Minsk, Odessa, Sevastopol, Smolensk, Briansk, Novgorod . . . Everything lay in ruins: hundreds and thousands of cities, towns and villages, factories and mills. Our most valuable monuments of culture were plundered or destroyed—picture galleries and palaces, libraries and cathedrals.

In the West they said at that time that Russia would not be able to rise even in a hundred years, that it was out of international politics for a long time ahead because it would focus on healing its wounds somehow. And today they say, some with admiration and others with open hostility, that we are a superpower! We revived and lifted the country on our own, through our own efforts, putting to use the immense potentialities of the socialist system.

And we cannot but mention one more aspect of the matter which is frequently ignored or hushed up in the West, but without which it is simply impossible to understand us, the Soviet people; along with the

41

economic and social achievements, there was also a new life, there was the enthusiasm of the builders of a new world, an inspiration from things new and unusual, a keen feeling of pride that we alone, unassisted and not for the first time, were raising the country on our shoulders. People thirsted for knowledge and culture and mastered them. They rejoiced at life, reared their children, and did their day-to-day chores. All this we did in an entirely new atmosphere which differed greatly from what had been before the Revolution, in an atmosphere of ease, equality and immense opportunities for the working people. We know very well what we received from socialism. In short, people lived and worked creatively at all stages of the peaceful development of our country. Letters which I receive from my compatriots say proudly: sure, we were poorer than others, but our life was more full-blooded and interesting.

Fourteen out of fifteen citizens living in the USSR today were born after the Revolution. And we are still being urged to give up socialism. Why should the Soviet people, who have grown and gained in strength under socialism, abandon that system? We will spare no effort to develop and strengthen socialism. I think that a minimum of the new system's potential has been tapped so far.

This is why we find strange proposals—some even sincere—to alter our social system and turn to methods and forms typical of a different social set-up. People who make such suggestions do not realize that this is just impossible even if there were someone wishing to turn the Soviet Union to capitalism. Just think: how can we agree that 1917 was a mistake and all the seventy years of our life, work, effort and battles were also a complete mistake, that we were going in the "wrong direction"? No, a strict and impartial view of the facts of history suggests only one conclusion: it is the socialist option that has brought formerly backward Russia to the "right place"—the place the Soviet Union now occupies in human progress.

We have no reason to speak about the October Revolution and socialism in a low voice, as though ashamed of them. Our successes are immense and indisputable. But we see the past in its entirety and complexity. Our most tremendous achievements do not prevent us from seeing contradictions in the development of our society, our errors and omissions. And our ideology itself is critical and revolutionary by nature.

And when we seek the roots of today's difficulties and problems we do this in order to comprehend their origin and to draw lessons for present-day life from events that go deep into the 1930s.

The most important thing now for us in the past history is that through comprehension of it we come to perceive the origins of perestroika. Our history shaped up under a strong influence of attendant factors. But it is our history, and the sources of perestroika lie in it.

But why did everything that made perestroika necessary happen? Why has it been delayed? Why did the obsolete methods of work persist so long? How did the dogmatization of social consciousness and theory occur?

All this needs explanation. And, in analyzing and explaining, we find much proof that the Party and society saw the negative processes growing. Furthermore, awareness of a need for change acutely manifested itself more than once. But the changes did not go all the way and were inconsistent under the weight of the "legacy of the past" with all its dominant attributes.

A major landmark in our history was the 20th CPSU Congress[1]. It made a great contribution to the theory and practice of socialist construction. During and after, a great attempt was made to turn the helm in the country's advance, to impart an impulse to liberation from the negative aspects of socio–political life engendered by the Stalin personality cult.

The decisions taken by the Congress helped through major political, economic, social and ideological measures. But the possibilities that emerged were not used to the full. The explanation is the subjectivist methods adopted by the leadership under Khrushchev. Economic management was dominated by improvization. That leadership's wilful and changing ideas and actions kept society and the Party in a fever. Ambitious and unfounded promises and predictions again produced a gap between words and deeds.

That was why at the next stage, whose hallmark was the October

---

[1] *The 20th Congress of the CPSU* was held in Moscow on 14–25 February 1956. The Congress approved the Directives for the Sixth Five-Year Plan for the country's economic development for 1956–60, spelled out the principle of peaceful coexistence between states with different social systems as it applies to the current epoch, and condemned the personality cult of Stalin and its consequences.

1964 Plenary Meeting of the CPSU Central Committee[1], the first step was to overcome these extremes and to combat these extremes. A line towards stabilization was taken. And it was a well-justified line. It received the support of the Party and the people. Some positive results appeared. The decisions that were formulated and adopted were more considered and better substantiated. The start of the economic reform of 1965[2] and the March 1965 Plenary Meeting of the Central Committee devoted to agriculture were major initiatives aimed at positive changes in the economy. But, having produced a substantial though temporary effect, they petered out.

The atmosphere of complacency and the interrupted natural process of leadership change gave rise to stagnation and retardation in the country. These I have described above. The situation, meanwhile, demanded more and more insistently important decisions to refine the mechanism of economic and social management.

What conclusions have we drawn from the lessons of history?

First, socialism as a social system has proved that it has immense potentialities for resolving the most complex problems of social progress. We are convinced of its capacity for self-perfection, for still greater revelation of its possibilities, and for dealing with the present major problems of social progress which arise as we approach the twenty-first century.

At the same time, we realize that improving socialism is not a spontaneous process, but a job requiring tremendous attention, a truthful and unbiased analysis of problems, and a resolute rejection of anything outdated. We have come to see that half-hearted measures will not work here. We must act on a wide front, consistently and energetically, without failing to take the boldest steps.

One more conclusion—the most important one I would say—is that we should rely on the initiative and creativity of the masses; on the active participation of the widest sections of the population in the implementation of the reforms planned; that is, on democratization and again democratization.

---

[1] *This Plenary Meeting*, held on 14 October 1964, relieved Nikita Khrushchev of his duties as First Secretary of the CPSU Central Committee. Leonid Brezhnev was elected to this post.

[2] *The economic reform of 1965* was aimed at improving the mechanism of economic activity in industry and construction with the emphasis on profit.

What Inspired Us to Launch Perestroika

It is wrong, and even harmful, to see socialist society as something rigid and unchangeable, to perceive its improvement as an effort to adapt complicated reality to concepts and formulas that have been established once and for all. The concepts of socialism keep on developing; they are being constantly enriched as historical experience and objective conditions are taken into consideration.

We have always learned, and continue to learn, from Lenin's creative approach to the theory and practice of socialist construction. We are using his scientific methods and mastering his art of analyzing concrete situations.

As perestroika continues, we again and again study Lenin's works, especially his last.

The classics of Marxism–Leninism left us with a definition of the essential characteristics of socialism. They did not give us a detailed picture of socialism. They spoke of its theoretically predictable stages. It is our job to show what the present stage should be like. We'll have to actually go through this stage, for the classics teach us the approach, not the techniques.

This new stage confronts us with a need to sort out many theoretical issues and established ideas of socialism, relying on Lenin's heritage and methods. Such a review is all the more important since Lenin's ideas were not always adhered to in the years after his death. The specific situation in the country made us accept forms and methods of socialist construction corresponding to the historical conditions. But those forms were canonized, idealized and turned into dogma. Hence the emasculated image of socialism, the exaggerated centralism in management, the neglect for the rich variety of human interests, the underestimation of the active part people play in public life, and the pronounced egalitarian tendencies.

Take the pattern of economic management. The specific historical situation in which the Soviet Union developed, and our extreme conditions, could not but influence that pattern. The threat of war, the bloodiest and the most devastating wars in a history which

45

would have been difficult even without them, and the two postwar rehabilitation efforts all naturally gave rise to strict centralism in management. As a result, the democratic basis of our management system shrank.

Now, back to how this paradox developed. Let us now see why it emerged. As young Soviet Russia started building a new society, it was all alone against the capitalist world, facing a need to quickly overcome economic and technological backwardness, and create an up-to-date industry practically from scratch. That was done with unprecedented alacrity.

To do that, we had to drastically increase the proportion of savings in our national income. The bulk of the money was allocated to the development of heavy industry, the defense industry included. The question of what that priority cost us was never asked, or at best remained in the background. The state spared no expense, and the people were willing to make sacrifices for the sake of their country's rapid progress, for the sake of its defense capabilities, its independence and its socialist choice.

The management system that developed was meant to meet those objectives. It was severely centralized, every assignment regulated down to the last detail. It strictly posed tasks and allotted budget sums. And it fulfilled its mission.

We can't wholly ascribe such management to objective conditions, however. There were mistaken premises and subjective decisions. We have to bear them in mind, too, as we evaluate today's problems. Be that as it may, the management system which took shape in the thirties and forties began gradually to contradict the demands and conditions of economic progress. Its positive potential was exhausted. It became more and more of a hindrance, and gave rise to the braking mechanism which did us so much harm later. Methods for extreme situations were still being used.

The dogmatism here stimulated the development of a "spend-away" economy,[1] which gained great momentum and continued to exist until the middle eighties. Herein lie the roots of the notorious

[1] *"Spend-away" economy*—one of the manifestations of extensive management of the economy when growth is achieved mostly through the construction of new plants and factories and the employment of more workers, which leads to increased production costs without any rise in product quality.

"gross-output approach,"[1] which has until recently dominated our economy.

It was in these conditions that a prejudiced attitude to the role of commodity–monetary relations and the law of value under socialism developed, and the claim was often made that they were opposite and alien to socialism. All this was combined with an underestimation of profit-and-loss accounting, and produced disarray in pricing, and a disregard for the circulation of money.

In the new conditions the narrow democratic basis of the established system of management began to have a highly negative effect. Little room was left for Lenin's idea of the working people's self-management. Public property was gradually fenced off from its true owner—the working man. This property frequently suffered from departmentalism and localism, becoming a no man's land and free, deprived of a real owner. Ever increasing signs appeared of man's alienation from the property of the whole people, of lack of coordination between public interest and the personal interests of the working person. This was the major cause of what happened: at the new stage the old system of economic management began to turn from a factor of development into a brake that retarded socialism's advance.

Speaking of the political aspect of the braking mechanism, one cannot fail to see that a paradoxical situation developed: an educated and talented people committed to socialism could not make full use of the potentialities inherent in socialism, of their right to take a real part in the administration of state affairs. Of course, workers, farmers and intellectuals have always been represented in all bodies of authority and management, but they were not always drawn into the making and adoption of decisions to the extent required for the healthy development of socialist society. The masses had been prepared for more active political effort, but there was no room for this, although socialism grows stronger precisely because it involves ever greater numbers of people in political activity.

The braking mechanism in the economy, with all its social and ideological consequences, led to bureaucracy-ridden public structures and to expansion at every level of bureaucracy. And this bureaucracy

[1] *"Gross-output approach"*—unbalanced planning and production which emphasizes the "weight" and "quantity" of products instead of improvement of their quality and adjustment of supply to real demand.

acquired too great an influence in all state, administrative and even public affairs.

It goes without saying that in these conditions Lenin's valuable ideas on management and self-management, profit-and-loss accounting, and the linking of public and personal interests, failed to be applied and develop properly. This is only one example of ossified social thought that is divorced from reality.

Perestroika set new tasks for our policies and our social thought. They included putting an end to the ossification of social thought, in order to give it wider scope and to overcome completely the consequences of that monopoly on theory typical of the period of the personality cult. At that time the forms of the development of socialist society that had come into being under extreme conditions were made by Stalin's authority into something absolute, and were regarded as the only possible forms for socialism.

A drastic change must be made in social and political thought. And here we must learn from Lenin. He had the rare ability to sense at the right time the need for radical changes, for a reassessment of values, for a revision of theoretical directives and political slogans.

Here is a most striking example. In April 1917, when Lenin came back to Russia, he wasted little time in assessing accurately the situation, tendencies and possibilities of development in the country after the February revolution.[1] He not only correctly determined the only possible tactics of the Party and the Soviets, but also set forth a new strategic task, that of preparing the Party and the masses for a socialist revolution. Otherwise the gains achieved in overthrowing the autocracy could well have been lost. Such a change in tactics was unexpected even for many seasoned Bolsheviks. This is the kind of dialectics in political thinking that we are learning about as we carry out our perestroika.

Both then and afterwards, it often happened that the Party was too slow in understanding new ideas. It was difficult at times, with even persons most committed to the cause of the revolution revealing misunderstanding. But Lenin and his associates had the ability to convince people, to explain things, and return again and again to the

---

[1] *The February bourgeois–democratic revolution* of 1917 overthrew tsarism. A provisional government was set up, which had to share power with the Soviets of Workers', Peasants' and Soldiers' Deputies.

same issue, to fire others with energy and to win over those who hesitated and doubted. Lenin himself found it hard sometimes. He once bitterly wrote in a letter, referring to those who were unable to stand the tension and were seeking an easy life in the revolution: "there were trying times, sometimes very trying, but I would not for a world exchange the smallest bit of that period for a whole life in company with shallow persons and philistines."

I have mentioned several times, referring to Lenin, that if you take up particular issues without seeing the general perspective, you will keep bumping into this general perspective all the time. Taking this as our guideline, from the very start of perestroika, especially at the June 1987 Plenary Meeting of the CPSU Central Committee, we attached prime importance to a conceptual approach. Of course, we sought to make methods less chaotic. In order to make a substantial gain, it is not at all necessary to begin by turning everything upside down and then to start correcting all the mistakes.

New tasks have to be tackled, with no ready-made answers. Nor are there such answers today. Social scientists have not yet offered us anything cohesive. The political economy of socialism is stuck with outdated concepts and is no longer in tune with the dialectics of life. Philosophy and sociology, too, are lagging behind the requirements of practice. Historical science must undergo a major revision.

The 27th CPSU Congress and Plenary Meetings of the Central Committee have opened up new opportunities for creative thought and have given a powerful impulse to its development. No revolutionary movement is possible without a revolutionary theory—this Marxist precept is today more relevant than ever.

Perestroika is a Revolution

Perestroika is a word with many meanings. But if we are to choose from its many possible synonyms the key one which expresses its essence most accurately, then we can say thus: perestroika is a revolution. A decisive acceleration of the socio–economic and cultural development of Soviet society which involves radical changes on the way to a qualitatively new state is undoubtedly a revolutionary task.

I think we had every reason to declare at the January 1987 Plenary Meeting: in its essence, in its Bolshevik daring and in its humane social thrust the present course is a direct sequel to the great accomplishments started by the Leninist Party in the October days of 1917. And not merely a sequel, but an extension and a development of the main ideas of the Revolution. We must impart new dynamism to the October Revolution's historical impulse and further advance all that was commenced by it in our society.

Of course, we don't equate perestroika with the October Revolution, an event that was a turning point in the thousand-year history of our state and is unparalleled in force of impact on mankind's development. And yet, why in the seventieth year of the October Revolution do we speak of a new revolution?

Historical analogy may be helpful in answering this question. Lenin once noted that in the country of the classical bourgeois revolution, France, after its Great Revolution of 1789–93, it took another three revolutions (1830, 1848 and 1871) to carry through its aims. The same applies to Britain where, after the Cromwellian Revolution of 1649, came the "glorious" Revolution of 1688–9, and then the 1832 reform was necessary to finally establish the new class in power—the bourgeoisie. In Germany there were two bourgeois-democratic revolutions (1848 and 1918), and in between them the drastic reforms of the 1860s, which Bismarck carried out by "iron and blood."

"Never in history," wrote Lenin, "has there been a revolution in which it was possible to lay down one's arms and rest on one's laurels after the victory." Why then should not socialism, called upon to carry out even more profound socio–political and cultural changes in society's development than capitalism, go through several revolutionary stages in order to reveal its full potential and finally crystalize as a radically new formation? Lenin repeated the following thought more than once: socialism would consist of many attempts. Each attempt would in a certain sense be one-sided, each would have its own specifics. And this applies to all countries.

Historical experience has shown that socialist society is not insured against the emergence and accumulation of stagnant tendencies and

50

even against major socio–political crises. And it is precisely measures
of a revolutionary character that are necessary for overcoming a crisis
or pre-crisis situation. The most important thing here is that socialism
is capable of revolutionary changes, because it is, by its very nature,
dynamic.

In the spring of 1985, the Party put this task on the agenda. The
gravity of accumulated and emerging problems, and the delay in their
understanding and solution necessitated acting in a revolutionary way
and proclaiming a revolutionary overhaul of society.

Perestroika is a revolutionary process for it is a jump forward in the
development of socialism, in the realization of its essential characteristics. From the outset we realized that we had no time to lose. It is
very important not to stay too long on the starting line, to overcome
the lag, to get out of the quagmire of conservatism, and to break
the inertia of stagnation. This cannot be done in a evolutionary
way, by timid, creeping reforms. We simply have no right to relax,
even for a day. On the contrary, day after day we must add to our
effort, build up its pace and its intensity. We must withstand the
stresses, what cosmonauts call big overloads, at the initial phase of
restructuring.

A revolution should be constantly developed. There must be no
marking time. Our own past illustrates this. We still feel the aftermath
of slowing down. Therefore we now need redoubled courage and
boldness. Should we again get stuck, we are in for trouble. Therefore
—only forward!

Of course, acting in a revolutionary way does not imply a headlong
dash. Cavalry attacks are far from being always appropriate. A revolution is governed by the laws of politics, by the art of the possible.
Bypassing its stages and getting ahead of ourselves must be avoided.
Now the main task is to create a basis for advance to qualitatively new
frontiers. Otherwise you may make a mess of the whole thing and
discredit the great cause.

In accordance with our theory, revolution means construction, but
it also always implies demolition. Revolution requires the demolition
of all that is obsolete, stagnant and hinders fast progress. Without
demolition, you cannot clear the site for new construction. Perestroika
also means a resolute and radical elimination of obstacles hindering
social and economic development, of outdated methods of managing

51

the economy and of dogmatic stereotype mentality. Perestroika affects the interests of many people, the whole of society. And, of course, demolition provokes conflicts and sometimes fierce clashes between the old and the new. There are no bombs exploding or bullets flying, of course, but those who are in the way resist. And inaction, indifference, laziness, irresponsibility and mismanagement are also resistance.

That's understandable. The atmosphere in our society has grown tense as the perestroika effort has gone deeper. We have heard some people say: was there any point in starting all this at all?

Some people do not even accept the word "revolution" as applied to this effort. Some are scared even by the term "reform." But Lenin was not afraid to use this word and even taught the Bolsheviks themselves to go in for "reformism" whenever that was required to carry forward the cause of the Revolution in the new conditions. Today we need radical reforms for revolutionary change.

One of the signs of a revolutionary period is a more or less pronounced discrepancy between vital interests of society whose front ranks are ready for major changes, and the immediate, day-to-day interests of people. Perestroika hits hardest those who are used to working in the old way. We have no political opposition, but this does not mean there is no confrontation with those who, for various reasons, do not accept perestroika. Everyone will probably have to make sacrifices at the first stage of perestroika, but some will have to give up for good the privileges and prerogatives which they do not deserve and which they have acquired illegitimately, and the rights which have impeded our progress.

The question of interests has always been a key issue for the Party at crucial moments. It would be appropriate to recall how Lenin fought for the Brest Peace Treaty[1] in the troubled year of 1918. The Civil War was raging, and at that moment came a most serious threat from Germany. So Lenin suggested signing a peace treaty with it.

The terms of peace that Germany peremptorily laid down for us were, as Lenin put it, "disgraceful, dirty." They meant annexing a

---

[1] *The Brest Peace Treaty*—a peace treaty between Soviet Russia and the countries of the Quadripartite Alliance (Germany, Austria–Hungary, Turkey and Bulgaria), signed on 3 March 1918, in Brest-Litovsk. It was annulled by the Soviet government on 13 November 1918.

vast tract of territory with a population of fifty-six million. It seemed impossible to accept them. Yet Lenin insisted on a peace treaty. Even some members of the Central Committee objected, saying that the workers, too, were demanding that the German invaders be rebuffed. Lenin, however, kept calling for peace because he was guided by vital, not immediate, interests, the interests of the working class as a whole, of the Revolution and the future of socialism. To safeguard them, the country needed respite before going ahead. Few realized that at the time. Only later was it easy to say confidently and unambiguously that Lenin was right. And right he was, because he was looking far ahead; he did not put what was transitory above what was essential. The Revolution was saved.

It is the same with perestroika. It meets the vital interests of Soviet people. It is designed to bring society to new frontiers and raise it to a qualitatively new level. We shall have to make sacrifices, which will not be easy. The established habits and ideas are disintegrating before our eyes. The disappearance of something customary provokes protest. Conservatism does not want to give way, but all this can and must be overcome if we want to meet the long-term interests of society and every individual.

We actually faced the issue of the relationship between immediate and long-term interests when we began introducing state quality inspection.[1] To improve the quality of products we instituted an independent body for ensuring that products met existing standards. At first many workers' earnings dropped, but the improved quality was needed by society and workers regarded the new measure with understanding. There were no protests from them. On the contrary, workers now say: "It is shameful to get what you have not earned." At the same time, they want managers, engineers and technical personnel to assume the same attitude. So state quality inspection has become a good testing ground for perestroika. It revealed people's attitudes to work and human reserves which could be utilized for perestroika. State quality inspection has become a litmus test confirming once again that the Soviet working class as a whole totally supports

---

[1] *State quality inspection*—a system for controlling the quality of products. It is independent of the management of an enterprise, and subordinate to the USSR State Committee for Standards. It was introduced on 1 January 1987, at 1,500 industrial enterprises. Its further extension has been planned.

the restructuring, and is ready to promote it, fulfilling in practice its role as the vanguard class of the socialist society.

Like revolution, perestroika is not something you can toy with. You must carry things through to the end and make progress every day so that the masses can feel its results and the process can continue gathering momentum both materially and spiritually.

When we call our measures revolutionary, we mean that they are far-reaching, radical and uncompromising, and affect the whole of society from top to bottom. They affect all spheres of life and do so in a comprehensive way. This is not putting new paint on our society or dressing up its sores, but involves its complete recovery and renewal.

Politics is undoubtedly the most important thing in any revolutionary process. This is equally true of perestroika. Therefore we attach priority to political measures, broad and genuine democratization, the resolute struggle against red tape and violations of law, and the active involvement of the masses in managing the country's affairs. All this is directly linked with the main question of any revolution, the question of power.

We are not going to change Soviet power, of course, or abandon its fundamental principles, but we acknowledge the need for changes that will strengthen socialism and make it more dynamic and politically meaningful. That is why we have every reason to characterize our plans for the full-scale democratization of Soviet society as a program for changes in our political system.

Hence we must—if we want perestroika to succeed—gear all our work to the political tasks and methods of leadership. The most important element in the activities of Party organizations and Party personnel is political work among the masses, political education of the working people and the raising of the level of people's political activity. The original meaning of the concept of "socialism," above all, as an ideological and political movement of the masses, a grass-roots movement whose strength lies primarily in man's consciousness and activity, has again come to the fore.

Revolution is an unparalleled phenomenon. And like a revolution, our day-to-day activites must be unparalleled, revolutionary. Perestroika requires Party leaders who are very close to Lenin's ideal of a revolutionary Bolshevik. Officialdom, red tape, patronizing attitudes and careerism are incompatible with this ideal. On the other hand, courage, initiative, high ideological standards and moral purity, a constant urge to discuss things with people and an ability to firmly uphold the humane values of socialism are greatly honored. The revolutionary situation requires enthusiasm, dedication and self-sacrifice. This particularly applies to the leaders. We still have a long way to go to achieve this ideal. Too many people are still "in the state of evolution," or, to put it plainly, have adopted a wait-and-see attitude.

A "Revolution from Above"? The Party and Perestroika

There is a term in historical science and also in political vocabulary: "revolution from above." There have been quite a few such revolutions in history. But they should not be confused with *coups d'état* and palace revolutions. What is meant is profound and essentially revolutionary changes implemented on the initiative of the authorities themselves but necessitated by objective changes in the situation and in social moods.

It may seem that our current perestroika could be called a "revolution from above." True, the perestroika drive started on the Communist Party's initiative, and the Party leads it. The Party is strong and bold enough to work out a new policy. It has proved capable of heading and launching the process of renewal of society. The Party started the effort with self-improvement. I spoke frankly about it at the meeting with Party activists in Khabarovsk, in the summer of 1986. We must begin with ourselves, I said. Everyone must assume the responsibility: in the Politburo, in local bodies, and in grass-roots Party organizations. We must be better than we are. We shall help those who can't improve themselves. The main thing is to be conscientious. We have grown accustomed to many practices when there was no openness. This applies to both the rank and file and high officials.

I don't mean to say people should be coaxed, like candidates do in some countries during election campaigns. Our people don't like it. They must know the truth. One mustn't be afraid of one's own people.

Openness is an attribute of socialism. But there are still some people, in the higher echelons too, who speak about socialist ethics for all and of a surrogate kind for themselves: that is, something that suits their selfish ends. That won't do.

In short, the restructuring effort started with the Party and its leadership. We began from the top of the pyramid and went down to its base, as it were. Still, the concept of "revolution from above" doesn't quite apply to our perestroika, at least it requires some qualifications. Yes, the Party leadership started it. The highest Party and state bodies elaborated and adopted the program. True, perestroika is not a spontaneous, but a governed process. But that's only one side of the matter.

Perestroika would not have been a truly revolutionary undertaking, it would not have acquired its present scope, nor would it have had any firm chance of success if it had not merged the initiative from "above" with the grass-roots movement; if it had not expressed the fundamental, long-term interests of all the working people; if the masses had not regarded it as their program, a response to their own thoughts and a recognition of their own demands; and if the people had not supported it so vehemently and effectively.

The very nature of restructuring implies that it must go on at every work place, in every work collective, in the entire management system and in Party and state bodies, including the Politburo and the government. The restructuring concerns all, from rank-and-file communist to Central Committee Secretary, from shopfloor worker to minister, from engineer to Academician. It can be brought to a successful end only if it is truly a nationwide effort. But in any case, everyone must work honestly and conscientiously, sparing no efforts and abilities. Such a movement will gradually involve more and more people.

When a serious and thought-out approach is suggested, it will always meet with support and understanding among the working people. This is exactly how we've been trying to act over the past two and a half years. Maybe we have not yet fully realized ourselves or shown the people the full complexity of the situation in which the country has found itself and what is to be done. But we have said the most essential thing and received support and approval in response.

The weaknesses and inconsistencies of all the known "revolutions from above" are explained precisely by the lack of such support from below, the absence of concord and concerted action with the masses. And, since all these things were lacking, a greater or lesser degree of coercive pressure from above was needed. This led to deformities in the course of changes, and hence their high socio–political and moral "cost."

It is a distinctive feature and strength of perestroika that it is simultaneously a revolution "from above" and "from below." This is one of the most reliable guarantees of its success and irreversibility. We will persistently seek to ensure that the masses, the "people below," attain all their democratic rights and learn to use them in a habitual, competent and responsible manner. Life convincingly confirms that at sharp turns of history, in revolutionary situations, the people demonstrate a remarkable ability to listen, understand and respond if they are told the truth. This is exactly how Lenin acted at even the most trying moments after the October Revolution and during the Civil War, when he went to the people and talked to them frankly. This is why it is so important that perestroika maintains a high level of political and labor energy amongst the masses.

It is often said in the West that perestroika will run into difficulties, and that that will displease our working people. What should I say to that? Of course there will be difficulties in such a great undertaking. And if we come across legitimate discontent or protest, we will make a serious effort, above all, to ascertain the reasons behind such things. Administrative zeal cannot help in such cases. The bodies of authority, and public and economic organizations must learn to work so as not to give any pretexts for such manifestations and so as to resolve in good time the questions that may arouse such reactions as they occur. If the authorities do not tackle specific problems of common con-cern, the people will try to do it themselves. It is when the people keep speaking at meetings and appealing to the higher authorities, but the latter let it all pass, that unusual actions begin to take place at grass-roots. They are a direct result of shortcomings in our work.

There is only one criterion here: we will listen to and take into consideration everything that strengthens socialism, whereas the trends alien to socialism we will combat, but, I repeat, within the framework of the democratic process. Not to play at revolutionism, not to be carried away, not to fuss or overindulge in administrative methods is one of the principles of the true Leninist revolutionary spirit.

When asked if we are not pushing it too hard, we reply: no, we are not. There is no reasonable alternative to a dynamic, revolutionary perestroika. Its alternative is continued stagnation. Upon the success of perestroika depends the future of socialism and the future of peace. The stakes are too high. Time dictates to us a revolutionary choice and we have made it. We will not retreat from perestroika but will carry it through.

When Jimmy Carter, whom I met this summer, asked me, "Are you confident in the success of your efforts at economic and political reforms in the Soviet Union?" I replied:

"We have started a major and difficult undertaking in the political, economic, social and spiritual spheres. Restructuring concerns all groups of society. This is not an easy task. We have gone through certain and, possibly, the most important phases of restructuring. We have proposed the policy of change and we see that it is approved by society. And it is being implemented. Many problems are cropping up, of course.

"The West has at once begun speaking of some kind of opposition, but that is not serious. We have started a major restructuring. We are recasting our attitudes and thinking and our whole way of life, and are dispeling stereotypes. The atmosphere in society has changed a great deal. Society has been put into motion. We are getting great support and pushing things on, relying on that support. If we had not been confident of the correctness of this policy, my colleagues and I would not have proposed it.

"Now we have the experience of the first two years, the experience of practical implementation of this policy, our confidence in the correctness of what we are doing has increased considerably. We will proceed along this road no matter how hard it may be. Of course, there will be different stages along that road. We will reach some goals within a short time. Other tasks will take several years to accomplish. There are remote goals, too. We will press ahead."

The Soviet people are convinced that as a result of perestroika and democratization the country will become richer and stronger. Life will get better. There are, and will be, difficulties, sometimes considerable, on the road of perestroika, and we are not concealing that. But we will cope with them. Of that we are sure.

2

Perestroika Gets Under Way: The First Conclusions

Two and a half years have passed since the policy of perestroika began. We have a theoretical conception of it and a specific program, both of which are being continuously developed, clarified, and enriched with new approaches and ideas. This demands great creative efforts from the leaders of the Party and the state, and involves discussions. After the 27th CPSU Congress[1] and several Plenary Meetings of the Central Committee, the problems and the course of perestroika are being enthusiastically discussed by all sectors of Soviet society. The program of perestroika has already found expression in a series of state legislative acts approved by parliament—the Supreme Soviet of the USSR.

Parallel with this, day-to-day practical work to implement the strategy of perestroika has been going on. We have amassed certain, if limited, experience. There are initial encouraging results but there have also been errors and miscalculations. Today we see more clearly our possibilities and weak points. We still believe that we are at the initial stage. Nevertheless, perestroika has already become part of our life, involving the masses. In this sense it is already a reality.

I SOCIETY IS PUT IN MOTION

How It All Began

When we speak about what has been done over the two and a half years, we usually mean the time both before the Congress and after it.

[1] *The 27th CPSU Congress* was held in Moscow 25 February—6 March 1986.

60

The CPSU congresses hold a special place in our history, marking as it were, milestones on our way. For many reasons the 27th Congress had to give answers to the most urgent issues of the life of Soviet society. The time for holding it was determined by the Party Rules[1]. The preparation of a new edition of the Party Program[2] was under way, and the plans for the Twelfth Five-Year-Plan period and for the period ending in the year 2000 were being drawn up. The difficulty was that the political directives for the Congress began to be shaped in conditions which changed dramatically after the 1985 March[3] and April Plenary Meetings of the CPSU Central Committee. New processes had begun both within the Party itself and in society as a whole.

The process of grasping, of comprehending the ideas of the Plenary Meeting was not easy. New ideas were born in discussions that were held at all levels—in the Politburo, the Central Committee, local Party organizations, the scientific community, and work collectives. Lively debates, and sometimes polemics started in the media. The country's past also began to be assessed critically. Thousands of people—workers, farmers, and intellectuals—eagerly took part in these debates—at meetings of their work collectives, in the press and in letters to the highest Party and government bodies which contained both criticism and suggestions. Different, and sometimes directly opposite points of view were expressed on many specific problems, and an eager search for a way out of the existing situation was openly launched. We consider such plurality of opinion both natural and useful. It became clear that preparation for the 27th Congress should be based on new approaches, though less than a year was left before the time for which it was scheduled.

Of course, the Congress could have been postponed. This opinion was persistently expressed, and convincing arguments were voiced. But the approaches of the stagnation period that had affected all of us were felt to be behind that. A point of view which, in my opinion, most accorded with the situation—that we should hold the Congress

---

[1] *The Rules of the CPSU*—the Party's main law which determines the rights and duties of its members, the Party's organizational structure and the principles of inner-Party democracy.

[2] *The Program of the CPSU*—the Party's main document, which sets forth its theoretical and ideological foundations, the principles of its activities, and the goals which it strives to achieve.

[3] *Special Plenary Meeting of the CPSU Central Committee* held 11 March 1985 which elected Mikhail Gorbachev General Secretary of the CPSU Central Committee.

on schedule and draw all healthy forces of society into the preparation for it—ultimately prevailed.

The 27th Congress adopted major resolutions which are of tremendous importance for the future of the USSR. It formulated the guidelines for the Party's work to implement the concept of acceleration of social and economic development advanced by the April Plenary Meeting of the Central Committee. Yes, it was a congress to which its delegates brought not only their concerns and truth but also their thoughts, plans and determination to give a fresh and powerful impetus to the development of socialism.

It was a courageous congress. We spoke openly about the shortcomings, errors and difficulties. We emphasized the untapped potential of socialism, and the Congress adopted a detailed long-term plan of action. It became a congress of strategic decisions.

But at the time we failed or were just unable to fully realize the dramatic character and scope of the processes under way. Now we can see better, and it is clear that we have to resolutely continue the work started in the pre-Congress period and at the Congress itself, and simultaneously to study more deeply the society we live in. To do this, we had to return to the sources, to the roots, to better assess the past, and to decide on our priorities and on ways to accomplish them. Without understanding this we could lose our way.

Even nearly a year after the 27th Congress some people in various strata of society and in the Party itself continued to think that perestroika was not a long-term policy but just another campaign. Many local officials kept the active supporters of perestroika in check, warning those of them who were too demanding: wait, comrades, don't make a fuss, and everything will blow over in a year or two. They sincerely believed that everything would go full circle, as had been the case more than once before. There were also self-styled skeptics who would chuckle in the office corridors: we've been through different periods, and we'll live through this one as well. Concern over the fate of perestroika was growing in society: won't things slip back into the same old rut?

At the January Plenary Meeting we self-critically analyzed the causes of the complex and contradictory situation. We did not strive to only criticize the past and name an official or two. Does the essence of the matter lie only in naming someone? What was needed was assessments of phenomena and an analysis of processes and tendencies. And we sought to do this. I am sure that if the January Plenary Meeting had confined itself to criticizing the past it would not have fulfilled its mission. We need lessons and criticism not for squaring accounts but for our present and our future.

If at the January Plenary Meeting we had not proposed a constructive program of action, if we had not said the main thing—what was to be done, what additional forces should be activated to eliminate the braking mechanism, and how an effective mechanism of acceleration could be created—this would have meant marking time. If the Plenary Meeting had not indicated the direction for us to follow, if it had not proposed democratization as the main motive power of perestroika, it would have been completely pointless.

The main idea of the January Plenary Meeting—as regards ways of accomplishing the tasks of perestroika and protecting society from a repetition of the errors of the past—was the development of democracy. It is the principal guarantee of the irreversibility of perestroika. The more socialist democracy there is, the more socialism we will have. This is our firm conviction, and we will not abandon it. We will promote democracy in the economy, in politics and within the Party itself. The creativity of the masses is the decisive force in perestroika. There is no other, more powerful force.

The months that have passed since the Plenary Meeting have shown that we acted correctly. Our generation faces the tremendous task of restructuring the whole country. Perhaps we will not cope with everything but we will have time for advancing the acceleration process. We will lay the foundations and I am sure that the entire Soviet society will join in the process of perestroika.

But even when the newest democratic mechanism has been tried out and the moral levers have begun to be used in full, the task will not become simpler. In fact, I think the amount of work will increase and that it will become ever more complex; it is clear that its forms and methods will have to be altered more than once because we will have to work in new political, economic, moral and cultural conditions.

Perestroika Gains Momentum

I hope by now I've succeeded in showing you that Soviet society has been set in motion, and that there's no stopping it. But we do not encourage unrealistic expectations. Some people hope that everything will immediately change of its own accord, without requiring any special effort. Many think like this: new leaders have emerged, so everything will change now, everything will be all right. It's a mistake, however, to think that from now on it will be an easy ride downhill. On the contrary, we are still climbing uphill, and we have a long way to go before perestroika gains momentum.

Perestroika is only just getting off the ground. So far we have only been shaping the mechanism of acceleration. Until recently we were engaged more in learning what was what, in exploring approaches and in gathering ideas and recommendations. Now we all have to forge ahead together. It is quite another matter that different people have different ideas of perestroika itself and of the role they have to play in it.

There are not many outspoken opponents of perestroika, but there are, however, people who support the innovations but believe that perestroika should not affect them, only those at the top—in the Party, state and economic bodies, other sectors, adjoining enterprises, co-workers in the shop, on the farm or at the construction site—in short, anyone but themselves. In a talk I had with workers at the big VEF[1] radio engineering plant in Riga during my visit to the Latvian Soviet Socialist Republic I considered it necessary to tell them that difficulties are one thing, but if they were going to be interested only in what is happening "at the top" and not make use of their own resources, perestroika would slow down, start wheel-spinning and wind up as a half-hearted measure.

There are also people who do not know how to work in the new way, in the context of perestroika. They have to be taught and they have to be helped.

[1] *VEF*—an electrical engineering plant in Latvia.

There is also the problem of sluggishness, of inertia. The practice of waiting for instructions from above on every matter, of relying on top-level decisions has not yet been done away with. Not that this is surprising, for this is the way it used to be from workshops to ministries, and it is still having its effect today, even in the upper echelons of administration. The point is that people grew unaccustomed to thinking and acting in a responsible and independent way. Herein lies another big problem.

The main task is to get the whole of society involved in the process of restructuring. Socialism in our society is developing on its own basis. We are not suggesting that perestroika should be carried out with a different people, party, science, literature, and so on. This is not so. We are carrying it out together, through a nationwide effort. The entire intellectual potential must be brought into play. I can see from my own experience that all of us are changing in the course of perestroika. It would be unfair to deny someone the right to experience their own perestroika, to act differently today from how he did yesterday, to proceed today from a realization of the situation and the goals which have been put forward by our time.

We Have No Ready-Made Formulas

Politics is the art of the possible. Beyond the limits of the possible begins adventurism. It is for this reason that we appraise our possibilities carefully and soberly and map out our tasks taking this into consideration. Taught by bitter experience, we do not run ahead of ourselves on our chosen path, but take account of the evident realities of our country.

The greatest difficulty in our restructuring effort lies in our thinking, which has been molded over the past years. Everyone, from General Secretary to worker, has to alter this thinking. And this is understandable, for many of us were formed as individuals and lived in conditions when the old order existed. We have to overcome our own conservatism. Most of us adhere to correct political and ideological principles. But there is a substantial distance between a correct stand and its realization.

It sometimes even happens that during the discussion of an issue in the Politburo we seem to draw substantiated conclusions and take innovative decisions, but when it comes to choosing methods for implementing them, we end up trying to use old methods to accomplish new tasks.

In politics and ideology we are seeking to revive the living spirit of Leninism. Many decades of being mesmerized by dogma, by a rule-book approach have had their effect. Today we want to inject a genuinely creative spirit into our theoretical work. This is difficult, but it must be done. Creative thought seems to be consolidating.

We realize that there is no guarantee against mistakes, the worst of which would be to do nothing out of fear of making one. We know the mistake of doing nothing from our own experience. Many of our troubles derive from it. Our opponents in the West have noticed this weakness, which was particularly manifest in the late seventies and early eighties, and were on the verge of consigning the Soviet Union to the "ash-heap of history." But their requiem was clearly premature.

I am pleased that there's a growing understanding, both within the Party and in society as a whole, that we have started an *unprecedented* political, economic, social and ideological endeavor. If we are to implement everything we have planned, we must also carry out *unprecedented* political, economic, social and ideological work in both the internal and external spheres. Above all, we bear an *unprecedented* responsibility. And we are aware of the need for large-scale and bold efforts, especially at the first stage.

Many things are unusual in our country now: election of managers at enterprises and offices; multiple candidates for elections to Soviets in some districts; joint ventures with foreign firms; self-financed factories and plants, state and collective farms; the lifting of restrictions on farms producing food products for enterprises and run by them; wider cooperative activities; encouragement of individual enterprise in small-scale production and trade; and closure of non-paying plants and factories operating at a loss; and of research institutes and higher educational establishments working inefficiently. A press that is more incisive, taking up "taboos," printing a rich variety of public points of view, and conducting an open polemic on all vital issues concerning our progress and perestroika. All that is natural and necessary, although all these things do not come easily, nor are they understood readily both among the public at large and among Party members.

I don't think that the past two and a half years have been the most difficult period for the CPSU. It has, however, been one of the most serious, requiring a high sense of responsibility, maturity and loyalty to ideals and basic goals. A particular tendency may or may not suit us, but we try to view things soberly and realistically. Only in this way can we submit a policy to the people and advance goals that they will understand and will lead them forward.

Certainly, the leadership has also had some differences of opinion about how stagnation should be overcome and how things should be handled in the future. There is nothing surprising about this. Quite the contrary, it would be strange, to say the least, if there were no such differences and if everybody thought and spoke exactly the same. A conflict of opinions generates thought. But we are at one insofar as the main thing is concerned—we are unanimous in our belief that perestroika is indispensable and indeed inevitable, and that we have no other option.

All the Soviet people, the entire Party, including the Central Committee and its Politburo, and the government are in a process of restructuring. In this revolutionary work we, the members of the Politburo, are gaining experience in resolving the problems facing our society. The same is taking place in the republics, regions and work collectives involved in perestroika. In tackling the new tasks the whole nation is being put to the test of perestroika. Most importantly, the very climate of our society has changed. The process of releasing the Soviet people's social and political activity is under way. People have become bolder and are displaying a keener sense of civic duty. There is much that has piled up in previous years which they want to speak about openly.

The novelty of an uncommon situation has been growing. If somebody told us in April 1985 that in two years we would have what is actually taking place today, we would most likely have disbelieved it or would even have found it unacceptable. But what has actually been the case? The fact is that something we would have certainly set our faces against or would have been noncommittal about just a year ago is becoming not only a common subject of discussion but a natural component of everyday life. Society is changing, it is all in motion.

67

We are living through no ordinary period. People of the older generation are comparing the present revolutionary atmosphere with that of the first few years after the October Revolution or with the times of the Great Patriotic War. But my generation can draw a parallel with the period of the postwar recovery. We are now far more sober and realistic. So the enthusiasm and revolutionary self-sacrifice that increasingly distinguish the political mood of the Soviet people are all the more valuable and fruitful.

At the June 1987 Plenary Meeting of the Central Committee I spoke about the danger of allowing a discrepancy to develop between the growing activity of the masses and the surviving outdated methods and style in the activities of government agencies, managerial bodies and even Party organizations. We are taking determined steps to overcome this discrepancy. However, one can look at this situation from a different angle. It would have been far worse if the passivity of the people and their failure to live up to the requirements of perestroika had posed the main obstacle. Fortunately, that is not the case. Pressure from the working people and their outspokenness are mounting and even outpacing the actual rate of restructuring.

Direct communication and letters have become the major "feedback" linking the Soviet leadership with the masses. Letters arrive at the editorial offices of newspapers and magazines (many of which get published), and addressed to the government, the Supreme Soviet and, in particular, the Party Central Committee.

And here is a point worthy of note. There were many letters to all kinds of institutions in earlier times, but what has now changed is the very character of the letters. Fewer of them are so-called "personal requests" asking for help in obtaining an apartment or a pension, in assisting a wrongly convicted person, or reinstating somebody at his place of work. Although there are still some of that kind this is not their main purpose today. The majority contain reflections and expressions of concern about the nation's future. It is as if what has been painfully withheld in the long years of silence and estrangement has been finally given vent. The new situation encourages people to speak up. And they want to relate their thoughts, ideas and troubles not just to a friend or relative, but to the nation's leaders. Some letters are truly heartfelt.

Having read the original manuscript of this book, my publishers asked me to quote from the most typical ones. Here is one from A. Zernov, a 33-year-old worker living in the Yakut Autonomous Republic, in the Far East.

"Though I am not a Party member, I consider it my duty to write to you and thank you for awakening in us ordinary workers a sense of civic responsibility. The people have been waiting for these changes . . .

"I'll be frank with you. At first many people reacted to the general course of perestroika with suspicion. Not that it ran counter to our wishes—not at all. People simply knew from bitter experience that too often good slogans did not square with reality. However, we quickly realized that perestroika was not a short-term campaign but a necessary process historically. And the most important thing was that we saw it affected all spheres of our society.

"Our life has become far more meaningful. People have begun to take a genuine interest in the situation in the country, to put forward proposals on how to improve work, and to make critical remarks. Discussions of 'sticky' production problems now start up all by themselves in work collectives. It's embarrassing that our products are of such poor quality! We are robbing ourselves . . .

"Thank you. It is difficult to write and express gratitude to a person you don't know, but, on the other hand, we don't feel uneasy about thanking a doctor who has cured us of a grave illness. You have cured us of civic passivity and indifference and have taught us to believe in our own powers, in justice and in democracy . . . Many people didn't use to take Central Committee Plenary Meetings or even Party congresses seriously. Now even my seven-year-old son yells to me whenever he sees you on television: 'Daddy, come quick. Gorbachev's speaking.'

"The future belongs to us. As for mistakes, no one is guaranteed against them. We were the trailblazers; we had no one to learn from, so we are learning from our own mistakes."

Here is a letter from Lithuania. It comes from V. A. Brikovskis, who wrote after the January 1987 Plenary Meeting of the Central Committee.

"My heart is so filled with impressions that I simply have to share them with somebody else. For the first time in so many years we can see in the Party and government leadership people with human faces instead of stone-faced sphinxes. This alone is a great achievement.

"What do people think about your policy?

"I shall not lie to you, dear Mikhail Sergeyevich, because that could only harm our common cause. I'll tell you the whole truth.

"I shall not speak about the privileged section of society. Everything's clear here. Many would like to continue living as if in a drug-induced sleep, in a land of milk and honey.

"I want to speak about the proletarians, the people for whom this perestroika was started. Unfortunately, there is no deep understanding of your policy among them and there is still little trust in it. But this should not seem surprising. Brains do not thaw out quickly after such a long and terrible 'winter.' It will be a long and painful process.

"But everything will work out in the end.

"I am a devout Catholic. Every Sunday I go to church and pray that God refrain from punishing the world for our sins. I know you are an atheist, but through your efforts you have shown that some believers have something to learn from you. And I want you to know that every Sunday I am in church from 9 a.m. to 1 p.m., praying for you and your family."

The following letter is from B. Dobrovolsky, a schoolteacher from Kishinev, in the republic of Moldavia:

"We young people are to continue Lenin's cause, the great cause of the Soviet people. You are doing a great job, so let's make sure that it does not become a Sisyphean task. Don't be offended by the tone of my letter: it comes from my being deeply hurt by the fact that some people do not understand the latest decisions of the Party and your personal contacts with the people. Let me tell you right away that I do. I approve of your meetings with working people and of the honest and open discussion of our problems and troubles. But my only wish is for these discussions to produce results. Not all people understand and accept your Leninist style of work: work among the people, work for the people, work in the name of the people. Sometimes I argue about this until I'm hoarse.

"Many people—I mean the generation born in the thirties, forties and fifties—have become ossified. And I am not afraid of using this word. At meetings they all (some of them are now small or even big bosses) say yes. To what? To everything. They say yes to renewal. They say yes to perestroika. It's always 'yes' and 'we want.' They are ready to bare their chests in ardor. But what is this in reality? Falsehood. I have tried to find out why. Why don't you believe a man who does not spare his life, health and nerves for us? Do you think it's easy to wake up a nation of many millions which has been lulled to sleep for decades? Do you think it is easy to promote initiative when many people have to look up the meaning of this word in the dictionary? Do you think it's easy to get you all moving?

"I am talking to you honestly about matters of principle. I am speaking on behalf of a whole generation of young Soviet people who have received a higher education."

Here is another letter, this time from G. Vardanian who lives in Georgia:

"You may remember me. Once when you still worked in the Stavropol Territory, you held a conference with those who were the first to introduce the rate-plus-bonus system and the team contract among farm-machine operators. At that time I worked as head economist on the collective farm named 'The Road to Communism' in the Alexandrovsky District. You talked with me for a long time, asking many questions about our life, the general mood on the farm and our work . . .

"All your initiatives in foreign and domestic policy inspire me and all honest people because they are consonant with our aspirations and concerns. It is painful for me to say, however, that not all people agree with you.

"I can't blame them. I will tell it to you straight, as you so like to do, that the problem lies with the local leaders: they were made in the image of former leaders and it is now very difficult to remold them.

"We can tell that things are hard for you. But we beseech you: do not take even one step backwards. There must be no change of mind or even the slightest retreat. Don't pay any attention to those who do not agree with you. The nation is rejoicing and is ready to make sacrifices for the sake of the goals you have set. This is what I wanted to tell you."

Finally, here is a letter from K. Lasta, a woman from Leningrad:

"All of us who are helping you must fight against every manifestation of the hated old practices, such as red tape, corruption, conformism, obsequiousness and fear of the powers that be. This is now the duty of everyone who does not want to return to the past. And everyone

71

also now has the duty to work at his place the way you work at yours, sparing no effort. For everyone can see how much energy, time, emotional strength and health the colossal, superhuman load you have placed upon your shoulders demands of you. Building is always difficult, but it is even more difficult to build on a site which must first be cleared of dirt. I hope it will make things a little easier for you if I tell you that a huge number of ordinary people stand by you, love you and care for you."

I could quote letters indefinitely. But this whole book would not be big enough for them all. In many of them people write about how perestroika has begun—or hasn't begun—at their factory, collective farm, construction site or office. They tell me what they are doing to become active in it, and analyze particular and general causes of the difficulties that arise along the way.

These letters—and there are thousands upon thousands of them— testify to the great confidence in the Party and government leadership. Regained confidence! And that is a great force, an invaluable asset. What strikes one in the letters is unfettered thinking, a high degree of political culture, and an urge to live and work as bid by conscience.

We in the Politburo discuss these letters, gathering them together at regular intervals. That helps the country's leadership to keep abreast of the course of events, to assess its policies properly and readjust them, and to work out modern methods for handling things.

There is one thing common to all the letters—unreserved and passionate support for perestroika. Even pointed and scathing judgments are imbued with a desire to help it forward. Yet, as the reader will have noticed from what I've quoted above, there is also a note of anxiety lest perestroika should go the way of the reforms of the fifties and sixties and start dying down. People are urging us not to retreat! Not a step backwards! But to move forward and on with greater courage and determination!

In short, we must be able not only to readjust our policies in line with the reaction of the masses and with the way they are reflected in the public mind, but we must ensure feedback, that is, encourage the people to give us ideas, suggestions and advice, including via direct contact with them.

Now everybody is getting used to it. But at first there were some "compassionate" people who cautioned against the danger of

Gorbachev getting "oxygen poisoning" during one of his outdoor chats with people, the danger of him being told something unwelcome, something the men in the Kremlin should not know. There have been some comments and, perhaps, there are still some, to the effect that direct informal meetings are nothing short of wooing the people. I have a different, in fact, opposite view on this subject. There are no hints, recommendations and warnings that are more valuable than those you get straight from the people.

In general, the people have become more forthcoming at such meetings. How was it before? You would put a question to someone but he would remain silent, perhaps out of fear or mistrust. True, there was also some demagogy: what are they thinking of over there in Moscow? This is bad, that is not good. But there were no suggestions. Now an interesting and serious conversation always gets going. Workers and farmers are becoming more optimistic; intellectuals and professional people have been speaking out in an authoritative and demanding way. But the loudmouths have quietened down somewhat and are wary of meddling in serious and constructive discussion. Whenever they do meddle people cut them short.

I have already spoken about the impression I got from a meeting with people in October Square in Krasnodar in the summer of 1986. What a substantive conversation it was, what problems people raised! I was really pleased to see them so zealously supporting the Central Committee line. And then I realized how bitter the people are, and how many suggestions and recommendations they have for their leaders.

I did not intend to make a speech in the Kuban area[1] (Krasnodar is its capital). I just went there to have a look at the way things were going there and to see with my own eyes how an economic experiment of national importance was getting under way—a whole district had begun to operate on the principle of self-financing and self-repayment. And after numerous conversations, I found it necessary to speak in public. I think what I said proved useful for other regions of our country as well, because it was prompted by the very realities of life. Consultations and meetings with the people are really indispensable. One can't achieve much by injunction.

[1] *Kuban*—an area in the western part of the Northern Caucasus whose population is for the most part descendent from those Cossacks who a few centuries ago were resettled there.

The experience we have already gained in carrying out perestroika is once more bearing out Lenin's idea that revolutions are a great and most effective school of political education and enlightenment for the masses. Perestroika is a revolution, and the most peaceful and democratic one at that. It is within the confines of the democratic process that we shall proceed to overcome the erroneous positions we are encountering and will yet encounter in the course of this renewal of society, and even the most outspoken resistance. We don't have any significant groups of the population whose long-term interests would be irreconcilable with perestroika.

The difficulties we are experiencing in the democratization process are largely of our own making. We are all products of our time, of a certain pattern of things and habits. Therefore we say that we all have to change ourselves, including those in the Politburo, in government and other top echelons of leadership. Some manage to do it easily and quickly, others find it difficult and are asking to be retired or to be transferred to a different job.

The people are getting rid of their erstwhile apathy and becoming fully involved in public life. And that finds various forms of expression. Some make biting speeches at meetings, others stage rallies or street processions. Generally, the democratic process does not rule out the possibility of such grass-roots activities. We have already traveled some way from the times when such things caused official fear and incurred administrative bans. We do not yet have enough ethic of debate, sometimes a speaker at the dais is interrupted by someone sitting on the podium, and some people in their articles tend to settle old scores with others or tag offensive labels on them. But there is a steadily growing understanding that democracy is incompatible with excessive, bureaucratic regimentation of social life. Of course, no self-respecting society can allow anarchy, a free-for-all or chaos. Neither can we. Democracy also implies law and order, and the strictest observance of the laws by authorities and organizations, as well as by all citizens.

More Light to Glasnost!

The new atmosphere is, perhaps, most vividly manifest in glasnost. We want more openness about public affairs in every sphere of life. People should know what is good, and what is bad, too, in order to multiply the good and to combat the bad. That is how things should be under socialism.

It is important to be aware of all that is positive and constructive, to use it, to make it an asset of all the people, the entire Party, so that the shoots of new attitudes can be used in the conditions of perestroika.

Truth is the main thing. Lenin said: More light! Let the Party know everything! As never before, we need no dark corners where mold can reappear and where everything against which we have started a resolute struggle could start accumulating. That's why there must be more light.

Today, glasnost is a vivid example of a normal and favorable spiritual and moral atmosphere in society, which makes it possible for people to understand better what happened to us in the past, what is taking place now, what we are striving for and what our plans are, and, on the basis of this understanding, to participate in the restructuring effort consciously.

Democratization of the atmosphere in society and social and economic changes are gaining momentum largely thanks to the development of glasnost. It goes without saying that the policy of the Party is the basis of this process. Things will not start changing, however, if the political course is not pursued in a way understandable to the masses. The people should know life with all its contradictions and complexities. Working people must have complete and truthful information on achievements and impediments, on what stands in the way of progress and thwarts it.

People might be said to have developed a taste for glasnost. And not only because of their natural desire to know what is taking place, and who is working how. People are becoming increasingly convinced that glasnost is an effective form of public control over the activities

75

of all government bodies, without exception, and a powerful lever in correcting shortcomings. As a result, the moral potential of our society has been set in motion. Reason and conscience are beginning to win back ground from the passiveness and indifference that were eroding hearts. Naturally, it is not enough to know and to tell the truth. Acting on the knowledge of the truth and of understanding it is the main thing.

We have come to realize the necessity of learning to overcome the inveterate discrepancy between the reality and the proclaimed policy. It is this major shift in the moral sphere that makes up the emotional content and the essence of the present socialist revolutions in our society.

We have begun drafting bills that should guarantee glasnost. These bills are designed to ensure the greatest possible openness in the work of government and mass organizations and to enable working people to express their opinion on any issue of social life and government activity without fear.

When beginning the restructuring process, the CPSU Central Committee relied on two powerful real forces—the Party committees and the mass media. I can even say that the Party might not have reached the present level of discussion about the entire package of perestroika issues—and the process of perestroika is very vast, diversified and contradictory—if the mass media had not joined it actively, and in an appropriate manner, immediately after the April 1985 Plenary Meeting of the CPSU Central Committee.

The Central Committee highly appreciates the contribution the media have been making to perestroika. Why so? Because everything depends on the people. People are in the vanguard of the struggle, and perestroika develops through them. That is why the way people think, the level of their civic awareness and their civic stand are of decisive importance.

Our socialist society, which has resolutely embarked on the road of democratic renewal, has a vital stake in active participation by every citizen—every worker, every collective farmer, every scientist and every professional—in both the discussion of our plans and their implementation. And the mass media are playing and will continue to play a tremendous role in this. Naturally, they are not the only channel for expressing the people's will, for reflecting their views

76

and moods. But they are the most representative and massive rostrum of glasnost. The Party wants every citizen to voice his opinion confidently from that rostrum; the voice of citizens should not only make known the discussions that are taking place in the country but also be a guarantor of democratic control over the correctness of decisions and their conformity with the interests and requirements of the masses and, at the next stage, over the fulfilment of the decisions.

The current democratization process is reflected not only in publications, it is increasingly influencing the activities of the mass media. Gradually, as though thawing, our newspapers, magazines, radio and television are uncovering and handling new topics. One of the signs of the general revitalization is that our press is increasingly preferring dialogue to monologue. Formal reports are giving way to interviews, conversations, "round-table" discussions, and discussions about letters from readers. True, there is a tendency sometimes to limit the number of contributing writers to three to five people. This is nothing but professional arrogance. It is much more useful to diversify the authorship so that all citizens have a say, so that socialist pluralism, as it were, is represented in each publication in its entirety. It is certainly a good thing when a professional writer defines his position. It is much more interesting, however, to read conversations and interviews with workers, secretaries of district Party committees, chairmen of collective farms, scientists and cultural personalities. They are the carriers of live ideas. Or take the letters—what wonderful documents they are! They are truly moving.

Not everyone, however, likes the new style. This is especially true of those who are not used to living and working in the conditions of glasnost and broad criticism, who cannot and do not want to do this. It is they who voice discontent with our mass media and sometimes even demand that glasnost be constrained, curbed.

We do not regard it as negative that there are debates on whether there is not too much criticism, whether we need such broad openness, and whether democratization will have undesirable consequences. These debates, in a way, demonstrate concern for the stability of our society. Democracy and glasnost may be drowned in rhetoric and their meaning distorted. There are people who are seemingly all for the innovations, but when it comes to action they attach all sorts of conditions and reservations to the development of democracy, criticism and glasnost.

It is no longer a question of whether the CPSU Central Committee will continue the policy of glasnost through the press and the other mass media and with the active participation of citizens. We need glasnost as we need the air.

I would like to stress once again that the policy of broadening glasnost and developing criticism and self-criticism, rather than playing at democracy, is a matter of principle for our Party. We regard the development of glasnost as a way of accumulating the various diverse views and ideas which reflect the interests of all strata, of all trades and professions in Soviet society. We won't be able to advance if we don't check how our policy responds to criticism, especially criticism from below, if we don't fight negative developments, don't prevent them and don't react to information from below. I cannot imagine democracy without all this.

On the other hand, the criteria and character of criticism are also changing in the conditions of restructuring and democratization. Criticism is, first and foremost, responsibility, and the sharper the criticism, the more responsible it should be, for each article on a social topic is not only a self-expression by a certain person or a reflection of somebody's complexes or ambitions, but a matter of public importance. Democratization is introducing substantial corrections into the relationships between those who criticize and those who are criticized. These should be relations of partnership built on mutual interest. A dialogue is more appropriate in such instances, while all sorts of condescending lecturing and didactics and especially courtroom tones are absolutely inadmissible. And the latter can be found even in articles written by good and respected authors. No one has the right to a final judgment.

One thing is obvious: criticism should always be based on the truth, and this depends on the conscience of the author and the editor, on his sense of responsibility to the people.

The press must become even more effective. It should not leave in peace loafers, profit-seekers, time-servers, suppressors of criticism, and demagogues; it should more actively help those who are selflessly working for perestroika. A lot here depends on the local Party committees. If the Party committee reorganizes its work, the press does so, too.

I want to emphasize that the press should unite and mobilize people rather than disuniting them and generating offence and a lack of confidence. Renewal of society also means striving to assert the dignity of man, his elevation and his honor. Criticism can be an effective instrument of perestroika only if it is based on absolute truth and scrupulous concern for justice.

To uphold the fundamental values of socialism is a tradition of our press. Any fact, whether it is the burning issue of today or some unfortunate event of the past, may become the subject of analysis by the press. What values you defend, whether the people's destiny and future are of concern to you is what matters the most. It so happens, sometimes, that an author brings a sensational fact, a topical fact, out in a newspaper and begins to dance around it, imposing on others his own ideas and likes. In my opinion, any honest, open talk, even if it arouses doubts, should be welcomed. But if you try to fit somebody else's suit on us, beware! Glasnost is aimed at strengthening our society. And we have a lot to assert. Only those whom socialist democracy and our demands for responsibility prevent from satisfying their personal ambitions, which are, anyway, far removed from the people's interests, can doubt this.

Of course, this is not a call to put a ban on criticism or to switch to half-truths and give up critical analysis. The interests of deepening socialist democracy and enhancing the political maturity of the people require fuller use of the mass media for discussing public and state issues, broadening control by the public, active striving for greater responsibility, for stronger discipline at work, for observance of social-ist law and order, and against violations of the social principles and ethical standards of the Soviet way of life. We seek to organize this work in such a way that the mass media can act as a free, integral and flexible force nationwide, a force capable of promptly tackling the more topical events and problems.

Glasnost, criticism and self-criticism are not just a new campaign. They have been proclaimed and must become a norm in the Soviet way of life. No radical change is possible without it. There is no democracy, nor can there be, without glasnost. And there is no present-day socialism, nor can there be, without democracy.

79

There are still quite a few officials who continue to react painfully to criticism in the media and assess articles or broadcasts from the angle of personal taste, past experience, wrong interpretation of the interests of society, or simply do not understand the role of the press in the socialist society of today. Sometimes, they try to scare the critics by warning of the possible reaction to a critical article on the part of the West. The West, they claim, is eager to hear our self-criticism in order to turn it against us, to discredit the socialist way of life. I cannot say anything definite about others, but I myself do not fear criticism. A critical review of our own experience is a sign of strength, not weakness. Such an approach accords with the principles of socialist ideology.

But there exists, also, another, "quiet" method of suppressing or avoiding criticism, when officials agree in public with it, and even applaud it and promise to take effective measures, but in actual fact are in no hurry to draw practical conclusions. They hope that everything will end in talk, "sink into the sand," and their sins will not be recalled any longer. For such people the important thing is to repent in proper time.

Let me just reiterate what I said at the January Plenary Meeting: the attitude to criticism is an important indication of a person's attitude to perestroika, to everything new taking place in our society.

We will do all in our power to prevent anyone from either suppressing criticism or sidestepping it. Criticism is a bitter medicine, but the ills that plague society make it a necessity. You make a wry face, but you swallow it. And those who think that criticism need only be dosed out at intervals are wrong. People who are inclined to believe that stagnation has fully been overcome and it's time to take it easy are just as wrong. A slackening of criticism will inevitably harm perestroika.

Perestroika and the Intelligentsia

The intelligentsia has enthusiastically supported the restructuring. I will take the liberty of one digression here. Dedicated to socialist values, the intelligentsia, an organic part of Soviet society with a deep

80

sense of patriotism, is our great and, perhaps, unique achievement, our inestimable spiritual capital. Our intelligentsia has had a difficult history. Many intellectuals, including democratically-minded ones who censured the tsarist regime and even fought against it, were frightened by the Revolution and were swept away by the wave of white emigration[1] abroad, where they gave their talent and knowledge to other peoples. This was a great loss for our fledgling Soviet society.

The intelligentsia, including intellectuals in the Bolshevik Party, suffered enormous, at times irretrievable, losses because of violations of socialist legality and the repressions of the 1930s. This, too, was a formidable blow to the country's intellectual potential.

Nevertheless, the Soviet intelligentsia continued to form and grow, mirroring the objective laws governing the development of socialism and its vital needs. The Leninist cultural revolution[2] ultimately turned our semi-literate and simply illiterate country into one of the most educated countries in the world.

In the period of stagnation, however, a paradoxical situation took shape in which our society was unable to adequately use its enormous cultural and creative potential. Again, the reason was that the development of democracy had been artificially slowed down. All manner of bans, and a fear of new, creative approaches could not fail to have their effect.

I recall a meeting in June 1986 with the personnel of the apparatus of the CPSU Central Committee. It concerned perestroika. I had to ask them to adopt a new style of working with the intelligentsia. It is time to stop ordering it about, since this is harmful and inadmissible. The intelligentsia has wholeheartedly welcomed the program for the democratic renewal of society.

Congresses of creative unions[3] of film-makers, writers, artists, composers, architects, theatrical figures and journalists have been held. They were marked by heated debate. All the congresses sincerely

---

[1] *White emigration*—a general term for all those who left Russia after the 1917 October Revolution and during the Civil War of 1918–22. A large number of them actively fought against the Soviet government in the Civil War and engaged in subversive activities against the Soviet Republic. Many emigrants later took Soviet citizenship and some of them came back to their homeland.

[2] *The cultural revolution*—the elimination of illiteracy in the Soviet Union in the 1920s–30s, the mastering of modern culture by the broad popular masses.

[3] *Creative unions*—voluntary societies of intellectuals that unite writers, architects, composers, actors, artists, journalists, film-makers, etc.

supported perestroika. The participants severely criticized themselves; many former top union officials were not elected to leading bodies, nor were the loudmouths. Instead, eminent, authoritative people were elected to head the unions.

I told those who found the debates too heated that they should not be surprised or become indignant, that these congresses should be accepted as a normal, albeit new, phenomenon. Democratization is taking place everywhere, acquiring acute forms at times. Someone objected, claiming that it would be difficult to work in an environment where each individual is his own philosopher, his own foremost authority, and believes that only he is right. I replied that it is far worse to be dealing with a passive intelligentsia, and with indifference and cynicism.

Emotional outbursts are an inevitable part of any complicated endeavor. This has always been the case in revolutionary times. Today it is as if we are going through a school of democracy again. We are learning. We still lack political culture. We do not even have the patience to hear out our friends. All this is sure to pass. We will master this science, too. The thorniest issues have to be discussed with due respect for one another. Even the most extreme viewpoint contains something valuable and rational, for the person who upholds it honestly and who cares for the common cause in his own way reflects some real aspects of life. For us this is not an antagonistic, class struggle; it is a quest, a debate on how we can really get going with the restructuring effort and make our progress solid and irreversible. So I don't see any drama in polemics, in comparing viewpoints. This is normal.

Group prejudices and intolerance have indeed surfaced among writers in view of the new openness. There was a moment when passions were running high in the literary community. We brought home to them the view of the Central Committee, namely that it would be very sad if the creative and artistic intelligentsia squabbled instead of consolidating, and its members started using openness, frankness and democratism to settle old scores and take vengeance for criticism. The worst thing that can happen is if, in these revolutionary times, the creative intelligentsia allows itself to get bogged down in trifles, if it gives vent to personal ambitions and expends its energies on senseless high words rather than creative endeavor. The Central

82

Committee urged writers to rise above their emotions, convenient habits and stereotypes. Elevate yourselves and think of the people and society, we said. Let the intelligentsia's sense of responsibility also manifest itself in its creative unions, taking care, above all, of society's spiritual development.

The intelligentsia is imbued with a sense of civic responsibility, and it has eagerly shouldered a large share of the restructuring effort. Our intelligentsia has, along with the Party, got down to change. Its public-spirited stand is manifesting itself more and more strongly, and we have a vested interest in this activity; we appreciate everything —the way it joined the effort after April 1985, its enthusiasm and its desire to help the restructuring of society. We hope that this contribution by the intelligentsia will continue to grow. The intelligentsia is rising to a new level of thinking and responsibility. Its guidelines coincide with the political course of the CPSU and the interests of the people.

II NEW ECONOMIC AND SOCIAL POLICY IN ACTION

How has perestroika been developing in the economy?

I must say, frankly, that all our efforts toward changing the structure of the national economy, transferring it on to the track of intensive development, and accelerating scientific and technological progress prompted even more urgently the need for a radical reform of the economic mechanism and for restructuring the entire system of economic management.

Socialism and public ownership, on which it is based, hold out virtually unlimited possibilities for progressive economic processes. For this, however, we must each time find the most effective forms of socialist ownership and of the organization of the economy. Of prime importance in this respect is for the people to be the true master of production, rather than a master only in name. For without it, individual workers or collectives are not interested, nor can they be interested, in the final results of their work.

It is Lenin's idea of finding the most effective and modern forms

83

of blending public ownership and the personal interest that is the groundwork for all our quests, for our entire concept of radically transforming economic management.

Economic Reform: The June 1987 Plenary Meeting of the CPSU Central Committee

In carrying out a radical economic reform, it was important to preclude the repetition of the past mistakes which in the 1950s, 1960s and 1970s doomed to failure our attempts to change the system of economic management. At the same time, those attempts proved to be incomplete and inconsistent for they emphasized certain issues, while ignoring others. Speaking frankly, the solutions that were offered then were not radical, they were halfway measures, which not infrequently missed the essence of the matter.

I would say that the concept of economic reform, which we submitted to the June Plenary Meeting, is of an all-embracing, comprehensive character. It provides for fundamental changes in every area, including the transfer of enterprises to complete cost accounting, a radical transformation of the centralized management of the economy, fundamental changes in planning, a reform of the price formation system and of the financial and crediting mechanism, and the restructuring of foreign economic ties. It also provides for the creation of new organizational structures of management, for the all-round development of the democratic foundations of management, and for the broad introduction of the self-management principles.

There is an inner logic in any complex process, and it reflects interrelationships between certain measures, between certain concrete steps. A natural question arose before us: Where to begin! What is the starting point in restructuring management?

In our planned economy, it would seem logical, at first sight, to start restructuring from the centre, to determine the structure and functions of central economic bodies, then go over to the middle management level, and then, finally, to enterprises and amalgamations, the primary level. That might be correct from the viewpoint of abstract logic, but reality and accumulated experience dictated a different approach and a different logic: we should start with enterprises and amalgamations, the main link in the economic chain. We should start with finding the most effective economic model for them, then create the optimum economic conditions, extend and consolidate their rights, and only on that basis introduce fundamental changes in the activity of all higher echelons of economic management.

As we determined that sequence of the restructuring effort, we bore in mind that it is there, at enterprises and amalgamations, that the main economic processes are taking place, that material values are being created, and scientific and technological ideas are materializing. It is the work collective that gives a tangible shape to economic and social relations, and it is in the work collective that personal, collective and social interests of people are interlinked. The work collective largely determines the social and political atmosphere countrywide.

We also took into consideration our past experience, in which repeated attempts to reform the upper management levels without support from below were unsuccessful because of the stubborn resistance of the management apparatus, which did not want to part with its numerous rights and prerogatives. We have recently encountered that resistance, and still encounter it now. Here too, as in all other areas of restructuring, we must combine what comes from above with the movement from below, i.e., give the restructuring effort a profoundly democratic nature.

What is the main shortcoming of the old economic machinery?

It is above all the lack of inner stimuli for self-development. Indeed, through the system of plan indices, the enterprise receives assignments and resources. Practically all expenses are covered, sales of products are essentially guaranteed and, most importantly, the employees' incomes do not depend on the end results of the collective's work: the fulfilment of contract commitments, production quality and profits. Such a mechanism is likely to produce medium or even poor quality work, whether we like it or not. How can the economy advance if it creates preferential conditions for backward enterprises and penalizes the foremost ones?

We can no longer run our affairs like that. The new economic mechanism must put matters right. It must become a powerful lever, a motivating force for resourceful quality performance. Every enterprise must proceed from real social demands to determine production and

85

sales plans for itself. Those plans must be based not on numerous detailed assignments set by higher bodies, but on direct orders placed by government organizations, self-accounting enterprises and trade firms for specific products of appropriate quantity and quality. Enterprises must be put in such conditions as to encourage economic competition for the best satisfaction of consumer demands and employees' incomes must strictly depend on end production results, on profits.

We included all these principles of economic management and its specific forms in the draft Law on the State Enterprise (Amalgamation) which was discussed nationwide in work collectives, at meetings of workers and trade-union locals, and in the media. The draft law evoked the interest of the entire nation. The people felt that their opinion was needed. A special group of government officials, scientists and representatives of various state agencies considered the submitted proposals, amendments and additions. Everything that was rational and reasonable was included and considerably improved it.

Most corrections were meant to extend the work collective's rights. The general demand was not to retreat under the influence of inertia, but to go on firmly. It was felt that the new law should not be overburdened by numerous instructions which could emasculate it and bring it to a standstill. The USSR Supreme Soviet has adopted the law which will enter into force on 1 January 1988.

True, the press carried some proposals which went outside our system. There was an opinion, for instance, that we ought to give up planned economy and sanction unemployment. We cannot permit this, however, since we aim to strengthen socialism, not replace it with a different system. What is offered to us from the West, from a different economy, is unacceptable to us. We are sure that if we really put into effect the potential of socialism, if we adhere to its basic principles, if we take fully into consideration human interests and use the benefits of a planned economy, socialism can achieve much more than capitalism.

We attach primary importance to the Law on the State Enterprise in our economic reform. We use it as a yardstick for our other steps and measures. We consider them from the point of view of how fully they conform to this law and contribute to its practical implementation.

In preparing the Plenary Meeting, the Politburo spent several months examining the results of a comprehensive and strictly objective analysis of the activities of the Council of Ministers of the USSR, Gosplan[1], Gossnab[2], Minfin[3], Gosbank[4], economic ministries and departments and industrial management bodies. Ordinances were drafted to govern the operation of central agencies so as to make it (and their official functions) strictly consistent with the Law on the State Enterprise, not contradict it in any way. They were discussed at the Plenary Meeting, finalized, adopted and implemented.

The June Plenary Meeting of the CPSU Central Committee, its decisions, and the "Basic Provisions for Radical Restructuring of Economic Management" it adopted, are, in effect, completing the construction of a modern *model* of socialist economy to meet the challenge of the present stage of national development.

The Plenary Meeting and the session of the Supreme Soviet of the USSR that followed it developed and consolidated the policy of promoting the people's active involvement in economic and production processes, closely combining the interests of the state with those of the individual and the work collective, and of making the Soviet working people the true master.

Of course, we will still have things to complete or, perhaps, re-do. No society can ever have any system of economic management replaced overnight by a different, even a more advanced one, as if it were a kind of mechanical contrivance. We will have to adjust a dynamic and flexible mechanism sensitive to changes in production and capable of being constantly modernized, accepting what is advanced and rejecting what has outlived itself. The main danger here is stopping the belief that since decisions have been taken they will always be relevant in their present form.

By drawing up a program for a radical economic reform, we have laid the foundations for a full-scale offensive, this time in every area of the process of accelerating and extending the restructuring. The decisions taken provide the organizational and economic prerequisites for attaining the targets of the current five-year plan and the long-term

[1] *Gosplan (USSR State Planning Committee)*—a government agency in charge of long-term and current planning of the country's economic and social development and control over the fulfilment of those plans.
[2] *Gossnab*—USSR State Committee for Material and Technical Supply, a government agency.
[3] *Minfin*—USSR Ministry of Finance.
[4] *Gosbank*—State Bank of the USSR, the country's main bank.

objectives up to the year 2000. The task now in hand is to bring the new machinery of economic management into full operation competently and without delay.

This is, perhaps, the most crucial moment in the restructuring of the economy and management. The stage of constructive work has started. Now everything must be translated into reality. The emphasis now is on actually doing what we have concentrated our efforts for— and that is the hallmark of this juncture.

On to Full Cost Accounting!

The essence of what we plan to do throughout the country is to replace predominantly administrative methods by predominantly economic methods. That we must have full cost accounting is quite clear to the Soviet leadership.

True, there are some obstacles. Two of them, at least, are large. The first is that we have to do this in the context of the already endorsed five-year plan, that is, make it fit in. This particular aspect has a serious effect on the process of transition. So what are we to do, after all: stick to the five-year plan or drop it? There is only one answer to this question: we must reach the five-year-plan targets! This is an extremely difficult five-year-plan period: extensive forward-looking research is being conducted, great structural changes are taking place, many social issues are being resolved, and, along with all that, many innovations must be introduced in the course of this period. These are trying times for the factory managers: they have a heavy burden of problems that have built up and at the same time they have to change over to self-financing.

Another obstacle is that some of the more important components of the new management mechanism are not yet ready and will not be put into effect at once. It will take two or three years to prepare a reform of price formation and of the finance and crediting mechanism, and five to six years to go over to wholesale trade in the means of production. A lot has still to be decided about determining the functions of ministries, the reorganization of territorial administration, and the reduction of personnel.

Therefore we shall have a very complicated transition period, during which both the old and the newly introduced mechanisms will coexist. But full cost accounting will be introduced without delay. We will energetically follow this path gaining experience in the process. We will try out and test everything.

Whenever I meet people working in industry or even ministers, I tell them: never flinch; search and try things out. The people have so much wisdom and so keen a sense of responsibility that you can and must act boldly and confidently. Well, suppose we make mistakes. So what? It is better to rectify them than sit and wait.

A New Concept of Centralism

In the course of perestroika a new concept of democratic centralism is taking shape. It is important to have its two sides correctly balanced, bearing in mind that at different stages different aspects will be highlighted.

The situation now stands as follows: there are many people who are calling for stronger centralism. Balance sheets, proportions, the need for incomes to correspond to the mass of commodities and volume of services, structural policies, state finances, defense—all these require a firm centralized principle. All our republics and all our peoples should feel that they are placed in equal conditions and have equal opportunities for development. In this lies the guarantee of Soviet society's stability. That is why we do not want to weaken the role of the center, because otherwise we would lose the advantages of the planned economy.

At the same time, one cannot fail to see that the central authorities are overburdened with minor work. We will relieve them of current duties, for, by dealing with them, they lose sight of strategic matters.

Much of what we justly criticized at the January and June Plenary Meetings is due in the first place to omissions at the center: it could not sense dangerous trends in time, failed to find solutions to new problems, etc. All reorganization of the central apparatus and its functions, I repeat, will be strictly matched against the Law on the State Enterprise. Centralism in the conditions of perestroika has nothing in common with bureaucratic regulation of the many-faceted life of production, scientific and design collectives. We have yet to divide the functions of the center and localities, to change the essence of ministries' work, and their very purpose.

We are contemplating democratizing planning. This means that plan-making—not formal but actual—will begin within enterprises and work collectives. It is they who will be planning the production of their output, on the basis of social needs expressed in target figures and government contracts and on direct economic contract ties with consumers.

The State Planning Committee will have to give up detailed regimentation and day-to-day monitoring of the work of ministries and departments, and the latter will have to do the same with regard to enterprises. The activities of enterprises (wage funds, profit distribution, payments into the budget, etc.) will be regulated by long-term economic normatives; this will, in effect, be self-regulation.

We envisage broadening openness at all stages of planning, and introducing wide discussion of state and regional social, economic, scientific, technological and ecological problems. With a view to finding optimum solutions, the principle of variability will be introduced in the planning system.

As distinct from the previous practice, the central bodies will control the enterprises in a limited number of areas—in the fulfilment of state orders, profits, labor productivity and general indicators of scientific and technological progress and the social sphere. The fulfilment by enterprises of contract obligations and state orders for the more important products, types of work and services is becoming a major criterion of the activities of enterprises. The composition and volume of state orders will gradually be reduced with the saturation of the market in favor of the growing direct ties between manufacturers and consumers. When we have acquired the necessary experience, we will place state orders on a competitive basis, applying the principle of emulation, or socialist competition.

The system of material and technical supplies will undergo radical changes. The emphasis will be on a transition from forming funds to centralized distribution of resources, to wholesale trade.

In short, the advantages of planning will be increasingly combined with stimulating factors of the socialist market. But all this will take place within the mainstream of socialist goals and principles of management.

The broadening of the rights and economic autonomy of enterprises, the changing of the functions of central economic and sectoral departments and the transition from predominantly administrative methods to mainly economic methods of management call for radical changes in the managerial structure.

Earlier, the improvement of management was often accompanied by the establishment of new organizational elements, which resulted in the swelling of the apparatus, its becoming bulky, unwieldy and bureaucratic. We realize that the rates of economic restructuring are in no small degree held back by the bulky nature and inadequate efficiency of the management apparatus. So we intend to make heavy cuts in the managerial apparatus and, when necessary, will simplify its structure and enlarge sectoral ministries. We already have some experience of doing this. For example, agriculture and the processing of its produce were managed in our country by seven all-Union ministries and departments. We amalgamated all these departments into Gosagroprom[1], at the same time cutting their managerial staff by almost half. In another case, we chose to enlarge some ministries by merging them. This is how we will proceed in future, taking each case on its individual merits.

It is now clear to everyone that given the present scale of the economy, no ministerial or departmental apparatus, however qualified, can take upon itself the solution of absolutely every question, nor can it replace the thought and initiative of work collectives. Redistribution of rights between the central departments and the enterprises is not proceeding smoothly. The apparatus of the ministries and ministers themselves are unwilling to give up the habit of deciding minor matters themselves. They are used to that practice, which makes it so much easier for them. Any transfer of rights from the center to the localities is, in general painful, although, I repeat, the necessity of this is obvious to all, to both ministers and staff. They realize that this action benefits the cause, but, nevertheless, narrow departmental and sometimes group interests are put above those of society and the people.

There is one more way of perfecting economic management.

---

[1] *Gosagroprom (USSR State Agro–Industrial Committee)*—the central organ of state management of the country's agro–industrial complex, which was formed in 1985.

91

Experience shows that there is potential for achieving maximum efficiency at the points where industries meet. But to expect that the State Planning Committee will be able to trace all inter-sectoral links and choose an optimum variant is to harbor an illusion. The ministries are even less in a position to do so. It was this that put on the agenda the question of setting up agencies to manage large economic complexes. As can be seen, the management system will undergo great changes. We intend to act resolutely, but also in a balanced way, without unnecessary fuss.

Goal: World Technological Standards

While restructuring our planning and economic activities and extending the rights of the enterprises, we have also tackled the questions of scientific and technological progress. The branches that are in the forefront of this progress are being lent additional financial and material support. To this end a target-oriented national program has been mapped out, and funds allocated.

During the Twelfth Five-Year-Plan period[1], we will renew the greater part of fixed assets in machine-building. The amount set aside for these purposes will be almost double that spent in the previous five years.

Analysis of industry's performance has shown mistakes in the investment policy. For many years our policy had been to build more and more enterprises. The construction of workshops and administrative buildings absorbed vast sums. The existing enterprises, meanwhile, remained at the same technological level. Of course, if good use is made of everything available in two or three shifts, the targets of the Twelfth Five-Year Plan can be met using the existing equipment. But obsolescent equipment would in one way or another drag us backward, since it would mean we would be unable to put out modern products. Old machinery must be given up. This is why we are so drastically changing our structural and investment policies.

In 1983, I visited ZIL[2]. It was a time of active preparations for the

[1] *The Twelfth Five-Year-Plan period*—the current five-year development period (1986–90).
[2] *ZIL*—the Moscow I.A. Likhachev Motor Works.

modernization of that plant, one of the first such projects of the Soviet automotive industry. In 1985, I again visited ZIL and asked how modernization had progressed. It turned out that sights had been set on the average technological level, with reliance on equipment made five to seven years earlier. One could not, therefore, expect substantial advances in technology. Besides, a larger workforce would be required. Focusing on outdated techology does not lead to appreciable intensification of production; it merely consolidates the time-lag. As it transpired, the collective had come up with another, more advanced version, but it had not been supported and work on it had been discontinued. We backed the decision of the plant collective to go back to this plan for the ZIL modernization. A new plan for retooling has been drawn up, and is being successfully implemented. ZIL will become a really modern enterprise.

Generally speaking, drastic changes in technology and equipment take time. As we say, "Moscow was not built in a day." If we had set the task of deciding everything at one go, we would have had to modernize production by using outmoded, obsolescent equipment. It would have been tantamount to marking time.

Then we took a look at what equipment we had and whether it met world standards. It was discovered that only a lesser part of it was on that level. The conclusion suggested itself: rather than preserve our technological backwardness for many years, we would do better to pass through the pains of developing new equipment now and then, through advances in machine-building, make a breakthrough to the newest technologies. That "then" does not necessarily imply a remote future. No, structural modernization of Soviet machine-building must be combined with vast efforts to turn the scientific potential to good account. This is the most vital and urgent task for us, even a top priority. We have found ourselves in this situation technologically because we underestimated our scientific potential and placed too great a reliance on external ties.

As I see it, we accepted the policy of *détente* with too radiant hopes; I would say, too trustingly. Many thought it would be irreversible and open up unbounded possibilities, in particular for expanding trade and economic relations with the West. We even discontinued some of our research and technological developments, hoping for the international division of labor, and thinking that some machines would be more advantageous to buy than to manufacture at home. But what happened in reality? We were seriously punished for our *naïveté*. There came a period of embargoes, boycotts, bans, restrictions, intimidation of those trading with us, etc. Some Western politicians even publicly anticipated the collapse of the Soviet system. But they ranted in vain.

Certainly, we have drawn the necessary conclusions, started the necessary research and development and the production of what we once proposed to purchase, so Western firms will ultimately be the losers. Incidentally, I think all this noise about bans and restrictions is aimed not only against the USSR, but also, in very large measure, against rival non-American firms.

On the whole, the various US "sanctions" and "embargoes" and other bans helped clarify a great deal. As they say, every cloud has a silver lining. We have drawn lessons from the decisions taken by the US and some other Western countries to refuse to sell the Soviet Union advanced technology. That is perhaps why we are now experiencing a real boom in the fields of information science, computer technology and other areas of science and technology.

We decided to put a firm end to the "import scourge," as our economic executives call it. To these ends we are putting into operation the great potential of our science and mechanical engineering.

It is a paradox that many achievements of Soviet scientists were introduced in the West more quickly than in our own country, for instance, rotary conveyor lines. We were also slow in another case. We were the first to invent continuous steel casting. What came of it? Now eighty percent of the steel produced in some countries is cast by our method, but much less, in our country. The path in our country from a scientific discovery to its introduction in production is too long. This enables enterprising foreign industrialists to make money out of our ideas. Of course, such a situation does not suit us. There must be reciprocity in exchanges. Evidently, the situation is going to change. And, indeed, of late it has.

Considerable work is being done to invigorate scientific and techno-logical progress. We are launching target-oriented programs, prompt-ing work collectives and economic and other scientists to work in a creative way, and have organized twenty-two inter-sectoral research and technological complexes headed by leading scientists. The priority of the day is, as I said, the development of Soviet mechanical engineering. The June 1986 Plenary Meeting of the CPSU Central Committee proposed a program for radical modernization in mechanical engineering. It set a target unprecedented in the history of Soviet industry, that of reaching in the next six to seven years world standards as regards major machinery, equipment and instruments. The emphasis, it was decided, would be placed on machine tool-building, instrument-making, electronics and electrical engineering. The iron-and-steel and chemical industries are also being modernized on a wide scale.

Wishful thinking is a most dangerous occupation. And yet all the changes under way hold out much promise. Recently, I visited the town of Zelenograd not far from Moscow, where some research organizations and enterprises of the electronics industry are concentrated. I was gratified to hear scientists and specialists say that in a number of fields we are not trailing behind or even keeping level with the US, but are ahead in some ways. So the West's technological arrogance has proved of benefit to us. The task now, which is no less difficult, is to translate these results into practice.

Living Tissue of Perestroika

Perestroika embraces an immense range of diverse problems and tasks related to what has remained from the past, what should be done now, immediately, and what still lies in store for us. Although I run the risk of repeating myself, I would like to offer the reader a multi-colored picture of perestroika, to invite him to look into the kaleidoscope of everyday life in which the living tissue of our future is formed. We are preparing the masses for radical changes. This implies that the necessary economic and psychological conditions should be furnished, because it is not easy to break old habits and do away with concepts of social forms that have established themselves in definite historical conditions.

The accusations of righteous individuals are still being heard. Look at those who point their finger with indignation at disorder, at shortages and at flaws. And if somebody starts doing something worthwhile but unusual, these pseudo-socialists scream that he is undermining the foundations of socialism! This is also among the realities of perestroika. We must patiently argue with such fighters for "pure" socialism, ideal and unsullied in its abstract form, to prove that it has nothing to do with real life.

Lenin never believed that the road to socialism would be straight. He knew how to change slogans when life required it. And he was never a slave to resolutions once they were adopted. He was not afraid to stimulate individual labor activity, when the state and the public sector were weak. And today, in the course of the restructuring effort, some individuals are afraid of the measures being implemented to develop cooperatives, and promote individual labor activity, contracts and self-financing; they're worried that we're weakening the "foundations" and engendering petty proprietors. They feel that by introducing various forms of contracts we might be undermining collective farms. But what about the fact that shops are lacking many goods? This is what we should sound the alarm about, and not cry in panic: "Help, socialism is in jeopardy!"

We believe that combining personal interests with socialism has still remained the fundamental problem. We are referring, of course, to personal interests in the broad, and not just in the material, sense. What we need is not "pure," doctrinaire, invented socialism, but real, Leninist socialism. Lenin was very clear on this point—since we have enormously developed industry and power, there is nothing to be afraid of. Drawing on this strength, we can effect socialist transformations in a planned fashion. This is genuine socialist work. This was true then and it is even more true today, for our society is now economically and politically strong. Lenin never lost track of the real state of affairs; he was guided by the interests of the working people.

I am convinced that the most effective forms of organizing production on the basis of full cost accounting will take root quickest in the agro–industrial complex. For one thing, our collective farms have long-standing traditions. For another, rural folk are enterprising and resourceful. All this makes for greater mobility and flexibility when applying cost accounting, self-sufficiency and self-financing.

The collective contract has proven itself well in agriculture from the standpoint of labor organization and remuneration. A household contract system[1] is now being set up, and the first results are encouraging.

In early August 1987, I was in the Ramenskoye District outside Moscow, where I spoke with members of a team which has been operating on a contract basis applying intensive technology for five years. They grow seed potatoes, and last year the five of them brought the state farm enormous profits. Amazing things happen when people take responsibility for everything themselves. The results are quite different, and at times people are unrecognizable. Work changes and attitudes to it, too.

The individual in our society wants to be part of everything, and this is a good thing. He does not like situations where his opinion is not sought, where he is looked upon merely as manpower and his human and civic qualities are not appreciated. The collective contract and the democracy which is linked with it are precisely what supports a person's sense of being a citizen and a master.

Today, we have large collective farms and sovkhozes[2] in many agricultural areas. Large work teams, sections and complexes have been organized. They are somewhat divorced from the land, and this affects end results. Today, we must ensure a more solid and direct connection with the interests of the individual through collective, family and rental contracts within the framework of these collective and state farms. Then we will combine the advantages of a large collective economy with the individual's interests. This is exactly what we need. If we act in this way we can make impressive strides in solving the problem of foodstuffs within two or three years.

If personal interests are disregarded, nothing will come of the effort, and society will only stand to lose. For this reason it is imperative to strike a balance of interests, and we are doing so through the new economic mechanism, through greater democracy, through the atmosphere of openness, and through public involvement in all aspects of restructuring.

[1] *Collective contract*—a work method under which a team of workers carries out some work all the way through under a contract with the administration of its own enterprise or with any other organization. In this case, the pay of each participating worker directly depends on his working efficiency. *Household contract*—a collective contract by a family.

[2] *Collective farm*—a farming cooperative. *Sovkhoz*—a state farm.

97

The first thing that has to be ensured is an atmosphere that encourages the restructuring effort and renders the individual socially active and responsible. This is the atmosphere of openness, of discussing all matters, even the most difficult, with the people, so as to resolve them all together. To achieve this we need real public involvement in administration. That is why we say that democratization is the cornerstone of the restructuring effort. Such forms as the new management mechanism, election of managers, and setting up of work-collective councils at the work team, factory shop and enterprise level have been legitimately introduced. It is evident from the example of collectives of contractual and family-run farms how our people have missed the proprietary role. They want not only to earn more, which is entirely understandable; they want to do it honestly. They want to earn, not scrounge from the state. This desire is totally in a socialist spirit, so there should be no restrictions—whatever a person earns he should receive. At the same time, we should not allow a person to receive what he has not earned.

The Social Policy of Restructuring

We proceed from the assumption that only the strong social policy proclaimed by the 27th Congress of the CPSU can ensure success for perestroika. The standards of living should be raised and the housing situation eased; more foodstuffs should be produced and the quality of commodities improved; public health services should be further developed; the reform of the higher and secondary schools should be accomplished, and many other social problems should be resolved.

Tackling the current and long-term tasks, the June Plenary Meeting of the CPSU Central Committee of 1987 paid special attention to questions of increasing the production of foodstuffs and consumer goods and expanding housing construction.

Large-scale measures are being implemented. We are building more housing. For us, this is a nationwide task. More money will be invested in tackling it. We must help people get more and better housing, both in urban and in rural areas.

People must have a good quality of life. If this problem is solved, the work collective becomes stabilized. People appreciate more the changes that take place in their city or village, in production, in the conditions of work and in the very nature of work than how fast their wages grow.

The current passiveness of leaders who fail to use the opportunities available for solving social problems is particularly intolerable. This is explained, on the one hand, by the old habit of approaching these issues on the basis of a so-called principle of the residual, when only what is left after satisfying the needs of production is earmarked for social purposes. On the other hand, it is a result of the psychology of dependence, which has struck deep roots. Cost accounting and self-financing are putting an end to all this. The economic mechanism itself calls for an active, reasonable and enterprising approach, for acting in a proprietary manner.

Our achievements in education are universally known. They are impressive when compared to the most developed countries. Nevertheless, we are carrying out a school reform. What made us do it? To begin with, the new demands modern society is placing on people. Besides, the stagnation phenomena in our society have affected our educational system as well: in education, too, there were manifestations of complacency in results achieved, which immediately affected everything else.

Now, after a nationwide discussion, we have adopted programs for a radical transformation of higher and secondary schools. The main direction of efforts is training young people for future work with a view to meeting the requirements of scientific and technological progress and getting rid of everything of secondary importance which gives people little except unnecessary burdens. The humanistic education of the young, the aim of which is a proper upbringing and the acquisition of adequate cultural standards, is being improved. Colleges and secondary schools lay emphasis on stimulating creative methods of instruction and education and fostering initiative and independence in secondary and higher school collectives. The new tasks call for restructuring the material base and, most importantly, for teachers to attain a new level in their work. Those who upgrade their skills will be encouraged materially. The programs have the necessary financial backing, and their realization is proceeding.

Guidelines for improving the country's public health services are currently under nationwide discussion. When the discussion is over, the guidelines will be submitted to thorough examination by the CPSU Central Committee and the government and then by the Supreme Soviet of the USSR. This comprehensive project will require vast investments and large-scale effort. We have found the financial and material resources for its first stage, which will be carried out in the last years of the Twelfth Five-Year-Plan period and during the Thirteenth Five-Year-Plan period.

Intensification of social production suggests a new attitude to efficient employment and requires that the labor force be regrouped. While working in this direction, we must thoroughly scrutinize how the principle of social justice is implemented. The widespread practice of equalizing has been one of the prime deformities in the past few decades, resulting in the development of attitudes of dependence, consumerism and a narrow-minded philosophy of the type: "It is none of our business, let the bosses have the headache."

This is how the 27th Congress of the CPSU formulated the problem of social justice: under socialism, work is the foundation for social justice. Only work determines a citizen's real place in society, his social status. And this precludes any manifestation of equalizing.

Equalizing attitudes crop up from time to time even today. Some citizens understood the call for social justice as "equalizing everyone." But society persistently demands that the principle of socialism be firmly translated into life. In other words, what we value most is a citizen's contribution to the affairs of the country. We must encourage efficiency in production and the talent of a writer, scientist or any other upright and hard-working citizen. On this point we want to be perfectly clear: socialism has nothing to do with equalizing. Socialism cannot ensure conditions of life and consumption in accordance with the principle "From each according to his ability, to each according to his needs." This will be under communism. Socialism has a different criterion for distributing social benefits: "From each according to his ability, to each according to his work." There is no exploitation of man by man, no division into rich and poor, into millionaires and paupers; all nations are equal among equals; all people are guaranteed jobs; we have free secondary and higher education and free medical

100

services; citizens are well provided for in old age. This is the embodiment of social justice under socialism.

Today, when social justice is the point at issue in our country, much is said about benefits and privileges for individuals and groups of individuals. We have benefits and privileges that have been established by the state, and they are granted on the basis of the quantity and quality of socially useful work. There are benefits for people in the sphere of production and in the sphere of science and culture. For instance, we take special care of our eminent scientists, academicians and writers. Honorary titles are conferred on people for outstanding contributions to socialist construction. Thus, Heroes of Socialist Labor, award-winning scientists and cultural personalities enjoy certain extra benefits. There are also certain benefits for people in various industries and for those working in different regions (above all, in the north and remote areas), for servicemen, diplomats, etc. I believe this practice is justified, for it is in the interests of society as a whole. It, too, is based on the importance and size of a citizen's contribution.

But if there are privileges which have not been established by the state but which some people, abusing their official powers, "establish" for themselves, we ban them as unacceptable.

And there is one more aspect to the issue. Many of our organizations, institutions and enterprises run services facilities. A public catering system operates at large enterprises practically everywhere. Besides, in most cases enterprises shoulder the expenditures of maintaining public catering organizations. It is done jointly by the management and the trade union committee, as a result of which meals cost less.

Our country has an extensive network of medical institutions which provide health care services to people at their places of work. It comprises not only outpatient clinics but also holiday homes and after-work health-building centers situated near an enterprise or in recreation zones and health resorts. Many enterprises run their own shops, food-ordering services, dress-making establishments, and so on. A veritable services sphere of their own, you could say.

This is true not only of industrial enterprises. For instance, the Academy of Sciences, the Writers' Union or other organizations of this kind, have health centers, holiday hotels and summer cottage

101

settlements. The trade unions (by the way, the richest organizations in our country) and Party and Soviets' organizations also have such services. This situation has developed historically.

To be sure, the existence of such forms of services can generate, and does generate, problems, especially when the quality of the services provided to the entire population is much lower than at the aforesaid organizations and institutions. Such phenomena are naturally criticized by the working people. These issues should be solved in the course of furthering the programs we adopted.

We will firmly continue the struggle against drinking and alcoholism. This social evil has been deeply rooted in our society for centuries and has become a bad habit. Hence it is not easy to combat. But society is ripe for a radical turn around. Alcohol abuse, especially in the past two decades, has increased at an alarming rate and threatens the very future of the nation. The working people constantly remind us of the need to intensify our efforts to combat this evil. Some even demand prohibition countrywide. But we realize that it is inexpedient to introduce prohibition on a state scale. And we reply: if you want, introduce prohibition in your family, area or district. In thousands of villages and settlements the working people have decided at general meetings to end the sale and use of alcoholic beverages. The campaign continues. The per capita consumption of alcohol has dropped by half over the past two years. However, moonshining has gone up. It is impossible to resolve this issue by administrative measures alone. The most reliable way to get rid of such an evil as alcoholism is to develop the sphere of recreation, physical fitness, sport and mass cultural activities, and to further democratize the life of society as a whole.

III ALONG THE ROAD OF DEMOCRATIZATION

Our Main Reserve

One of the prime political tasks of the restructuring effort, if not the main one, is to revive and consolidate in the Soviet people a sense of responsibility for the country's destiny. A certain alienation, caused by

102

weakened ties between state and economic bodies, work collectives and rank-and-file workers, and by the underestimation of their role in the development of socialist society, still has a disturbing effect.

The human factor in the broadest sense is our main priority. We are doing all in our power to bring it into play, above all by enhancing the social thrust of all our plans. All I want to add is that we are working for a balance between two aspects—the economy and the social sphere. If the interests of this sphere are disregarded for the sake of economic development rates alone, interest in the results of labor is lost. This affects labor productivity and undermines the economy. On the other hand, the social sphere must not be built in such a way that the base is eroded, since then the very possibility for dynamic social development is undermined. Therefore, we have to find the golden mean that would make for harmonious socio–economic development. The correlation between these two aspects is not static; it is constantly changing. Today the social policy is being advanced to the forefront.

The moral aspect is of tremendous importance. If we do not effectively revive socialist values and a socialist atmosphere in our work collectives and in society as a whole, we will fail to carry through the restructuring drive. We can propose the right policies and effective mechanisms, but we won't accomplish anything if society does not improve through consolidation of the moral values of socialism, above all social justice, distribution according to labor input, uniform discipline, laws, rules and requirements for all.

We are also activating the human factor by improving the system of management, its mechanism. What is cost accounting in these terms? It is not only the rights of a work collective, but also its responsibility. If we say that you will live the way you work, it means we give the people the responsibility for their own future. A work collective naturally develops a reciprocal desire to have the right to run their enterprise and working process, the results of which determine the collective's incomes and life. Here, too, we have two sides of one process. In other words, cost accounting is linked with self-management, with the autonomy of work collectives.

We are taking a new view of the correlation between one-man management and the participation of work collectives in handling production tasks. This is a topical issue. There will be no progress

103

without workers' involvement in management through the corresponding mechanisms—at the work team, factory shop, plant and integrated works level. Furthermore, a work collective must have the right to elect its manager. And the latter receives the right to one-man rule on behalf of the collective, uniting everybody by his willpower.

Elections of economic managers are direct democracy in action. Initially people were frightened by this, claiming that we had gone too far, that things could come to a bad end. But those who reason that way forget the main point, that common sense always prevails. Group interests, a practice of covering up for one another, will somewhere make themselves felt. But basically everyone wants his work team, factory shop, enterprise, collective or state farm to be headed by dependable, intelligent managers capable of leadership, of opening up vistas for improving production and life. Our people understand this, and they certainly do not need weak management. They need people who are talented, considerate, yet demanding in a fair way.

People want to see changed attitudes on the part of the plant manager, shop superintendent and foreman. People expect a moral example and they expect it particularly from their superiors. There are several such examples. Where there is a good manager, there is success. He takes care of people. Everyone wants to talk with him. He need not raise his voice in giving out orders. He may look quite ordinary, but he sees and can explain everything. It is now extremely important to be able to explain the situation. People will agree to wait if they see why some of their demands cannot be satisfied fully right away.

We are also invigorating the human factor with the aid of more democratic procedures, better ideological work and a healthier moral climate in society. Far from everyone has come to fully realize the crucial character of the times. Much effort is required if perestroika is to win over those who are still sizing it up or are well suited by today's state of affairs.

The many routine notions cannot be removed in one stroke. Psychological habits that have become ingrained over the years cannot be abolished by any decree, even the most formidable. Regrettably, we have yet to fully rid ourselves of outdated forms of working with people, forms which are linked with our tendency towards ideological campaigns and grandiloquent twaddle. A lengthy, intense struggle is needed here, a struggle against red tape, unwarranted splendor, abstract slogans, and recurrences of pompous ostentation. The important thing is not to yield to illusions of wellbeing, not to allow bureaucratism and formalism to constrain the life-giving sources of the people's initiative.

In my talks with people in the street or at the workplace I constantly hear: "Everybody supports perestroika here." I am convinced of the sincerity and fairness of these words, yet I reply every time that the most important thing right now is to talk less about perestroika and do more for it. What is needed is greater order, greater conscientiousness, greater respect for one another and greater honesty. We should follow the dictates of conscience. It is a good thing that people understand this. What is more, they accept it with their minds and hearts. This is very important. There is a policy, there is a government that is fighting for this policy, and there are people that support it. This is the most important thing. Everything else will work out; the restructuring campaign will make headway and yield results. The chief impression I get from personal meetings with the Soviet people is how deeply they have sensed the political and moral meaning of perestroika.

Observance of Law—An Indispensable Element in Democratization

Observance of law is a matter of principle for us and we have taken a broad and principled view of the issue. There can be no observance of law without democracy. At the same time, democracy cannot exist and develop without the rule of law, because law is designed to protect society from abuses of power and guarantee citizens and their organizations and work collectives their rights and freedoms. This is the reason why we have taken a firm stand on the issue. And we know from our own experience what happens when there are deviations from these principles.

From the very beginning of Soviet rule Lenin and the Party attached

105

paramount importance to the maintenance and consolidation of law. This is only natural, because the political reality of the emerging new society required this: we had to consolidate the new system of government, abolish private ownership of the means of production, nationalize the land, give working people control of production, and protect the interests of workers and peasants from counter-revolution. All that had to be justified and formalized in laws. Otherwise the revolutionary process would have faced chaos and it would have been impossible to consolidate our acquisitions, ensure the normal functioning of the Soviet system of government and establish new principles in public life.

That purpose was fulfilled by the Soviet government decrees. From the very start they proclaimed legitimacy as a fundamental principle guiding the life of society in the Soviet Union and announced the task of enlisting the participation of millions of working people in running their country and teaching them, as Lenin put it, "to fight for their rights." This idea ran through the first Soviet Constitution of 1918 and the subsequent resolution "On the Strict Observance of Laws" passed by the All-Russia Congress of the Soviets.

After the Civil War, legislative work was intensified. Its aim was legally to codify the socialist transformations. Laws and the work of the bodies responsible for the observance of law and for administering justice became a major instrument in building a new state and legitimizing everything achieved as a result of economic, social, cultural and other activities. Lenin's demand that there must be one set of laws for the whole of the country and that "we must not budge *an inch* from our laws" was strictly observed.

However, mention should be made of the period which we call the personality cult period. It has affected our laws and their orientation and, especially, their observance. The emphasis on strict centralization, administration by injunction, and the existence of a great number of administrative instructions and restrictions belittled the role of law. At some stage this led to arbitrary rule and the reign of lawlessness, which had nothing to do with the principles of socialism or the provisions of the 1936 Constitution. Stalin and his close associates are responsible for those methods of governing the country. Any attempts to justify that lawlessness by political needs, international tension or alleged exacerbation of class struggle in the country are wrong. Violations of law had tragic consequences which we still cannot forget or forgive. The 20th Party Congress made a very harsh assessment of that period.

This found reflection in legislation. Democratic principles were restored, law and order consolidated and codification of legislation carried out. Nationwide discussion of draft laws and other important questions began to be practiced. In the past quarter century millions of people have taken part in the discussion of about thirty major national draft laws. They expressed their opinion on the latter, and suggested amendments and additions.

However, a subsequent period of stagnation was also linked with weakening law enforcement. Elements of arbitrary conduct and violation of law appeared again, including on the part of some leaders. Courts, procurators' offices, and other bodies called upon to protect public order and combat abuses were often ruled by circumstances, and found themselves in a dependent position and forfeited their principled stand in the struggle against law violators. Cases of corruption became more frequent in the law-enforcement machinery itself.

Now that we have launched perestroika, and have resolved to do away with the negative phenomena of the past and to give a fresh impetus to the development of socialist democracy, we have seen the need for far-reaching transformation both in the sphere of our legislation, and in the perfection of socialist legality as a whole. This need was also highlighted by radical changes in the mechanism of economic management and social development. This is part and parcel of the democratization of all aspects of our society. The measures which we are adopting in the field of legislation and law are becoming a support in the restructuring process. We are doing this work in the context of reforms in the economic, social and cultural spheres, considering the wishes of the working people, and the results of public opinion polls.

Perestroika requires greater organization in society, and conscious discipline of citizens. I'll put it this way: the deeper the restructuring, the more strictly and consistently the principles of socialism should be implemented, and the rules of life of socialist society codified in its Constitution and laws observed.

Perestroika sets higher demands as to the very content of legislative acts. Law should resolutely protect the interests of society, prohibiting what may prejudice national interests. This is an axiom. But, setting up this rigid framework, law is also called upon to make room for the initiative of citizens, work collectives and their organizations. Activity and initiative developing within the framework of law should be given every support and encouragement. We have lost too much trying to list all rights of enterprises in different instructions. In fact, it was implied that any undertaking which went beyond these instructions should have been treated as unacceptable. Meanwhile, experience has demonstrated that what we need is not a total legislative regulation of diversified phenomena of social life, but sound rationality, and constant fostering of and support for the worker, workforce, and all forms of popular initiative. Let's strictly observe the principle: everything which is not prohibited by law is allowed.

A whole series of important legislative acts have already been adopted in the course of perestroika. They include the Law on the State Enterprise (Association), laws on changing the system of running the agro–industrial complex[1], on the school reform, individual labor, on combatting illicit incomes, alcoholism and drug-addiction. Laws to improve public health and environmental protection, and to enhance care for mothers and children have been issued.

We are paying special attention to consolidating the guarantees of the rights and freedoms of Soviet people. Decrees of the Presidium of the USSR Supreme Soviet make suppression of criticism punishable by law, and establish a procedure for compensation for damage caused to citizens by unlawful actions of government and public bodies and officials. A law on the procedure to be followed when appealing in court against illegal actions by officials which have impaired the rights of citizens has been adopted. A practice for subjecting important questions of political life to nationwide discussion has also now been legally sealed in a law adopted by the USSR Supreme Soviet in June 1987.

At the same time we realize that the restructuring will continue to demand more and more new steps in the sphere of legislation, law and order. Total codification of legislation is coming on the agenda:

[1] *The Agro–Industrial Complex of the USSR (AIC)* is a structural unit of the national economy, incorporating branches engaged in the production of agricultural products and their processing, transportation, storage and sale.

this should settle such modern tasks as enhancing economic efficiency, pursuing a strong social policy, revealing the potential of all institutions of socialist democracy; in other words, it should pave the way to *self-government* by the people.

Considerable changes are to be introduced into election legislation. The experiments during the election campaign of June 1987 have enabled more accurate determination of just how to tackle this rather complicated problem. Work is now under way on legislative forms linked with restructuring the system of managing the national economy, and with a higher role for local bodies of state authority and administration. The scope of the work is very great, considering that about 30,000 national normative acts are operating in our economy. Many of these require substantial changes, and quite often simply abrogation. Thousands have already been canceled following the introduction of the Law on the State Enterprise.

After recent congresses, the trade unions and the Komsomol[1] made proposals to elaborate draft laws on organized labor and youth. Preparations are under way for draft laws on labor, on cooperative activities, on expanding the range of questions decided at work collective meetings, on the size of pensions for workers, administrative staff and collective farmers, and on product quality standards.

We shall have to work a great deal on changes to our Criminal Code. It should also be closely tailored to the current stage of Soviet society's maturity. Perfection of this important part of our work in the field of legislation and law will take place in the context of the tremendous transformation linked with the restructuring and democratization.

It is especially important to enhance the role of courts as an elective body very close to the population, to guarantee the independence of judges, and to observe most strictly democratic principles in legal proceedings, objectiveness, contested election, and openness. The same goals are being served by the measures recently taken to enhance the supervision by the procurator's office over strict and uniform observance of laws, to expand the functions of State Arbitration in settling economic disputes, to adjust judicial services in the national economy, and to develop judicial education for the public.

---

[1] *The Komsomol* is the All-Union Leninist Young Communist League (YCL), a self-active public organization of Soviet youth which was founded in 1918.

In other words, work on a tremendous scale beckons, the goal being to consolidate the legal foundations of socialism. Law and legality are not just concomitants in the deepening of our democracy and acceleration of social progress. These are working instruments in the restructuring and a reliable guarantee of it being irreversible.

Perestroika and the Soviets

Now that perestroika is under way and democracy is being developed, a new dimension has been added to the question of combining the Party's political leadership with the role of state agencies, trade unions and other public organizations. For example, consider our Soviets. Perestroika has forced us to make it clear what role they should play in the ongoing reform. There can be no democratization of society while the Soviets are not involved in the process and their status and activity are not exposed to revolutionary transformations.

The Soviets in Russia are a phenomenon unique in the history of world politics. They are the fruit of direct, creative participation by the working people. Few people in the West, perhaps, know that the very idea of the Soviets, soon followed by the first steps in organizing them, was conceived long before the October 1917 Revolution—in 1905. Following the February 1917 Revolution that toppled the tsarist administration, the Soviets developed into bodies of power throughout Russia, though with limited powers as they coexisted with the Provisional Government[1]. Naturally, they formed the political basis for the new republic that emerged in October 1917. Our country was henceforth called the Soviet Republic.

If there had been no Soviets, we would not have won the Civil War. If there had been no Soviets, we would not have succeeded in rallying millions of people, notably workers and peasants, in so vast a country. If there had been no Soviets, nothing would have come of the New

---

[1] *The Provisional Government* was the central body of bourgeois-landowner power in Russia, formed after the February Revolution. It existed from 2(15) March to 25 October (7 November) 1917.

Economic Policy.[1] Their real powers lay in the fact that, once created by the masses, they expressed and safeguarded working people's interests. The underlying feature and the secret of their rapid, even spontaneous spread throughout the country was in the fact that they made decisions and implemented them on their own while being in the focus of the public eye, under open control of all those whom their moves might concern. It was a unique and efficient way to combine direct democracy and representative democracy.

However, when the command–economy system of management was propelled into existence, the Soviets were somehow pushed back. Quite a few issues were resolved without their participation, or just left undecided to grow into problems. This lessened the prestige of the Soviets. From that moment the development of socialist democracy began to slow down. Signs appeared that the working people were being alienated from their constitutional right to have direct involvement in the affairs of state. As a result, the principle of the socialist revolution—that power must not only be for working people but also be wielded by working people—was gravely impaired.

It must be confessed that under these conditions many economic managers began treating legitimate demands and recommendations of the Soviets without due respect. Everybody seemed to understand —and nobody officially denied it—that local Soviets must be fully in charge of their respective territories in all issues concerning development and should meet the everyday needs of the people. But the real capabilities of the Soviets, as compared to those of economic agencies, did not let them fulfil those functions. The directors and the managerial staff of many enterprises, particularly big ones, could afford to ignore persistent and fair demands from the Soviets to build housing, air and water purifying facilities, promote social and cultural programs,

[1] *The New Economic Policy (NEP)* was an economic policy worked out by Lenin and launched in 1921. Its chief content: to replace the "prodrazvyorstka," or requisitioning of food from the peasants for the needs of the cities and the army during the Civil War and when the very existence of the Soviet state was under a deadly threat, with a "tax in kind," whereby a peasant paid a definite share of his output in tax. NEP's immediate aim was exchanges between town and country, on the basis of commodity–money relations, thus quickly normalizing production and the food situation in the country. Concessions were to be given to foreign firms, but this aspect did not gain development. Private enterprise in small-scale production and retail sales was also allowed. Enterprises were switching over to the cost-accounting system. NEP was conceived as a transitional, but relatively long period, during which a socialist transformation of society was gradually prepared and began to be effected.

develop public transport networks, provide better comforts in their areas, etc.

It cannot be said that the working people and Party agencies were totally unconcerned. Attempts were made to remedy the situation and change the existing order. But these attempts were too weak, due not so much to objective as subjective reasons. In the past fifteen years fourteen resolutions were adopted on improving the activity of the Soviets. Good though these resolutions were, the issue never got off the ground, because the economic, political and ideological environment of the braking mechanism fully resisted a greater role for the Soviets, which were basically the bodies incarnating broad democracy and openness.

We can well see now that as a result of the propagation of command–economy methods of management and supervision, whereby bureaucratic attitudes prevailed in many areas of public and government work, we have underused the capabilities of the Soviets to benefit the people. The dwindling role of the Soviets gave rise to what we see as a replacement of the functions and activities of government and administrative agencies by those of Party agencies.

For its part, "substitution" of the Soviets by Party agencies strongly influenced the Party political work. As Party officials directed their efforts toward economic affairs and management, cadres were recruited from among competent professionals, though often unskilled and inexperienced in matters of leadership. In short, a fault appeared in the functioning of the democratic machinery that owed its life to our socialist revolution.

So, in the course of the continuing drive for restructuring, we faced a formidable task—the need to restore completely the role of the Soviets as bodies of political power and as the foundation of socialist democracy. We are now renewing in full measure the prestige and powers of the Soviets, creating prerequisites for fully-fledged, efficient and creative work by them under the conditions of perestroika.

The January 1987 Plenary Meeting called on Party committees to keep strictly to the line of enhancing the role of the Soviets, avoiding interference in their affairs. It is also important that the heads and staffs of the Soviets should work with full vigor to eradicate inertia and overcome their habit of always looking to someone else and waiting for orders from above. The newly-adopted laws on the role of the Soviets at the restructuring stage encourage democratic attitudes by the Soviets and their executive bodies as they act. The pivot of their activities should be their closer link with the people. The new decisions let the Soviets arrange their work in such a way as to become the true bodies of popular government. They have been vested with extensive rights to coordinate and exercise control over the activity of all enterprises and organizations in their respective areas.

These are but the first few steps in restoring the revolutionary, democratic nature of the Soviets. The forthcoming All-Union Party Conference[1] is to consider and adopt appropriate resolutions on refinement of the electoral system and the work of the Soviets at all levels. Preparations for putting forward these proposals are well advanced. It is too early yet to evaluate them, but their chief importance is clear—they are aimed at furthering Soviet democracy.

The New Role of Trade Unions

What our country is undertaking and the issues it is tackling implies a re-evaluation of the role of trade unions in social affairs.

It should be said first and foremost that our unions are a formidable force. No labor law can be drafted unless endorsed by the All-Union Central Council of Trade Unions.[2] On all questions concerning labor laws, their enforcement and the safeguarding of the working people's rights the trade unions have the final say. If a manager fires a worker without asking the union for approval, a court of law automatically makes the decision invalid without any deliberation, inasmuch as the trade union has not been consulted for its opinion. No economic development plan, for one year or five years, is submitted to the Supreme Soviet unless approved by the trade unions. When the plans are in the making, the trade unions participate as well at all levels.

Social insurance, the running of sanatoriums and recreation resorts, tourism, physical training and sports, and the rest and recreation of

---

[1] *The 19th All-Union CPSU Conference* by decision of the June 1987 Plenary Meeting of the CPSU Central Committee will be convened on 28 June 1988, in Moscow.
[2] *The All-Union Central Council of Trade Unions (AUCCTU)* is the governing body of the Soviet trade unions in between their congresses.

113

children are all the responsibility of the trade unions. Consequently, they wield real power. But, alas, over the past few years there has been less trade union activity. On some issues, they have yielded their prerogatives to economic managers, while not enjoying some rights effectively enough.

So, having set about restructuring, we saw that the work of the trade unions could not be termed satisfactory. During my trip to the Kuban region, I reproached trade union leaders for pandering to managers, sometimes going so far as dancing to their tune. I asked them whether it was not high time they took a position of principle, and stood up for working people?

The new role of the trade unions in conditions of perestroika should consist primarily of giving a stronger social orientation to economic decisions, offsetting technocratic encroachments which have become widespread in the economy in the last few years. This means that the trade unions should be more active in elaborating the social sections of economic plans, and, if need be, setting forth and upholding their own alternative proposals.

Trade union committees should have teeth, and not be convenient partners for management. Bad working conditions at some enterprises, a poor health service, substandard locker rooms—trade union organizations seem to have got used to all this. But Soviet trade unions have the right to monitor managerial compliance with labor contracts, the right to criticize management, and even the right to demand that a director who fails to comply with the legitimate interests of the working people be removed from office.

It would be wrong to think that under socialism the working people do not need any protection. They should be protected even more, for socialism is a system for the working people. Hence the tremendous responsibility of the trade unions. All Soviet society is vitally interested in more vigorous work being undertaken by the trade unions.

Young People and Perestroika

Soviet *young people* offer enormous potential for the restructuring effort. It is the younger generation who will live and work in the remolded society. So naturally the organization of young people's work, studies and leisure is becoming a priority. Young people are searching for their place in the world. This is a difficult period in a person's life. It is a formative one as regards his family, occupational skills and political and civic views. He is coming into his own as an individual. For this reason a maximum amount of attention has to be paid to the young and the Komsomol (Young Communist League).

We have arranged things so that not a single important youth problem is tackled without the Komsomol's opinion being taken into consideration. This does not mean that we are pandering to the Komsomol. Not at all. We have to enhance its responsibility substantially. Nothing makes so effective an impact on the formation of the younger generation and its ability to take the country's present and future into its hands as trust, as involvement of the young in the real political and economic process. Patting young people on the back, talking down to them or playing up to them would not produce the desired results. The Komsomol and young people have to be given an opportunity to really show their worth. The young have to be free of petty guardianship and supervision; we should teach them by placing responsibility on them and by trusting them in real endeavors.

The January 1987 Plenary Meeting of the Central Committee called upon Party leaders to pay greater attention to the labor, ideological and moral steeling of young people. A didactic tone and regimentation are intolerable in work with young people. Whatever the reasons— distrust of the maturity of young people's aspirations and actions, elementary overcautiousness, a desire to make things easy for one's children—we cannot agree with such a stand. There are two prime areas in the life and work of the young. First, they have to master the entire arsenal of the ways to democracy and autonomy and breathe their youthful energy into democratization at all levels, and to be active in social endeavors. Acceleration and any progress at all are impossible without it. Each young person has to feel that he is involved in everything that is going on in the country. Second, the younger generation must be prepared to participate in the extensive modernization of our economy, above all through computerization and the introduction of new technologies and materials. Intellectual renewal and enrichment of society are what we expect of the young.

Young people are facing complex social problems. Many officials often call on them to go and work, say, at construction sites, but immediately forget about them when it comes to social questions. This is not the way to act. We support the idea of a youth law which would not repeat general propositions concerning all Soviet citizens but deal with the specific problems, rights and duties of youth. Such a law should define in more concrete terms the spheres of interaction between the Komsomol and state bodies, trade unions and other organizations as far as the work, studies, everyday life and leisure of young people are concerned. The law should enhance the responsibility of ministries and government departments for the solution of problems concerning the young.

The Komsomol Congress[1] which took place in 1987 has aroused a broad response nationwide. It has demonstrated that the Komsomol members are aware of their responsibility towards our country and people and are eager to take an active part in the process of social renovation. I liked the demanding atmosphere at the Congress. I have probably never experienced such a great desire to take part in a discussion as at that congress. There was live contact with a sympathetic audience which charged everybody with its energy.

There is every ground to believe that our young people wholeheartedly welcome the revolutionary changes, which have been started in the country, and that they are ready to promote them with their youthful energy and passionate dedication.

Women and the Family

Today it is imperative for the country to more actively involve women in the management of the economy, in cultural development and public life. For this purpose women's councils have been set up throughout the country.

The January Plenary Meeting also raised the question of promoting more women to administrative posts, especially since millions of women work in health care, education, culture and science. Many

[1] The 20th Congress of the Komsomol was held in April 1987.

116

women are also employed in the consumer, trade and service industries as well.

The extent of women's emancipation is often viewed as a yardstick to be used in judging the social and political level of a society. The Soviet state put an end to the discrimination against women so typical of tsarist Russia with determination and without compromise. Women gained a legally-guaranteed social status equal with men. We are proud of what the Soviet government has given women: the same right to work as men, equal pay for equal work, and social security. Women have been given every opportunity to get an education, to have a career, and to participate in social and political activities. Without the contribution and selfless work of women, we would not have built a new society nor won the war against fascism.

But over the years of our difficult and heroic history, we failed to pay attention to women's specific rights and needs arising from their role as mother and home-maker, and their indispensable educational function as regards children. Engaged in scientific research, working on construction sites, in production and in the services, and involved in creative activities, women no longer have enough time to perform their everyday duties at home—housework, the upbringing of children and the creation of a good family atmosphere. We have discovered that many of our problems—in children's and young people's behavior, in our morals, culture and in production—are partially caused by the weakening of family ties and slack attitude to family responsibilities. This is a paradoxical result of our sincere and politically justified desire to make women equal with men in everything. Now, in the course of perestroika, we have begun to overcome this shortcoming. That is why we are now holding heated debates in the press, in public organizations, at work and at home, about the question of what we should do to make it possible for women to return to their purely womanly mission.

Another problem is the employment of women in strenuous jobs that are hazardous to their health. This is a legacy of the war in which we lost huge numbers of men and which left us with an acute shortage of labor everywhere, in all spheres of production. We have now begun tackling this problem in earnest.

One of the most urgent social tasks for us—also a major task in the anti-alcohol campaign—is to improve the health of the family and enhance its role in society. We expect women's councils to be very active and take the initiative. They are just getting off the ground and can accomplish a great deal, for no other organization is so closely involved in private life and women's problems as they are.

Further democratization of society, which is the pivot and guarantor of perestroika, is impossible without enhancing the role of women, without women's active and specific involvement, and without their commitment to all our reforming efforts. I am convinced that women's role in our society will steadily grow.

The Union of Socialist Nations—A Unique Formation

We live in a multinational country. This is a factor of its might rather than of its weakness or disintegration. Tsarist Russia was called a prison of nations. The Revolution and socialism have done away with national oppression and inequality, and ensured economic, intellectual and cultural progress for all nations and nationalities. Formerly backward nations have acquired an advanced industry, and a modern social structure. They have risen to the level of modern culture, although some of them previously did not even have alphabets of their own. Every unbiased person is bound to acknowledge the fact that our Party has carried out a tremendous amount of work and has transformed the situation. Its results have enriched Soviet society, and world civilization in general.

All the nations and nationalities who inhabit our country made a contribution to the formation and development of our socialist homeland. Together they defended its freedom, independence, and its revolutionary gains against the invasions of its enemies. If the nationality question had not been solved in principle, the Soviet Union would never have had the social, cultural, economic and defense potential as it has now. Our state would not have survived if the republics had not formed a community based on brotherhood and cooperation, respect and mutual assistance.

All this does not mean, however, that national processes are problem-free. Contradictions are typical of any development, and they occur here as well. Regrettably, we used to stress our really

118

considerable achievements in the solution of the nationality problem, and assessed the situation in high-flown terms. But this is real life with all its diversity and all its difficulties.

The dialectics look like this: the growth of educational and cultural standards, alongside modernization of the economy, leads to the emergence of an intelligentsia in every nation; the growth of national self-consciousness and the growth of a nation's natural interest in its historical roots. This is wonderful. This was the aspiration of the revolutionaries of different nationalities who prepared our revolution, and who set out to build a new society on the ruins of the tsarist empire. It sometimes happens that in the process a certain section of people descend to nationalism. Narrow nationalist views, national rivalry and arrogance emerge.

But this is not the whole point. Still more important are the changes taking place in a society where one generation is replaced by others, and each of them should learn to live in a multi-ethnic state. This does not always come easily. Socialism, which has helped each nation to spread its wings, has all the conditions for solving nationality problems on the basis of equality and cooperation. It is important to act in the spirit of socialist principles, remembering that often the new generations do not even know how their nations have reached such heights. Nobody has told them of how internationalism has been working to their benefit, and for how many years.

Against the background of national strife, which has not spared even the world's most advanced countries, the USSR represents a truly unique example in the history of human civilization. These are the fruits of the nationality policy launched by Lenin. But how difficult it was at the start, how incredibly arduous were the first steps in building a harmonious multi-ethnic state. The Russian nation played an outstanding role in the solution of the nationality question. Many people passed through a kind of renaissance or enlightenment under the Leninist nationality policy and in a very short period of time. And when someone responds to this with nationalist arrogance, withdraws into himself, and tries to pass his own values as being absolute, this is unfair, and cannot be accepted. This always becomes the subject of lively and thorough debates in Soviet society.

Every national culture is a treasure which cannot be lost. But a sound interest in everything valuable which each national culture has should not degenerate into attempts to shut off from the objective processes of interaction and *rapprochement*. It is also dangerous when the attitude of representatives of one nationality toward those of another betrays a lack of respect. I spent many years in the Northern Caucasus, a region inhabited by a host of nationalities. Not only is every town, settlement, or mountain village there inhabited by people of different nationalities, but so, too, is the entire region. The history of the Northern Caucasus contains several gloomy pages, but in the years of Soviet government the situation has radically altered. I would not idealize it, but relations between the nationalities who inhabit that multi-ethnic region are characterized by a respectful attitude, cooperation, *rapprochement* and cohesion. I know from my own experience that highlanders are very responsive to friendship, but at the same time very sensitive to any display of arrogance toward them. I can recall that the Karachai–Cherkess autonomous region—part of the Stavropol Territory—is populated by Karachais, Cherkess, Russians, Abazins, Nogais, Ossetians, Greeks and representatives of other nationalities, and that they all live in harmony with one another. This is so because equality and a fair approach to the solution of all problems form the foundation of their life. Where these principles have at times been departed from, the price has always been high. The cultures of all nationalities are being preserved and developed within this small autonomous region. Their traditions are being taken care of, and literature is being published in their native languages. This does not set them apart, bringing them, rather, closer together. It is not enough to proclaim equality of nations. It is necessary to ensure that all ethnic groups should know a meaningful lifestyle.

I'd like to say once again that if negative phenomena emerge in this highly sensitive sphere of human relations, they emerge not just by themselves, but as a consequence of red tape, and lack of attention to people's lawful rights. There is sometimes heated debate on the development of ethnic languages in this country. What can be said on this score? Even the smallest ethnicity cannot be denied the right to its own mother-tongue. After all, this is human culture in today's diversity, with its numerous languages, attire, rituals and manifestations. This is our common wealth. How can it be ignored? How can one allow it to be underrated?

But at the same time, in our vast multi-ethnic country we cannot

120

do without a common means of communication. The Russian language has naturally come to fulfil this role. Everybody needs this language, and history itself has determined that the objective process of communication develops on the basis of the language of the biggest nation. For example, though representatives of many ethnic groups came together in the United States, English became their common language. Apparently, this was a natural choice. One can imagine what would have happened if members of each nation moving to the US had spoken only their own tongues and refused to learn English! The same applies to this country, where the Russian people have proven by their entire history that they have a tremendous potential for internationalism, respect and good will to all other peoples. Experience has shown that two languages should be studied (apart from a foreign one)—one's mother-tongue and Russian—so as to communicate with others.

Any attempts to fuel passions on ethnic grounds can only complicate a search for reasonable solutions. We are not going to shun this or other problems which may crop up. We shall tackle them in the framework of the democratic process, consolidating our internationalist community of nations.

Lenin taught us to display extreme caution and tact in the nationality issue. There cannot and should not be any stereotyped patterns here. One thing is clear: when the fundamental interests of nations converge, when the principle of equality in everything forms the backbone of relations between peoples—and this is exactly how it is in Soviet society—then any emerging problems and misunderstandings can be settled, even in difficult situations. Of course, there are quite a few people in the West and, for that matter, in the East, who would like to undermine the friendship and cohesion of the peoples of the Soviet Union. But this is an entirely different matter and here Soviet law stands on guard, protecting the accomplishments of Leninist nationality policy.

Proceeding from these positions, we shall remain firmly committed to our principles. National feelings of people should be respected, and cannot be ignored. But speculating on them amounts to political irresponsibility, if not a crime. It is a tradition of our Party to combat any manifestations of nationalist narrow-mindedness and chauvinism, parochialism, Zionism, and anti-Semitism, in whatever forms they may be expressed. We remain committed to this tradition. Our entire experience shows that nationalist attitudes can be effectively countered by consistent internationalism, by internationalist education.

Meeting people during my tours of republics and national regions of the Soviet Union, I see for myself over and over again that they appreciate and take pride in the fact that their nations belong to one big international family, that they are part and parcel of a vast and great power which plays such an important role in mankind's progress. This is exactly what *Soviet* patriotism is all about. We shall continue to strengthen the union and fraternity of free nations in a free country.

Prestige and Trust

Perestroika has embraced all spheres of society. The process of perestroika is developing by solving problems and overcoming difficulties. The Party acts as the initiator and generator of ideas, the organizer and guiding force and, I would say, the guarantor of perestroika in the interests of consolidating socialism, in the interests of the working people. The Party has assumed a truly historic responsibility. In 1917, Lenin said: "Having started a revolution we must go all the way." The same is true for perestroika: the Party will go all the way.

The prestige of and trust in the Party have been growing. Although we are still at a stage of transition from one qualitative state to another, the Party bodies are trying not to assume the duties of economic and administrative organizations. This is far from easy: it seems such a well-trodden path—exert Party pressure and the plan is fulfilled! But the Party's goal is different: above all, to theoretically analyze processes, to sense critical points in the development of contradictions in time, to introduce corrections into strategy and tactics, to elaborate policy and define methods and forms for its realization, to select and place personnel, and to provide for perestroika both organizationally and ideologically. Only the Party could do all this.

Management and economic matters are the job of the government and other organizations that are responsible for these matters. This approach did not appear out of the blue; it was prompted by experience. The Party must do its job. And all others must do theirs. When this doesn't happen, Party guidance, ideological work and work with the cadres prove inadequate.

Our society has developed historically in such a way that everything taking place within the Party finds reflection in our country's life. Official opposition does not exist in our country. This places even greater responsibility on the CPSU as the ruling party. That is why we regard the further development of intra-Party democracy, the strengthening of the principles of collective leadership in work, and broader openness in the Party, too, as a top priority. The Central Committee demands that the people elected to high posts be modest, decent, honest, and intolerant of flattery and toadying. In the Party there can be no one who is beyond criticism or anyone who does not have the right to criticize.

It was clear to us that we had to begin by changing our thinking and mentality, the organization, style and methods of work, that we had to begin with people, above all, with executives.

We have with great resolve embarked on a course aimed at supporting resourceful, thinking and dynamic people capable of self-critically appraising a situation, of getting rid of formalism and dogmatic approaches in work, and of finding new, unorthodox solutions, people who can and want to move forward bodily and who know how to achieve success. Perestroika has given such people a great deal of space for their creative activity.

There is, of course, no need for total restaffing. Nor is that possible, in fact. Of course, there can be some changes in personnel at top and intermediate levels and at the level of a single enterprise as well. We need fresh forces. Indeed, this is already happening. Besides, there is also a natural process that makes itself known: some people have already reached the finishing line in their working life. Some are simply no longer strong enough to shoulder the burden of a new responsibility. That is understandable, and there is no point in being too dramatic about the situation.

Each period has its own demands, its own advanced people, and its own modes of approach. Those who are capable of reorganizing themselves and following new ways in political, organizational and ideological work will work and will have the support of the working people and Party organizations. The bulk of our forces is ready for this, if in different ways: some will accept the new demands more quickly, others may think twice. In principle, we proceed from the assumption that most are capable of resolving the problems of perestroika. And yet we cannot put up with a situation where everything continues to be done in the old way, without acceleration, that is, without going into higher gear.

Perestroika calls for competence and high professionalism. We cannot do without up-to-date and all-round training, without thorough knowledge in the fields of production, science and technology, management, economics, in the organization of work and work incentives, sociology and psychology. In short, we have to bring as much of the nation's intellectual potential as possible into play, and substantially increase its creative efficiency.

I want to emphasize once again the significance of the Party's activity in the realm of theory. There is a vast amount of work going on here as well. But in this area, too, we are striving for greater democracy and we won't allow a monopoly by a single person or group of persons. The Central Committee of the CPSU is calling on all creative forces in the Party and society to become involved in this work. If we allow everything to come from the center, or, worse still, from a single person or group of persons, we would be likely to slip into fossilized thinking. That would be a fatal blow to the program of perestroika, and, for that matter, to the development of society. The history of the CPSU has some sad and bitter lessons in this respect. You cannot have the role of social science and the creative forces in the Party confined to commenting on the decisions or speeches of high-placed individuals. We have chosen a different approach—we shall act in keeping with Lenin's principles and Lenin's traditions.

IV THE WEST AND RESTRUCTURING

We are always interested how perestroika is regarded outside the country, in particular in the West. Not because we are just curious, but because it is our duty as politicians. We see that the process of restructuring is evoking growing interest not only because it is interesting in itself and because it concerns the fate of a great nation. Restructuring in our society is justly regarded as an event of great international consequence. "What is happening in the Soviet Union concerns the whole world," wrote a West European newspaper.

I must note first of all that accompanying the genuine interest in our perestroika among the vast majority of people around the world is optimism and the sincere wish that the changes started in the Soviet Union are successful. The world expects much from our perestroika and is hopeful that it will positively affect the entire course of world developments and international relations as a whole.

As for the official circles and most of the mass media in the West, at first there was very little belief in the feasibility of the reforms we announced in April 1985. Caustic remarks were abundant: it is a change of teams, they said, and so the new team is hurrying to put forward its concepts and programs. It was alleged that Russians were emotional people and used to new leaders laying the present shortcomings at the doors of former leaders, while everything remained as before. With time, they said, criticism will fade away and they will forget about their new undertakings.

But this point of view did not last long. It has become starkly clear that restructuring is a historical reality and that it is gaining in strength. After the January 1987 Plenary Meeting of the CPSU Central Committee it was no longer possible to deny the fact that this country has actually entered a period of bold and far-reaching reforms.

The new motifs became even more pronounced in comments on the June 1987 Plenary Meeting of the Central Committee. They started admitting that the scale and scope of proposed reforms in economic management surpassed the forecasts of most Sovietologists. We see that many in the West did not expect such frank and in-depth discussion, such large-scale constructive measures. The epithet "half-way," which was used to define our activities up to June, seems to have become outmoded when describing the decisions of the June Plenary Meeting and the session of the USSR Supreme Soviet. We went far beyond the "chalk circle" to which the West limited our possibilities and intentions. And even before the Plenary Meeting, there was a wealth of assertions about "Gorbachev's campaign for reforms" losing momentum.

Now they are talking about a "second revolution," about the irreversible nature of restructuring, about our making a "fresh leap" on the basis of newly-established economic and legal reforms. In general, they now have the right feel of the importance of the June Plenary Meeting for the restructuring process. So it became even more necessary to determine an attitude toward restructuring. We are criticized for the pace of restructuring. For being too slow by the "left," and for taking leaps that are too great by the "right." But, it seems, all agree that the Soviet leadership is implementing reforms in earnest.

Western observers want to know about the consequences of restructuring, for the Soviet Union and the world, if the process continues. They want to know what would better suit the West: the success or failure of perestroika?

Evidently, there are several answers to these questions. Many competent specialists admit that social and economic development in Soviet society can be accelerated and that success in the current drive for restructuring will have positive international consequences. They justly reason that the world community can only stand to gain from the growing wellbeing of the Soviet people and further progress of democracy. The scope and scale of the social and economic programs undertaken by the Soviet Union bear evidence of, and offer material guarantees for, its peaceful foreign policy. Hence, a message to the leadership of the Western powers—don't be scared by perestroika, don't make it the subject of a psychological war, but rather promote it through the mechanism of economic ties and cultural and humanitarian exchanges; take seriously the Soviet initiatives for disarmament and an improvement of the international situation, and seek accords on these issues.

Leaving aside many evaluations and estimates that we see as disputable, we, on the whole, regard this position as realistic and welcome its predominantly constructive orientation. It fits into the drive to improve international relations, reflecting public sentiments.

Some politicians display foresight in recognizing that the West would commit a blunder of historic proportions by not responding to Moscow's positive message, by not ridding itself of erroneous views of the Soviet Union and of the hoaxes it has itself created.

But an entirely different idea is also being actively promoted in the Western media and political discussions. Attempts are still being made to discredit our policies and intentions. There have been several pessimistic forecasts and scares concerning dynamism in domestic and foreign policies. This shows, once again, just how strong the Cold War inertia is and how deep go the roots of anti-Sovietism in certain quarters. If it all boiled down to scholastic debates and an exercise in propaganda, one could well ignore it. Indeed, experience will ultimately prove where the truth lies. But the point is that thence comes the opportunity to frighten people with the idea that perestroika may allegedly lead to the growing economic and military capability of the Soviet Union and, therefore, to a growing "Soviet threat." If so, relations with the Soviet Union should be seen in the context of a prospective failure of perestroika and the general aim should be to impede and frustrate it in line with the principle employed by the rabid anti-Sovieteers: "The worse for the USSR, the better for the West."

The extreme right-wing quarters do not attempt to hide their hostile attitudes to perestroika, for it proves that their opinion that socialism has nothing attractive to show the "free world" is wrong. To these people, rejection of the worn-out dogma of Soviet "social immobility" is tantamount to an ideological catastrophe. For they would then have to revise the entire doctrine of anti-Sovietism and the ensuing political directives. The mythical "Soviet threat" that allegedly stems from the fact that the Soviet Union, unable to cope with its internal difficulties, embarks on expansion would vanish into thin air.

They have even tried to discredit openness and democratization. For example, they report false news from the USSR, quoting the Soviet press as the original source. But it soon transpires that nothing of the kind has ever been printed in Soviet publications. By so doing they aim to provoke us into restraining and containing openness and abandoning democratization, to cause us to be irritated with our media. Their goal is to thwart the processes inherent in perestroika and unthinkable without glasnost and democratization.

There have been increasing efforts to sow doubts among our citizens over the correctness of perestroika, and attempts to scare them with difficulties and incite unrealistic expectations. They hope to cause our people's mistrust toward the leadership, set some leaders against others, and split the Party and society.

Some politicians and media, particularly in the United States, have been trying to present perestroika as a drive for "liberalization" caused by Western pressure. Of course, one cannot help paying tribute to Western propaganda officials, who have skilfully played a verbal game of democracy. But we will believe in the democratic nature of Western

127

societies when their workers and office employees start electing the owners of factories and plants, bank presidents, etc., when their media put corporations, banks and their bosses under a barrage of regular criticism and start discussing the real processes inherent in Western countries, rather than only engage in an endless and useless argument with politicians.

Some critics of our reforms say that painful phenomena in the course of perestroika are inevitable. They predict inflation, unemployment, enhanced social stratification, i.e. the things which the West is so "rich" in. Or they suggest that the Central Committee is strongly opposed among Party and government officials. Or they say our army is against restructuring, and the KGB[1] has not had its say yet. They are ready to use anything to achieve their ends.

But I must tell our opponents a few disheartening things: today members of the Politburo and the Central Committee are unanimous as they have never been before, and there is nothing that can make this unanimity waver. Both in the army, in the State Security Committee, and in every other government department, the Party wields the highest authority and has a decisive voice politically. The drive for perestroika has only consolidated the Party's position, adding a new dimension to its moral and political role in society and the state.

However, I will say for the sake of justice that competent Western observers rightly see the socialist nature of our transformations and that they are aimed at consolidating socialism. But those who try to scare the Western public with perestroika are really afraid of its success, if only because it frustrates the chances of using the "Soviet threat" bugbear, of shadowing the real image of our country with a grotesque and ugly "enemy image," of continuing the senseless arms race under demagogic mottoes and waxing rich on it.

Indeed, if our development plans are accomplished successfully, how will they be able to take people in by telling them that socialism is not a viable system able to give its citizens food and clothes? The idea that our country is an "evil empire," the October Revolution a blunder of history and the post-revolutionary period a "zigzag in history," is coming apart at the seams. That kind of perestroika really does not suit some people.

[1] *The KGB*—the State Security Committee under the government of the USSR.

"Today, they recklessly try to slander and besmirch the current reforms in the USSR," wrote the West German magazine *Stern*, "saying that in actual fact they only consolidate the communist system and that the Kremlin wants one single thing—to make the system more efficient. But, by God, if the drive against corruption and poor management, and if greater freedom of thought consolidate the communist system, then, according to this logic, democracy would be the best nutrient medium for Marxism–Leninism!" I would like to add a few words to this eloquent quotation. If socialism is indeed entirely incompatible with democracy and economic efficiency, as its adversaries say, the latter would have no reason to worry about their future and their profits.

And if we criticize ourselves the way nobody has ever criticized us, West, East or anywhere else, that is only because we are strong and we do not fear for our future. We will withstand these criticisms; the people and the Party will withstand them. But when our reforms produce the expected results, then the critics of socialism will also have to undergo a "perestroika."

We have put them in a predicament, because we know our short-comings far better and write and speak about them with greater sincerity and competence than they do. Thus people in the West will gradually stop believing all the nonsense they are told about the Soviet Union. All that hardly promotes trust in the policies of Western countries.

In my discussions with Americans and people from other Western countries, I always ask bluntly if they want the Soviet Union to have a chance to direct more resources to its economic and social development through cuts in its military spending. Or, by contrast, does the West want to overstrain the Soviet Union economically by accelerating the arms race in order to frustrate the formidable work we have started and force the Soviet leadership to allocate more and more resources for unproductive purposes, for armaments? Does the whole idea really boil down to forcing the Soviet Union to focus entirely on domestic problems, thus allowing the West to dominate the rest of the world?

But there is another aspect to this issue. Those hoping to overstrain the Soviet Union seem too presumptuous about their own economic wellbeing. No matter how rich the USA is, it too can ill afford to throw away a third of a trillion dollars a year on armaments. A rise in arms spending triggers increases in the budget deficit. The US today borrows two-thirds of what it spends on arms. The US federal debt is, in fact, the Pentagon's debt, and will have to be repaid by many generations of Americans. There must be an end to the thread somewhere. But, anyway, it is the Americans' own business.

Occasionally I get the impression that some American politicians, while praising the capitalist system and their democracy, are nevertheless not very sure about either, fearing competition with the USSR in conditions of peace. That compels them to insist on having the war machine, whipping up tensions, etc. I feel that some observers will write, upon reading these lines, that, regrettably, Gorbachev has a poor knowledge of Western democracy. Alas, I do know a thing or two, enough anyway to hold a firm trust in socialist democracy and socialist humanism.

We will resolve the issues which we honestly discuss, and we will achieve the goals we have charted. The disposition of our people should also be taken into account. If they have been stung to the quick, so to speak, if their patriotic feelings have been involved, they will spare no effort to achieve their ends and will work wonders in doing so. The Soviet Union is a vast country rich in minerals and skilled manpower, and with great scientific resources. Nearly all workers have a complete secondary education. So do not rush to toss us on the "ash-heap of history"; the idea only makes Soviet people smile.

In my talks with a delegation of the House of Representatives last April, I said that the execution of our plans for renewal posed no threat—either political or economic, or any other—to the American people, or to any country. I said the same thing in the Kremlin in my address to the participants in the Forum for a Nuclear-Free World and the Survival of Humanity: we want to be understood, we hope that the world community will admit that nobody need be a loser and the whole world will gain from our desire to make our country better.

And so, neither the Soviet Union, nor its perestroika pose any threat to anyone, except, perhaps, by setting an example—if someone finds it acceptable. Yet again and again we are accused of wanting to implant communism all over the world. What nonsense! I would not care if these accusations were made by people who do not have too many scruples about what they write to earn their living. But the same things are, to this day, also pronounced publicly by seemingly responsible statesmen. And I was very much surprised to hear it two years after perestroika had been launched from a politician I used to respect. Why, I inquired? We know the Truman, Eisenhower and Reagan doctrines. But nobody has ever heard any statements from us about "implanting communist domination." Lenin said that we, the socialist state, would chiefly influence world development through our economic achievements.

The success of perestroika will show that socialism is not only capable of coping with the historic task of reaching the heights of scientific and technological progress but that it can handle it with a maximum of social and moral efficiency, by the methods of democracy, for the people and thanks to their own efforts, intellect, skills, talents, conscience and awareness of their responsibility to other people.

The success of perestroika will lay bare the class narrow-mindedness and egoism of the forces that are ruling the West today, the forces that are hooked on militarism and the arms race, and that are looking for "enemies" all over the globe.

The success of perestroika will help the developing countries find ways to achieve economic and social modernization without having to make concessions to neocolonialism or throwing themselves into the cauldron of capitalism.

The success of perestroika will be the final argument in the historical dispute as to which system is more consistent with the interests of the people. Rid of the features that appeared in extreme conditions, the image of the Soviet Union will gain a new attractiveness and will become the living embodiment of the advantages that are inherent in the socialist system. The ideals of socialism will gain fresh impetus.

I have on more than one occasion realized that my Western interlocutors grasp this only too well. A Western politician, who is by no means a communist, said: "If you do what you've conceived, this will have fantastic, truly global consequences."

It is probably not easy for a foreign reader to understand many of our difficulties. It is only natural. Each people and each country have a life of their own, their own laws, their own hopes and misconceptions, and their own ideals. Such diversity is wonderful; it needs to be developed, rather than stifled. I, for one, am sick of the attempts by some politicians to teach others how to live and what policy to conduct. They proceed from the arrogant assumption that the life and policy of their own country is an example and a model of freedom, democracy, economic activity and social standard. I think it would be far more democratic to assume that other nations can disagree with this point of view. In our complicated and troubled world it is impossible to measure everything by one's own yardstick. Attempts at military diktat as well as at moral, political and economic pressure are out of fashion today. Moreover, these attempts are dangerous; they irritate the world public, and, consequently, hinder progress toward peace and cooperation.

A correct understanding of perestroika is also the key to comprehending the foreign policy of the Soviet Union. The truth about perestroika accords with the interests of universal peace and international security. Calling upon the West to subject our work to a responsible, honest and unbiased scrutiny, we proceed not only from our own interests. The inability or unwillingness to grasp the essence of perestroika is either a starting point for misconceptions about our intentions in the world arena or another attempt to maintain and deepen mistrust in relations among countries and peoples.

The organic tie between each state's foreign and domestic policies becomes particularly close and practically meaningful at crucial moments. A change in the domestic policy inevitably leads to changes in the attitude to international issues. That is why now, in the conditions of perestroika, the uniformity of our activities at home and in the international arena is more striking and more tangible than ever before. The new concept of the Soviet foreign policy, its guidelines and practical actions are all an immediate projection of the philosophy, program and practice of restructuring.

The process of perestroika in the Soviet Union holds out fresh opportunities for international cooperation. Unbiased observers predict growth in the Soviet Union's share of the world economy and invigoration of foreign economic, scientific and technological ties, including those maintained through international economic organizations.

We are saying openly for all to hear: we need lasting peace in order to concentrate on the development of our society and to cope with the tasks of improving the life of the Soviet people. Ours are long-term and fundamental plans. That is why everyone, our Western partner–rivals included, must realize that our international policy of building a nuclear-weapon-free and non-violent world and asserting civilized standards in interstate relations is equally fundamental and equally trustworthy in its underlying principles.

132

PART TWO

New Thinking and the World

3

How We See the World of Today

Where We Are

We started perestroika in a situation of growing international tension. The *détente* of the 1970s was, in effect, curtailed. Our calls for peace found no response in the ruling quarters of the West. Soviet foreign policy was skidding. The arms race was spiraling anew. The war threat was increasing.

In ascertaining how to achieve a turn for the better, one had to ask the following questions. Why is this happening? What juncture has the world approached in its development? To do this we had to cast a sober and realistic glance at the world panorama, to get rid of the force of habit in our thinking. As we say in Russia, to look at things "with a fresh eye."

What is the world we all live in like, this world of the present generations of humankind? It is diverse, variegated, dynamic and permeated with opposing trends and acute contradictions. It is a world of fundamental social shifts, of an all-embracing scientific and technological revolution, of worsening global problems—problems concerning ecology, natural resources, etc.—and of radical changes in information technology. It is a world in which unheard-of possibilities for development and progress lie side by side with abject poverty, backwardness and medievalism. It is a world in which there are vast "fields of tension."

Everything was a great deal simpler many years ago. There existed several powers which determined their interests and balanced them if they so managed, and warred if they failed. International relations were built on the balance of the interests of these several powers. This is one domain, that is another, and that one is still another. But have a look at what has happened over the forty postwar years to the present.

The political tableau of the world includes the sizable group of socialist countries which have gone a long way in their progressive development over not so long a history; the vast tract of developed capitalist states with their own interests, with their own history, concerns and problems; and the ocean of Third World countries which emerged in the past thirty to forty years when scores of Asian, African and Latin American countries gained independence.

It seems obvious that every group of states and every country has interests of its own. From the viewpoint of elementary logic, all these interests should find a reasonable reflection in world politics. But this is not so. I have more than once told my interlocutors from the capitalist countries: let us see and take into account the realities— there is the world of capitalism and the world of socialism, and there is also a huge world of developing countries. The latter is the home of millions of people. All countries have their problems. But the developing countries have a hundred times more than other states and this should be taken into consideration. These countries have their own national interests. For decades they were colonies, stubbornly fighting for their liberation. Having gained independence, they want to improve their peoples' life, to use their resources as they like, and to build an independent economy and culture.

Is there a hope for normal and just international relations, proceeding exclusively from the interests of, say, the Soviet Union or the United States, Britain or Japan? No! A balance of interests is needed. For the time being, no such balance exists. For now the rich get richer and the poor get poorer. Processes which could shake the entire system of international relations are, however, taking place in the Third World.

No one can close down the world of socialism, the developing world or the world of developed capitalism. But there exists the view that socialism is an accident of history and one long overdue for the ash-heap. Then the Third World would become tame and everything would return full cycle, and prosperity would again be possible at the expense of others. An escape into the past is no reply to the challenges of the future, being merely adventurism based on fear and diffidence.

136

And we have not only read anew the reality of a multi-colored and multi-dimensional world. We have assessed not only the difference in the interests of individual states. We have seen the main issue—the growing tendency towards interdependence of the states of the world community. Such are the dialectics of present-day development. The world—contradictory, socially and politically diverse, but none-theless interconnected and largely integral—is forming with great difficulties, as if it is feeling its way through a conflict of opposites.

Another no less obvious reality of our time is the emergence and aggravation of the so-called global issues which have also become vital to the destinies of civilization. I mean nature conservation, the critical condition of the environment, of the air basin and the oceans, and of our planet's traditional resources which have turned out not to be limitless. I mean old and new awful diseases and mankind's common concern: how are we to put an end to starvation and poverty in vast areas of the Earth? I mean the intelligent joint work in exploring outer space and the world ocean and the use of the knowledge obtained to the benefit of humanity.

I could say a lot about the work we do at a national level in our country to help resolve these problems. I touched upon them to a certain extent when I discussed our perestroika. We will do whatever depends on us.

But the Soviet Union alone cannot resolve all these issues. And we are not ashamed to repeat this, calling for international cooperation. We say with full responsibility, casting away the false considerations of "prestige," that all of us in the present-day world are coming to depend more and more on one another and are becoming increasingly necessary to one another. And since such realities exist in the world and since we know that we in this world are, on the whole, now linked by the same destiny, that we live on the same planet, use its resources and see that they are not limitless and need to be saved, and nature and the environment need to be conserved, then such a reality holds for all of us. The necessity of effective, fair, international procedures and mechanisms which would ensure rational utilization of our planet's resources as the property of all mankind becomes ever more pressing.

And here we see our interdependence, the integrity of the world, the imperative need for pooling the efforts of humanity for the sake of its self-preservation, for its benefit today, tomorrow and for all time.

137

Last but not least, there is one more reality which we must recognize. Having entered the nuclear age when the energy of the atom is used for military purposes, mankind has lost its immortality. In the past, there were wars, frightful wars which took millions upon millions of human lives, turned cities and villages into ruins and ashes and destroyed entire nations and cultures. But the continuation of human-kind was not threatened. By contrast, now, if a nuclear war breaks out, every living thing will be wiped off the face of the Earth.

Even what is logically impossible, namely, that mankind can be annihilated many times over, has now become technically possible. The existing nuclear arsenals are so great that for every inhabitant of the Earth there is a charge capable of incinerating a huge area. Today, just one strategic submarine carries a destructive potential equal to several Second World Wars. And there are dozens of such submarines!

The arms race, just like nuclear war, is unwinnable. Continuing such a race on the Earth, and extending it into space, would accelerate the accumulation and modernization of nuclear weapons, the rate of which is already feverish. The world situation can become such that it would no longer depend on politicians but would become captive to chance. All of us face the need to learn to live at peace in this world, to work out a new mode of thinking, for conditions today are quite different from what they were even three or four decades ago.

The time is ripe for abandoning views on foreign policy which are influenced by an imperial standpoint. Neither the Soviet Union nor the United States is able to force its will on others. It is possible to suppress, compel, bribe, break or blast, but only for a certain period. From the point of view of long-term, big-time politics, no one will be able to subordinate others. That is why only one thing—relations of equality—remains. All of us must realize this. Along with the above-said realities of nuclear weapons, ecology, the scientific and techno-logical revolution, and informatics, this also obliges us to respect one another and everybody.

Such is our world—complex but not hopeless. We hold the view that everything can be resolved but everyone should rethink his role in this world and behave responsibly.

New Political Thinking

In the two and a half years which have passed since April 1985, we have gone a long way in comprehending the world situation and ways to change it for the better. I shall also write about the practical moves which we have made with a view to radically improving the international atmosphere. But now to the most important point.

Having adopted at the 27th Congress the concept of a contradictory but interconnected, interdependent and, essentially, integral world, we began to build our foreign policy on this foundation. Yes, we remain different as far as our social system, ideological and religious views and way of life are concerned. To be sure, distinctions will remain. But should we duel because of them? Would it not be more correct to step over the things that divide us for the sake of the interests of all mankind, for the sake of life on Earth? We have made our choice, asserting a new political outlook both by binding statements and by specific actions and deeds.

People are tired of tension and confrontation. They prefer a search for a more secure and reliable world, a world in which everyone would preserve their own philosophic, political and ideological views and their way of life.

We are looking at what is taking place with open eyes. We see that stereotypes persist and that the old outlooks have struck deep roots, nourishing militarism and imperial ambitions according to which other countries are regarded as targets for one's political and other activities and are deprived of the right to independent choice and independent foreign policy.

We do not propose to offer any super-radical methods for solving various regional problems, although such methods are also necessary in some instances. We do not wish to handle international affairs in a manner that would heighten confrontation. While we do not approve the character of current relations between the West and the developing countries, we do not urge that they should be disrupted. We believe these relations should be transformed by ridding them of neocolonialism, which differs from the old colonialism only in that its mechanism

139

of exploitation is more sophisticated. Conditions are required in which the developing countries can be masters of their own natural and human resources and can use them for their own good, rather than for somebody else's.

Normalization of international relations in the economic, information and ecological areas should be based on broad internationalization. By all indications, the West would like to keep things in the family, so to speak, within the Sevens, the Fives and the like. This probably explains the attempts to discredit the United Nations. It is alleged, for instance, that the UN is losing its meaning and that it is almost disintegrating. And this is said today, when there are so many changes in a world saturated with the diverse interests of numerous states and when finding a balance of these interests is a priority. In the circumstances, the role of the United Nations with its experience of streamlining international cooperation is more important than ever before.

It is true that the efforts of the United Nations have not always been successful. But, in my view, this organization is the most appropriate forum for seeking a balance of the interests of states, which is essential for the stability of the world.

I realize that everything cannot change overnight. I also realize that the West and we shall continue to have different approaches to specific situations. And, still, as I have already said, the nations of the world resemble today a pack of mountaineers tied together by a climbing rope. They can either climb on together to the mountain peak or fall together into an abyss. In order to prevent disaster, political leaders should rise above their narrow interests and realize the drama of the situation. That is why the need for a new comprehension of the situation and of its complacent factors is so urgent today.

It is no longer possible to draft a policy on the premises of the year 1947, the Truman doctrine and Churchill's Fulton speech. It is necessary to think and act in a new way. What is more, history cannot wait; people cannot afford to waste time. It may be too late tomorrow, and the day after tomorrow may never come.

The fundamental principle of the new political outlook is very simple: *nuclear war cannot be a means of achieving political, economic, ideological or any other goals*. This conclusion is truly revolutionary, for it means discarding the traditional notions of war and peace. It is the political function of war that has always been a justification for war, a "rational" explanation. Nuclear war is senseless; it is irrational. There would be neither winners nor losers in a global nuclear conflict: world civilization would inevitably perish. It is a suicide, rather than a war in the conventional sense of the word.

But military technology has developed to such an extent that even a non-nuclear war would now be comparable with a nuclear war in its destructive effect. That is why it is logical to include in our category of nuclear wars this "variant" of an armed clash between major powers as well.

Thereby, an altogether different situation has emerged. A way of thinking and a way of acting, based on the use of force in world politics, have formed over centuries, even millennia. It seems they have taken root as something unshakable. Today, they have lost all reasonable grounds. Clausewitz's dictum that war is the continuation of policy only by different means, which was classical in his time, has grown hopelessly out of date. It now belongs to the libraries. For the first time in history, basing international politics on moral and ethical norms that are common to all humankind, as well as humanizing interstate relations, has become a vital requirement.

A new dialectic of strength and security follows from the impossibility of a military—that is, nuclear—solution to international differences. Security can no longer be assured by military means—neither by the use of arms or deterrence, nor by continued perfection of the "sword" and the "shield." Attempts to achieve military superiority are preposterous. Now such attempts are being made in space. It is an astonishing anachronism which persists due to the inflated role played by militarists in politics. From the security point of view the arms race has become an absurdity because its very logic leads to the destabilization of international relations and eventually to a nuclear conflict. Diverting huge resources from other priorities, the arms race is lowering the level of security, impairing it. It is in itself an enemy of peace. The only way to security is through political decisions and disarmament. In our age genuine and equal security can be guaranteed by constantly lowering the level of the strategic balance from which nuclear and other weapons of mass destruction should be completely eliminated.

141

Perhaps this frightens some people. "What is to be done with the military-industrial complex then?" they ask. The jobs and wages of so many people are involved. This issue was specially analyzed in one of the most recent works of Nobel Prize laureate V. Leontyev, and he has proved that the militarists' arguments do not hold water from an economic standpoint. This is what I think: to begin with, each job in the military-industrial complex costs two or three times more than one in a civilian industry. Three jobs could be created instead. Secondly, even today sectors of the military economy are connected with the civilian economy, doing much for the latter. So, this is a starting point for utilizing their possibilities for peaceful purposes. Thirdly, the USSR and the USA could come up with large joint programs, pooling our resources and our scientific and intellectual potentials in order to solve the most diverse problems for the benefit of humankind.

The new political outlook calls for the recognition of one more simple axiom: security is indivisible. It is either equal security for all or none at all. The only solid foundation for security is the recognition of the interests of all peoples and countries and of their equality in international affairs. The security of each nation should be coupled with the security for all members of the world community. Would it, for instance, be in the interest of the United States if the Soviet Union found itself in a situation whereby it considered it had less security than the USA? Or would we benefit by a reverse situation? I can say firmly that we would not like this. So, adversaries must become partners and start looking jointly for a way to achieve universal security.

We can see the first signs of new thinking in many countries, in different strata of society. And this is only natural, because it is the way of mutually advantageous agreements and reciprocal compromises on the basis of the supreme common interest—preventing a nuclear catastrophe. Consequently, there should be no striving for security for oneself at the expense of others.

The new outlooks influence equally strongly the character of military doctrines. Those should be strictly the doctrines of defense. And this is connected with such new or comparatively new notions as the reasonable sufficiency of armaments, non-aggressive defense, the elimination of disbalance and asymmetries in various types of armed forces, separation of the offensive forces of the two blocs, and so on and so forth.[1]

Universal security in our time rests on the recognition of the right of every nation to choose its own path of social development, on the renunciation of interference in the domestic affairs of other states, on respect for others in combination with an objective self-critical view of one's own society. A nation may choose either capitalism or socialism. This is its sovereign right. Nations cannot and should not pattern their life either after the United States or the Soviet Union. Hence, political positions should be devoid of ideological intolerance.

Ideological differences should not be transferred to the sphere of interstate relations, nor should foreign policy be subordinate to them, for ideologies may be poles apart, whereas the interest of survival and prevention of war stand universal and supreme.

On a par with the nuclear threat, the new political mode of thinking considers the solution of other global problems, including those of economic development and ecology, as an indispensable condition for assuring a lasting and just peace. To think in a new way also means to see a direct link between disarmament and development.

We stand for the internationalization of the efforts to turn disarmament into a factor of development. In a message to the International Conference on this subject in New York in late August 1987, I wrote: "The implementation of the basic principle 'disarmament for development' can and must rally mankind, and facilitate the formation of a global consciousness."

The Delhi Declaration on Principles for a Nuclear-Weapon-Free

---

[1] Europe's socialist nations have resolutely embarked on this course. On 29 May 1987, in Berlin, a meeting of the Political Consultative Committee adopted a document of principled importance "On the Military Doctrine of the Warsaw Treaty Member-Countries." The document lays down the essence of the purely defensive character of this doctrine. "Never, and under no circumstance," it says, "shall we begin hostilities against any state or any alliance of states unless we ourselves come under an armed attack. We shall never be the first to use nuclear weapons. We have no territorial claims to any state either in Europe or outside it. The Warsaw Treaty member-countries do not look on any state or any people as an enemy: they are prepared to build relations with all countries without exception, on the basis of mutual consideration for the interests of security and peaceful coexistence."

The Warsaw Treaty countries do not strive to have more armed forces and armaments than is necessary for purposes of defense. They will strictly adhere to the principle of sufficiency in protecting their security. They have proposed to the NATO countries that everyone sits down together and compares the military doctrines of the two alliances in order to better understand each other's intentions. The answer to that proposal was silence.

and Non-Violent World, which was signed by Prime Minister Rajiv Gandhi of the Republic of India and myself in November 1986, contains words which I'd like to cite here as well: "In the nuclear age, humanity must evolve a new mode of political thought, a new concept of the world that would provide reliable guarantees for humanity's survival. People want to live in a safer and a more just world. Humanity deserves a better fate than being a hostage to nuclear terror and despair. It is necessary to change the existing world situation and to build a nuclear-weapon-free world, free of violence and hatred, fear and suspicion."

There are serious signs that the new way of thinking is taking shape, that people are coming to understand what brink the world has approached. But this process is a very difficult one. And the most difficult thing is to ensure that this understanding is reflected in the actions of the policy-makers, in their minds. But I believe that the new political mentality will force its way through, for it was born of the realities of our time.

Our Road to a New Outlook

We do not claim to be able to teach others. Having heard endless instructions from others, we have come to the conclusion that this is a useless pastime. Primarily, life itself teaches people to think in a new way. We ourselves have come gradually to it, mastering it stage by stage, reconsidering our customary views on the problems of war and peace, on relationships between the two systems, and pondering over global problems.

It was a long road. Thirty-odd years ago, the 20th CPSU Congress reached an important conclusion, to the effect that a new world war was not inevitable, and could be prevented. This implied that a future conflict could not just be postponed, and a "peaceful respite" prolonged, but that any international crisis could be settled by peaceful means. Our Party proclaimed its conviction in the possibility and necessity of eliminating the threat of war as such, of banishing war from the life of mankind. It was declared then that war is by no means an indispensable prerequisite for social revolutions. The principle of

144

peaceful coexistence was refined, with account taken of the changes brought about by the Second World War.

In the years of *détente* we tried to fill this principle with a concrete content on the basis of equitable international dialogue and co-operation. Those years saw the conclusion of a number of important treaties completing the "postwar" period in Europe, and an improvement in Soviet–American relations which influenced the entire world situation.

The very logic of *détente* was being prompted by the increasing realization that a nuclear war cannot be won. Proceeding from this fact, we declared five years ago to the whole world that we shall never be the first to use nuclear weapons.

A far-reaching conceptual turning-point was reached at the April 1985 Plenary Meeting of the CPSU Central Committee, and the 27th CPSU Congress. This was, to be precise, a turning towards a new way of political thinking, to new ideas about the correlation between class principles and principles common to humanity in the modern world.

A new way of thinking is not an improvization, nor a mental exercise. It is a result of serious reflections on the realities of today's world, of the understanding that a responsible attitude to policy demands scientific substantiation, and that some of the postulates which seemed unshakable before should be given up. A biased approach, *ad hoc* decisions for the sake of transient goals, and departures from a strictly scientific analysis of the situation cost us dear.

It can be said that we have conceived the new mentality through suffering. And we draw inspiration from Lenin. Turning to him, and "reading" his works each time in a new way, one is struck by his ability to get at the root of things, to see the most intricate dialectics of world processes. Being the leader of the party of the proletariat, and theoretically and politically substantiating the latter's revolutionary tasks, Lenin could see further, he could go beyond their class-imposed limits. More than once he spoke about the priority of interests common to all humanity over class interests. It is only now that we have come to comprehend the entire depth and significance of these ideas. It is they that are feeding our philosophy of international relations, and the new way of thinking.

One may argue that philosophers and theologists throughout history have dealt with the ideas of "eternal" human values. True, this is so, but then these were "scholastic speculations" doomed to be a utopian dream. In the 1980s, as we approach the end of this dramatic century, mankind should acknowledge the vital necessity of human values, and their priority.

Since time immemorial, class interests were the cornerstone of both foreign and domestic policies. It goes without saying that officially they were, as a rule, presented as the interests of a nation, state or alliance, and were covered up with references to the "universal wellbeing," or religious motives. However, Marxists and a good many other sober-minded people are convinced that in the final analysis the policy of any state or alliance of states is determined by the interests of prevailing socio–political forces. Acute clashes of these interests in the international arena have led to armed conflicts and wars throughout history. This is why the political record of mankind is largely a record of wars. Today, this tradition is leading directly into the nuclear abyss. We—all mankind—are in the same boat, and we can sink or swim only together. This is why disarmament talks are not a game which can be won by one side. All should win, or else all stand to lose.

The backbone of the new way of thinking is the recognition of the priority of human values, or, to be more precise, of humankind's survival.

It may seem strange to some people that the communists should place such a strong emphasis on human interests and values. Indeed, a class-motivated approach to all phenomena of social life is the ABC of Marxism. Today, too, such an approach fully meets the realities of a class-based society, a society with opposing class interests, as well as the realities of international life which are also permeated by the opposition. And up to the most recent time class struggle remained the pivot of social development, and still remains as such in class-divided countries. Correspondingly, Marxist philosophy was dominated— as regards the main questions of social life—by a class-motivated approach. Humanitarian notions were viewed as a function and the end result of the struggle of the working class—the last class which, ridding itself, rids the entire society of class antagonisms.

But now, with the emergence of weapons of mass, that is, universal destruction, there appeared an objective limit for class confrontation in the international arena: the threat of universal destruction. For the

146

first time ever there emerged a real, not speculative and remote, common human interest—to save humanity from disaster.

Changes were introduced in the spirit of the new outlook into the new edition of the CPSU Program adopted by the 27th Party Congress. Specifically, we deemed it no longer possible to retain in it the definition of peaceful coexistence of states with different social systems as a "specific form of class struggle."

It was an accepted belief that the source of world wars lay in contradictions between the two social systems. Before 1917, there was only one system in the world—capitalism—but it did not prevent world war between states belonging to that same system. There were other wars, too. And vice versa; during the Second World War, countries representing different systems fought in one coalition against fascism and eventually crushed it. The common interest of all peoples and states before the fascist menace outweighed the socio–political differences among them and provided a foundation for an anti-fascist, "supra-system" coalition. This means that today, too, in the face of a still worse danger, states belonging to different social systems can and must cooperate with one another in the name of peace.

In developing our philosophy of peace, we have taken a new look at the interdependence of war and revolution. In the past, war often served to detonate revolution. One may recall the Paris Commune which came as an echo of the Franco–Prussian war, or the 1905 Russian Revolution triggered by the Russo–Japanese war. The First World War provoked a real revolutionary storm which culminated in the October Revolution in our country. The Second World War evoked a fresh wave of revolutions in Eastern Europe and Asia, as well as a powerful anti-colonial revolution.

All this served to reinforce the Marxist–Leninist logic that imperialism inevitably generates major armed confrontations, while the latter naturally creates a "critical mass" of social discontent and a revolutionary situation in a number of countries. Hence a forecast which was long adhered to in our country: a third world war, if unleashed by imperialism, would lead to new social upheavals which would finish off the capitalist system for good, and this would spell global peace.

But when the conditions radically changed so that the only result of nuclear war could be universal destruction, we drew a conclusion about the disappearance of the cause-and-effect relationship between

147

war and revolution. The prospects of social progress "coincided" with the prospects of the prevention of nuclear war. At the 27th CPSU Congress we clearly "divorced" the revolution and war themes, excluding from the new edition of the Party Program the following two phrases: "Should the imperialist aggressors nevertheless venture to start a new world war, the peoples will no longer tolerate a system which drags them into devastating wars. They will sweep imperialism away and bury it." This provision admitting, in theory, the possibility of a new world war was removed as not corresponding to the realities of the nuclear era.

Economic, political and ideological competition between capitalist and socialist countries is inevitable. However, it can and must be kept within a framework of peaceful competition which necessarily envisages cooperation. It is up to history to judge the merits of each particular system. It will sort out everything. Let every nation decide which system and which ideology is better. Let this be decided by peaceful competition, let each system prove its ability to meet man's needs and interests. The states and peoples of the Earth are very different, and it is actually good that they are so. This is an incentive for competition. This understanding, of a dialectical unity of opposites, fits into the concept of peaceful coexistence.

Such are, in general outline, the main stages of our passage to a new philosophy of peace and to the comprehension of new dialectics of the common human and class interests and principles in our modern epoch.

Does this imply that we have given up the class analysis of the causes of the nuclear threat and of other global problems? No. It would be wrong to ignore the class heterogeneity of the forces acting in the international arena or to overlook the influence of class antagonism on international affairs and on the approaches to the accomplishment of all other tasks of mankind.

We see how strong the positions of the aggressive and militarist part of the ruling class are in the leading capitalist countries. Their main support comes from the powerful military–industrial complex whose interests are rooted in the very nature of the capitalist system and which extracts huge profits from arms production at the tax-payers' expense. And to make the people believe that all that money is not being spent in vain, they must be convinced of the existence of an "external enemy" which wishes to encroach upon their wellbeing and "national interests" in general. Hence the reckless and irresponsible power politics. How can this total reliance on strength be possible in our nuclear age when the existing stocks of weapons are so huge that even a minor part of these weapons can easily annihilate mankind? This is exactly what we call a mentality of the notorious "Cold War." This mentality, however, is still embedded in concrete economic interests of the arms corporations and in the influence on the policy wielded by the army, which refuses to give up its privileged position, and by the bureaucratic machinery serving militarism.

One might ask why we maintain and modernize our weapons and armed forces. I can give an accurate answer to this because I am Chairman of the Soviet Union's Defense Council. Ever since the October Revolution, we have been under permanent threat of potential aggression. Try getting in our shoes and see for yourself. A civil war with foreign forces involved, intervention by fourteen states, an economic blockade and cordon sanitaire, no diplomatic recognition (by the US up to 1933), armed provocations in the East and, finally, a devastating and bloody war against fascism which came from the West. Nor can we forget the plans for an atomic attack on the Soviet Union by the American military and the National Security Council. We also ask why the West was the first to set up a military alliance, NATO, and is always the first to develop new weapons systems. Or, why does the incumbent US Administration not want to stop nuclear arms testing and why is it pressing the Americans to squander colossal sums on the Star Wars program? These are not idle questions. Can all these facts be classified as peaceful aspirations? I repeat, try getting in our shoes and see how you would react.

For all that, we are sincerely prepared for disarmament, but only on a fair basis of equal security, and for cooperation along a very broad front. However, bearing in mind the bitter lessons of the past, we cannot take major unilateral steps for fear that they may serve as a temptation for the advocates of "global national interests." In our opinion, the most important thing to do now is to set the mechanism of humankind's self-preservation into motion and to bolster the potential of peace, reason and good will.

The "Hand of Moscow"

Probably the most hackneyed statement by a Soviet leader in the West is the angry exclamation by Nikita Khrushchev: "We will bury you!" It should be explained for the sake of foreign readers that in the late 1920s and early 1930s we had heated debates between farming experts and scientists which were described with bitter irony as a dispute on "who will bury whom." Khrushchev's exclamation, borrowed from these debates, was unfortunate in all respects, but it must be viewed in the context of his whole speech. It should not be taken literally. He was describing the competition between the two systems, and wanted to show that socialism does not fear being compared to capitalism, and that the future belongs to socialism. Khrushchev was an emotional man, and took it very much to heart that his sincere efforts and specific proposals to improve the international situation came up against a brick wall of incomprehension and resistance.

Let me tell you, this time from my own experience, that to negotiate with the West on disarmament problems one must have incredible patience, because economic interests are always involved. It should probably be added, too, that if we in the Soviet Union judged the policy of another state by individual statements made by its leaders, it would long since have been time to start shooting. But this does not happen. So people in the West must stop exploiting those few words by one who is no longer among the living, and must not present them as our position.

As for the mysterious White House book of quotations to which the West refers, deliberating about Lenin's "doctrine" of imposing communism throughout the world and plans for subduing the whole of Europe, I must say that no such doctrine was ever entertained by Marx, Lenin or any of the Soviet leaders. The so-called "quotations" sometimes used by high-ranking speakers are the fruit of crude falsification or at best ignorance.

This is what I want to say about the notorious "hand of Moscow." In accordance with Marxist theory, the future belongs to a society where there is no exploitation of man by man and no national and racial oppression. The future belongs to a society governed by principles of social justice, freedom and harmonious development of the individual. But every nation has the right to decide whether these principles are good for it and whether it wants to adopt them in restructuring its life. If it does, it is up to it to decide how fast and in what form it should do so.

"The victorious proletariat cannot impose on any other nation its own ideal of a happy life without doing damage to its own victory." This statement by Marx is an accurate definition of our attitude to all kinds of "exports of revolution." Revolutions, Lenin said, "ripen when millions of people realize that they can no longer live the old way." They "ripen in the process of historical development and break out when a certain combination of internal and external conditions arises." Any attempts to make a revolution "to order" or set a date for it were condemned by Lenin as "charlatanism."

The theory we call scientific socialism says that human society passes certain stages in its development. There was primitive society, then the slave-owning system and then feudalism. Feudalism gave way to capitalism and the twentieth century saw the birth of socialist society. We are convinced that these are natural steps on one historical ladder. This is the inevitable evolution of the world. Let the West think that capitalism is the highest achievement of civilization. It's their prerogative to think so. We simply do not agree with this. And let history decide who is right.

Revolutions and liberation movements emerge on national soil. And they arise when poverty and oppression of the masses become intolerable, when national dignity is humiliated and when a nation is denied the right to decide its own destiny itself. If the masses rise to struggle, it means that their vital rights are suppressed. And someone else's ambitions or a "hand of Moscow" have nothing to do with this. In short, this myth is a malicious lie.

International Implications of New Thinking

We do not consider new thinking as something fixed once and for all. We do not think that we have found the final truth which the

151

others merely have to accept or reject, that is, take a position which we would call erroneous. This is not so. For us, too, new thinking is a process in the course of which we continue to learn and gain ever new experience. Lenin said that even seventy Marxes would not be enough to analyze all the interrelated processes in world economy. Since then the world has become much more complex. The development of a new mode of thinking requires dialaogue not only with people who hold the same views but also with those who think differently and represent a philosophical and political system that is different from ours. For they also carry the historical experience, culture and traditions of their peoples; they are all part of world development and are entitled to their own opinion and to an active role in world politics. I am convinced that today's politicians must be aware of the intellectual potential of other countries and peoples, for otherwise their activities will be doomed to provincialism and a narrow national view, if not worse.

That is why we stand for a broad dialogue, for the comparison of views and for debate and discussion. This stimulates thought and prevents people from falling into the conventional ruts of thinking. The main thing, however, is that this helps internationalize the new mode of thinking.

Dialogue between people "from different worlds," people of different walks of life and with different views, is especially important. If they are united by a common concern for humankind's future, the disputes and numerous controversies between them do not prevent them from finding points of contact and coming to terms on the main issues. This is a good example for the whole world.

One can see this particularly clearly during meetings of scientists, writers and cultural personalities. Sincerity and competence characterize their concern and anxiety for the world's future, for man's destiny and potential, as well as their moral strength and their suffering for all those still living in conditions unfit for man. This is extremely important in an age when science and human intellect are unraveling the most obscure mysteries of Nature and life and are virtually determining the course of history. I would therefore say that the informal and lively dialogue of politicians, scientists and cultural personalities is an imperative.

The meetings with such people not only enrich one's theory and philosophy, but have also influenced the political moves and decisions that had to be taken in recent years. I well remember my meeting in November 1985 with a delegation from a Nobel Prize-winners' congress—George Wald (USA), Teo Knippenberg and Susan Gabrielle (Holland), Alois Anglaender (Austria) and Alexander Prokhorov (USSR). This meeting was also attended by Academicians Anatoly Alexandrov and Yevgeny Velikhov. Our discussion took place shortly before I went to Geneva for my first meeting with President Reagan. The scientists handed me an appeal from the participants in their congress and we had a very serious discussion about the possible consequences of the use of nuclear weapons, the importance of banning nuclear tests and the danger of militarizing space. We agreed that efforts for security through disarmament should be combined with efforts to guarantee man decent conditions of existence.

I remember the Nobel Prize winners saying that today it takes more courage to safeguard peace than prepare for war. That meeting gave the moral support for the stands we planned to take at the meeting with the US President.

Take another example. At the Moscow International Forum "For a Nuclear-Weapon-Free World and the Survival of Humanity"—a meeting unprecedented in the number of participants and their authority—I had the opportunity to feel the moods and hear the thoughts and ideas of an international intellectual élite. My discussions with them made a great impression on me. I discussed the results of the congress with my colleagues in the Politburo and we decided to make a major new compromise—untie the Reykjavik package and separate the problem of medium-range missiles in Europe from the other issues.

Yet another example. The Soviet Union repeatedly extended its unilateral moratorium on nuclear explosions. This, I should say, was the result of a serious study of numerous appeals to the Soviet leadership from various intellectuals from other countries. We took their worries and arguments seriously because we realized that responsible policy must take into account the opinion of what may be called the most authoritative part of the public. I think that a policy which does not display concern for mankind's future—and this concern should be a distinguishing mark of any true intellectual—is immoral and does not deserve respect.

A deep impression concerning the new outlook was made by the Issyk-Kul forum, which was attended by world-renowned cultural personalities invited there by Soviet writer Chinghiz Aitmatov. I met with them. The main theme of our discussion was humanism and politics, and the moral and intellectual aspect of political activities in the nuclear age. I said at the meeting that nations had learned from their past tragedies, had summoned their strength and collected their thoughts, and, overcoming hardships, difficulties and losses, rose again and moved ahead, each choosing its own way. What will happen if we fail to ward off the nuclear threat looming over our common home? I am afraid we won't be able to correct such a mistake. This is our most important task. That is why the intellectual and moral potential of the world's culture must be put at the service of politics.

The International Physicians for the Prevention of Nuclear War has come to exercise a tremendous influence on world public opinion within quite a short period of time. It was launched by American Professor Bernard Lown and our Soviet Academician Yevgeny Chazov. Tens of thousands of physicians from the Americas, Europe, Asia, Africa and Australia have joined it. I had met Professor Lown before, but this time, after their congress in Moscow, I met all the leaders of the movement. It is impossible to ignore what these people are saying. What they are doing commands great respect. For what they say and what they do is prompted by accurate knowledge and a passionate desire to warn humanity about the danger looming over it.

In the light of their arguments and the strictly scientific data which they possess, there seems to be no room left for politicking. And no serious politician has the right to disregard their conclusions or neglect the ideas by which they take world public opinion a stage ahead.

As far as the Soviet leadership is concerned, I must say we are eager to know the opinion (and even criticism) of all the different types of people in our world today. In our contact with them, we check out the potential of the new way of thinking and the realism of our policy. Now, whatever similarity and sometimes identity of views we discover through this contact provide evidence for us to see that our new modes of approach follow the same course as does the quest of the honest-thinking part of humanity.

It is natural for me as a communist to stay constantly in touch with the representatives of the communist movement in foreign countries.

Much has changed in these contacts in the past years. We are moving away from inter-party diplomacy which sometimes sugar-coated the truth or, worse still, dealt in Aesopian fables.

No matter what the opponents of communism think, communism originated and exists in the interests of man and his freedom, in order to defend his genuine rights, and justice on earth. Communism has a tremendous potential for humanitarianism. That is why our shared world outlook, and the ideas, assessments, considerations and mutual benevolent criticism, which we exchange with our friends in spirit, are indispensable. They help to develop a new way of thinking and to apply politically the rich accumulation of international experience which reflects the interests and sentiments of the working people.

We see the intensified international contacts between scientists, cultural personalities and intellectuals in general, and their professional movements, as an attempt to bring the best forces of their nations and peoples into their ranks, help them understand the contemporary world and express their opinion about its future so as to prevent the ultimate disaster.

This applies not only to disarmament, demilitarization of individual attitudes and of society itself, but also to such problems of common concern to humanity as the ecological danger, the energy and resource prospects, health care, education, foodstuffs, population growth, information aggression, etc. We find very many points of contact and very many useful things through exchanges with men of science and culture and authoritative members of the public on all of these matters.

I would say it has become imperative for politicians and representatives of science and culture to meet and keep up an exchange of views —it would seem this must become a natural thing for them to want in the present conditions.

I recently talked with an outstanding Latin-American writer, Gabriel Garcia Marquez. A great mind indeed. His range of thinking is global: reading just one of his books shows this. So it has turned out that, while talking about the restructuring under way in the Soviet Union, one can delve into any international and social problem of our times. For the whole world needs restructuring, i.e. qualitative change and progressive development. The opinion of such a man matters a lot. And it is precisely because it reflects the thoughts, cares and sentiments of millions—white, black, yellow, all people of the

155

Earth—that it inspires one. This means that what we have started to do at home may be of benefit to other peoples as well.

We welcome the direct influence of numerous and diverse public movements—trade union, women's, youth, anti-war or ecological movements—on international politics, an influence which has greatly increased in the last few years. They invade, with their imperative demands and their sense of responsibility, what was once solely the domain of diplomacy.

It is only fair that people should have first-hand information about the intentions of the statesmen on whom the course of events in the key areas of international life actually depends. I have met a delegation of the World Federation of Trade Unions. It is the biggest trade union center, having hundreds of millions of working people from many nations of the world behind it. The delegation handed me a document of the 11th World Trade Union Congress with an appeal to the US President and to myself. The significance of this document lies, in my view, in the fact that it represents the will of the working class, reflecting humankind's common interest in a safe peace. This document and the frank conversation I had with trade union leaders convinced me that the historic mission of the working class as a spokesman—through its own interests—for the interests of all social development is still alive, even now, when conditions have so radically changed.

I was deeply moved by the World Congress of Women which met in Moscow in June 1987. I was asked to speak there. It was a very representative forum—women from over 150 countries. What I felt when I heard the delegates speak and when I talked to them was an impressive personal involvement in what is going on in the world. Indeed, women, whose natural predestination is to preserve and continue the human race, are the most unselfish, self-sacrificing and numerous champions of the idea of peace. I gained much by attending this congress, both emotionally and politically.

Every day I receive scores of letters, messages and telegrams from all over the world—from politicians and public figures, mayors, MPs and businessmen and most of all from ordinary people, from couples, as well as families and children, plus many collective appeals. Some of them are really moving, containing verses, poems, drawings, small, hand-made souvenirs, diplomas from schools, groups and clubs, and even prayers. And behind these diverse human feelings and thoughts is an anxiety for the future of peace and the hope that humanity is worthy of something better than life under the threat of a nuclear holocaust.

However busy I may be, I try my best to answer these letters. The most important thing these messages and appeals show is confidence in the Soviet Union and in our present policies. We treasure this confidence and we will do all we can to justify it with our actions both at home and in international affairs.

Such communication with people from all over the world reinforces my conviction that the prospects for civilization are not hopeless, since the best minds and honest people think and worry about its present and future, and are ready to devote their talent, knowledge, time and emotional energy to preserving this world and building a better and more just one. So, while basing our policy on new thinking, we do not propose to confine ourselves to the ideas we are used to and to the political language that is typically ours. We have no intention whatsoever of converting everyone to Marxism. The new political thinking can, and must, imbibe the experience of all peoples and ensure the mutual enrichment and confluence of various cultural traditions.

For Honest and Open Foreign Policy

The Soviet leadership is striving to handle foreign affairs in a new way. *Dialogue* is the first thing I must mention in this context. One can hardly speak of achieving mutual understanding without it. Once we had embraced the principles of the new thinking, we made dialogue a basic instrument to test them out in international practice. Moreover, by means of dialogue we check how realistic our ideas, initiatives and international actions are. And we note with satisfaction that this word, though, unlike perestroika, not of Russian origin, has struck deep root in the diplomatic vocabulary in recent years. And political dialogue itself has come to play a more important role in international relations than ever before.

During the two and a half years I have been General Secretary, I

157

have had no less than 150 meetings and talks with heads of state and government, leaders of parliaments and parties—Communist, Social Democratic, Liberal, Conservative—and with politicians and public figures of various levels from Europe, the Americas, Asia and Africa. This has also become standard practice for many of my colleagues in the Soviet leadership. It is a great school for us. I think that such dialogue is useful for most of our interlocutors as well. It serves to shape and strengthen civilized international relations so essential to the modern world.

Furthermore, we want to return to the true, original meaning of the words we use in international contacts. In declaring our commitment to honest and open politics, we do mean honesty, decency and sincerity, and we follow these principles in our actions. By themselves, these principles are not new—we have inherited them from Lenin. What is new is that we are trying to free them of the ambiguities which are so widespread in the modern world. What is also new is that the present situation makes them mandatory for all.

We have, as a matter of fact, excluded all discrepancy between what we tell our foreign interlocutors behind closed doors and what we declare and do in public. I must confess I am not in favor of such intricate diplomacy whereby you fail to understand in the end what your partner wanted to say during a meeting or in an exchange of messages. I am in favor of an open, really working policy. It must not be a double-faced policy, for its predictability is an indispensable condition for international stability. There must be more light and more openness in international affairs and less tactical maneuvering and verbal juggling. No one can fool anyone else any longer. I keep repeating this to the people I talk to from the West. What is required of leaders today is a correct assessment of realities, a lucid mind and an increased sense of responsibility. That is to say, serious politics is required rather than playing at politics, or politicking.

I think the new style in international relations implies extending their framework far beyond the limits of the diplomatic process proper. Parliaments, along with governments, are becoming increasingly active participants in international contacts, and this is an encouraging development. It points to a trend toward greater democracy in international relations. The wide-scale invasion of this domain by public opinion, international and national public organizations is a sign of our times. Public, citizen diplomacy, a way of addressing the peoples directly, is becoming a standard means of interstate contact.

Using the methods of citizen diplomacy is no trick. We just proceed from the realization that the whole burden of the arms race, not to mention the possible consequences of international conflicts, rests on the people. We want the Soviet Union's position to be brought home to the peoples of the world.

At this point, I must touch on the acute and topical issue of the relationship between politics and propaganda. The response to our foreign policy initiatives has often been: "This is propaganda!" It has to be recognized that foreign policy proposals in this age of mass information and mass interest in international problems are always accompanied by propaganda. They must "impress." American leaders, for example, begin to advertize their intended international moves long before they announce them officially and always present them as "major," "historic," "crucial," etc. But what matters, after all, is the true character and purpose of the proposals: whether they are designed to be actually put into practice, whether they are realistic, whether they take into account the interests of all the parties concerned or whether they are propaganda and made just to arouse commotion. So I can declare with a full sense of responsibility that all our initiatives mean business, that they are, to quote Lenin, "slogans for action," not "slogans of propaganda."

At this point I can repeat with clear conscience what I said to *Time* magazine in August 1985. After all, if they really see nothing but propaganda in whatever we do, why not respond to it according to the principle of "tit for tat"? We suspended nuclear explosions. So why couldn't the Americans do the same in retaliation, and follow that up with yet another "propaganda blow" by suspending, say, the development of one of their new strategic missiles? And we would respond with just the same kind of "propaganda," and so on and so forth. Who, one may wonder, could stand to lose from this kind of "propaganda" competition?

Two and a half years is not such a long time. Judging by all the signs, the period we are talking about has proved to be full of great substance. What is the main thing here? Some people may say that the new political thinking is still making its way into world politics with difficulty. And this is true. Some may say that the inertia of the

159

old way of thinking is still stronger than the new trends. And this is also true. And still the main thing is that the difficult job of laying the ground for reshaping international relations has been done. And we believe that the world will be changing for the better. It is already changing.

4

Restructuring in the USSR and the Socialist World

The essence of our internationalist principle is: making important, meaningful decisions at home, and carefully weighing up what this will mean for socialism as a whole. It goes without saying that no socialist country can successfully move forward in a healthy rhythm without understanding, solidarity and mutually beneficial cooperation with the other fraternal nations, or at times even without their help.

On Real Socialism

When we embarked on the course of perestroika, we proceeded from the premise that restructuring was working, and would continue to work. To strengthen socialism as a whole in that restructuring is the cause of the whole Soviet people, and is designed to raise our society to a qualitatively new level. This is the first point.

The second point is that both the course we have chosen and the need to pick up our pace have made us look at how to develop cooperation with other socialist countries in a broad historical context. The resulting conclusion—and the fraternal parties have all reached this conclusion—is that greater dynamism should be imparted to our cooperation, that this sphere too is ready for a kind of restructuring. Our thoughts, and later our initiatives, were based on the following.

Over the postwar decades socialism has become a strong international formation and a major factor in world politics. A socialist form of economy functions in a large group of countries. The foundations have been laid for an international socialist division of labor. Multilateral organizations of socialist states have gained a varied experience of activity. Scientific and cultural exchanges have assumed

161

large proportions. Of course, this does not mean that the development of world socialism always proceeded successfully.

The initial economic level of countries that have taken the socialist path of development differed considerably. Even today it is far from identical. This is one of the difficulties in realizing socialism's overall potential and in perfecting the mechanisms of integration.

Socialism has gone through complicated phases of development. In the first postwar decades, only the Soviet Union had any experience in the building of a new society. It had to be responsible for everything that was happening, for good and bad. The character of economic relations with other socialist countries was also in line with this; these relations developed with emphasis on Soviet raw materials and fuel supplies and on the Soviet Union's aid in creating basic industries. In the field of state building, too, the fraternal socialist states largely relied on the Soviet example. To an extent, this was inevitable. Assertions concerning the imposition of the "Soviet model" distort this objective necessity of that time. The first socialist state's experience and help on the whole fostered the other countries' efforts to build a new society.

But it was not without losses, and rather serious ones at that. Drawing on the Soviet experience, some countries failed duly to consider their own specifics. Even worse, a stereotyped approach was given an ideological tint by some of our theoreticians and especially practical leaders who acted as almost the sole guardians of truth. Without taking into consideration the novelty of problems and the specific features of different socialist countries, they sometimes displayed suspicion toward those countries' approaches to certain problems.

On the other hand, there grew in a number of socialist countries tendencies towards a certain introversion, which gave rise to subjective assessments and actions. Moreover, the socialist nations have been a target of massive pressure from imperialism—political, military, economic and ideological—ever since their birth.

In some cases all this led to certain objective processes and to the emergence of problems that were not noticed in time by the ruling party and the leadership. As regards our friends in the socialist countries, they usually kept quiet, even when they noticed something of concern. Frankness was frowned upon, and could be "misunder-

162

stood," so to speak. Some socialist countries went through serious crises in their development. Such was the case, for instance, in Hungary in 1956, in Czechoslovakia in 1968, and in Poland in 1956 and then again in the early 1980s. Each of these crises had its own specific features. They were dealt with differently. But the fact is that a return to the old order did not occur in any of the socialist nations. I want to note here that it was not socialism that was to blame for the difficulties and complexities of the socialist countries' development, but, chiefly, miscalculations by the ruling parties. And, of course, the West can also be "credited" with helping, through its constant and stubborn attempts to undermine the development of the socialist states, to trip them up.

Through hard, and at times bitter, trials the socialist countries accumulated their experience in carrying out socialist transformations. The ruling communist parties' practice, as well as theoretical work, gradually produced a fuller and more precise idea of the methods, ways and means for a socialist transformation of society. Marx, Engels and Lenin, who theoretically substantiated the principles on which the concept of socialism is founded, did not seek to give a detailed picture of the future society. And this is in general impossible to do. This picture acquired its outlines and is still in the making as a result of the revolutionary creative work of all the socialist states.

There were also serious falterings in relations between socialist countries. Particularly grave was the disruption of the USSR's friendly relations with Yugoslavia, with the People's Republic of China and with Albania. In general there were enough bitter lessons. But communists learned. We are still learning today.

In general, an advantage of socialism is its ability to learn. To learn how to solve the problems being raised by life. To learn how to avert crisis situations which our opponents try to create and use against us. To learn how to resist attempts to stratify the socialist world and pit some countries against others. To learn how to prevent conflicts of interest between different socialist states, by harmonizing these interests and finding mutually acceptable solutions to the most complex problems.

What has world socialism achieved by the mid-1980s? Now we can safely state that the socialist system has firmly established itself in a large group of nations, that the socialist countries' economic potential

163

has been steadily increasing, and that its cultural and spiritual values are profoundly moral and that they ennoble people.

But in this case one may ask: if all is so well, why is perestroika exciting so much interest concerning relations between the socialist countries? Well, it's a legitimate question.

Generally speaking, the answer is simple enough: the initial phase of world socialism's rise and development is over, but the forms of relations which were established at that time have remained virtually unchanged. Furthermore, negative accretions in these relations were not examined with a sufficient degree of frankness, which means that not everything obstructing their development and preventing them from entering a new, contemporary stage was identified. Meanwhile, each socialist country, each socialist society, has accumulated considerable potential of its own in every field of life. Socialism's prestige and possibilities would be directly harmed if we clung to the old forms of cooperation or limited ourselves to them.

Indeed, beginning with the end of the 1970s, contacts between leaders of fraternal countries became more and more for show rather than for real business. There was less trust in them and their approach was more businesslike.

Now many things have changed. Over the past two and a half years the Soviet Union and its friends in the socialist community have jointly carried out great work. This needs to be, and is being, continued. The entire range of political, economic and humanitarian relations with the socialist countries is being cast anew. This is dictated by the objective needs of each country's development and by the international situation as a whole, rather than by emotions.

Toward New Relations

The role of the Soviet Union in the socialist community in the conditions of perestroika is determined by the objective position of our country. Whether things are going well in our country or whether they are going poorly, this inevitably affects everyone. But the level of interaction we are now reaching is the result of more than just the work we are doing at home. It is first and foremost the result of the joint activities and concerted efforts of the fraternal countries. And we have thoroughly discussed every aspect of cooperation with our friends and allies.

We all proceed from the premise that at this crucial stage in world development, socialism must show in full measure the dynamism of its political and economic system, a humane way of life. Socialist community relations are already being readapted to the requirements of the time. We are far from euphoric: the work is just gaining momentum. But the major goals have been defined.

What do these reference points imply? First of all, the entire framework of political relations between the socialist countries must be strictly based on absolute independence. This is the view held by the leaders of all fraternal countries. The independence of each Party, its sovereign right to decide the issues facing its country and its responsibility to its nation are the unquestionable principles.

We are also firmly convinced that the socialist community will be successful only if every party and state cares for both its own and common interests, if it respects its friends and allies, heeds their interests and pays attention to the experience of others. Awareness of this relationship between domestic issues and the interests of world socialism is typical of the countries of the socialist community. We are united, in unity resides our strength, and from unity we draw our confidence that we will cope with the issues set forth by our time.

Collaboration between the ruling communist parties is pivotal to cooperation between the socialist countries. Over the past few years we have had meetings and detailed discussions with the leadership of every fraternal country. The forms of this cooperation are also being renewed. A new, and probably key, link in this is the institution of multilateral working meetings between the leaders of fraternal countries. Such meetings enable us to confer, promptly and in a comradely manner, on the entire range of issues of socialist development and its domestic and foreign aspects.

The extension, in the complicated international situation, of the term of the Warsaw Treaty, by virtue of a unanimous decision, was a crucial event. Regular meetings of the Warsaw Treaty's Political Consultative Committee pave the way for an accumulation of the ideas and initiatives of its participants, and allow them to "synchronize their watches," so to speak.

165

What is intended is the harmonization of the initiatives of each fraternal country with a common line in international affairs. Experience has shown how important both components of the formula are. No fraternal country—and we attribute this to the USSR in full measure—can resolve its tasks on the international scene if it is isolated from the general course. Likewise, a coordinated foreign policy of our states can be efficient only provided the contribution of each country to the common cause is duly taken into account.

As far as economic relations are concerned, we have been developing them on the basis of consistent observance of the principles of mutual advantage and mutual assistance. We have reached an understanding that all of us are now in need of a breakthrough in science and technology and in the economic field. To this end, we have elaborated and adopted a comprehensive program for scientific and technological progress aimed at sharply increasing production efficiency, at doubling and even tripling productivity by the year 2000. Is this utopian? No. The socialist community has everything it needs to accomplish this task, including a formidable production capability, a vast number of research and engineering projects, as well as enough natural resources and manpower. Our plan-based system, too, enables us to channel considerable resources towards satisfying needs of prior importance.

The leaders of the member-states of the Council for Mutual Economic Assistance (CMEA), as a result of discussions, arrived at the conclusion that all structural components of the socialist system must function more efficiently. This is what all of us agree on. But it does not mean, of course, that these processes will proceed in an identical way in all socialist countries. For each nation has its own traditions, peculiarities and ways in which its political institutions function. In principle, all socialist countries are in one way or another going through the process of searching for renewal and profound transformations. But each country, that is its leadership and its people, decides independently what scope, scale, forms, rates and methods these transformations should have. There are no differences on that score; there are only specific features.

The French Prime Minister, Jacques Chirac, asked me: "Do you think the spirit of perestroika will bear its impact on all socialist states of Eastern Europe?" I said the influence is mutual. We borrow something from the experience of our friends and they take from us what they think suits them best. In short, it is a process of mutual exchange and enrichment.

Speaking honestly, it seemed to me that the point was raised out of more than a desire to know how we had been doing. It was to a certain extent prompted by rumors about some of our friends being in "disagreement" with the Soviet leadership's line towards perestroika. What can I say about this? We have no serious disagreements with our friends and allies. We are used to speaking frankly and in a businesslike manner. And, to my mind, we gain more from a critical and earnest evaluation of our moves and initiatives than from loud applause for just anything we have done. That's the first point. The second, and I will repeat it in this context, is that we do not claim we are the only ones to know the truth. Truth is sought in a joint quest and effort.

But let me say a few more words about economic affairs. We see direct links between companies and enterprises and specialization as the chief reserve and leverage for deepening our integration. It is exactly along these lines that we are restructuring our foreign economic activities and removing barriers preventing enterprises from finding appropriate partners in fraternal countries and deciding on their own how to cooperate with them. We are launching joint socialist companies, including those expected to meet our countries' needs for the most sophisticated goods more quickly. Such companies are being set up in services, construction and transport. The Soviet Union is prepared to offer them some lucrative orders. We are also prepared to consider the possibility of involving Western businessmen in the activities of such companies.

We hope to accelerate the process of integration in the forthcoming few years. To this end, the CMEA should increasingly focus on two major issues.

First, it will coordinate economic policies, elaborate long-term programs for cooperation in some crucial fields and promote major joint research and engineering programs and projects. In doing so it is possible and expedient to cooperate with non-socialist countries and their organizations, the EEC above all.

Second, the CMEA will focus on the development and coordination of normative standards for the integration mechanism, as well as on

167

legal and economic conditions for direct cooperation links, including, of course, the fixing of prices.

We want the CMEA to have less administrative regimentation, fewer committees and commissions, and to pay greater attention to economic incentives, initiative, the socialist spirit of enterprise, and to an increase in the involvement of work collectives in the process. We and our friends think that the CMEA must get rid of a surplus of paper work and bureaucratic muddle.

In no way does the CMEA infringe on the independence of any participating state and its sovereign right to be in charge of its own resources and capabilities and to do everything for the benefit of its people. The CMEA is not a supranational organization. In decision-making it relies on the principle of consensus, rather than on a majority vote. The only important thing is that any country's lack of desire or interest to participate in a project should not serve as a restraint on others. Anyone who wants to participate is welcome to do so; if not, one can wait and see how the others are doing. Every country is free to decide if it is prepared for such cooperation and how far it is going to be involved. I believe this is the only correct approach.

We also have a task of great magnitude concerning cooperation in the intellectual sphere. Change is imperative here too. In fact, each of the socialist countries is a social laboratory testing the various forms and methods of the socialist constructive effort. This is why, in our view, exchanging experience in socialist construction, and summing up such experience, is becoming increasingly significant.

We Soviet communists, as we consider the future of socialism, proceed from Lenin's idea that this future will be created through a series of efforts made by various countries. This is why we naturally believe that a good way to judge the earnestness of a ruling party is to look at how it uses its own experience, as well as the experience of its friends, and the world experience. As for the value of this experience, we have one criterion here: social and political practice—the results of social development and economic growth, and the strengthening of socialism in practice. Our science, our press and our specialists are now analyzing the experience of the fraternal countries on a much broader scale and much more actively so as to apply it creatively to Soviet conditions.

For their part, these countries show an immense interest in what is

168

happening in the USSR. I saw this when I met with the leaders of the socialist countries and with rank-and-file citizens during my trips abroad. Here is a small illustration. During my visit to Czechoslovakia, I had the opportunity to talk with people on the streets and in the factories of Prague; they would tell me: "What you're doing now is the right thing!" One young man noted: "So it boils down to: 'Speak the truth, love the truth, and wish others the truth.'" I added: "And act according to the truth. This is the most difficult science." I went on to say: "Life is harder than any school; not everything comes easy. Sometimes you have to retreat, and then advance. It is agonizing to think, analyze and re-analyze, but you shouldn't be afraid of this."

The general conclusion of the Soviet leadership is that we can reach a new level of friendship between the socialist countries by developing ties among their work collectives and their individuals as well as through an exchange of experience. Our ties in all spheres are becoming more vigorous. We've made a good start. The solid network of contacts along Party, state and public lines plays an important and even decisive part in the cooperation among the fraternal countries. We have various types of contacts—from those between enterprises, work teams, families, children's and youth organizations, universities and schools, creative unions and cultural figures and individuals, to permanent business ties between department officials, members of governments and Central Committee secretaries.

A few words about our relations with the People's Republic of China, where very interesting and in many respects fruitful ideas are being realized in the process of the "four modernizations." We view China as a great socialist power, and are taking definite steps to ensure that the development of Sino–Soviet relations takes place in a spirit of good-neighborliness and cooperation. There has already been a definite improvement. We believe that the period of alienation is past. We invite our Chinese comrades to work together with us to develop good relations between our two countries and peoples.

The current stage of historical development puts a strict demand on the socialist states: to pick up the pace, to move to the economically, scientifically and technologically most advanced positions, and convincingly to demonstrate the attractiveness of the socialist way of life.

We have been frank and self-critical in our assessment of the past development and have borne our share of the blame for failures in

169

the socialist community. Our friends were quick to respond. This has paved the way for restructuring relations, for bringing them to a new, contemporary level.

Together we have achieved a great deal in recent years in politics, economics and in the exchange of information. If everything is not yet successful, this does not make us nervous. We are working persistently, exploring fresh approaches. The main thing is that we are convinced of the importance of cooperation and the need to enhance it. At the current stage in history, which is in effect a turning point, the ruling parties of the socialist countries are aware of the great extent of their responsibility, nationally and internationally, and are persistently looking for further ways to accelerate social development. An orientation toward scientific and technological progress, people's creative endeavor and the development of democracy is the guarantee that in the coming period socialism will, contrary to the prophecies of all ill-wishers, reveal even more fully its real potential.

Revolutionary changes are becoming part and parcel of the vast socialist world. They are gaining momentum. This applies to the socialist countries, but it is also a contribution to the progress of world civilization.

5

The Third World in the International Community

The emergence into the international arena of over a hundred Asian, African and Latin American countries, which have embarked upon the path of independent development, is one of the great realities of the present-day world. We acclaim this twentieth-century phenomenon. This is a huge and diverse world with vast interests and difficult problems. We realize that the future of civilization hinges on how this world develops.

The responsibility for these dozens of countries with their aggregate population of many millions, and the responsibility for harnessing their enormous potential for the benefit of world progress, does not lie with them alone.

On the one hand, in the Third World we see examples of rapid, albeit uneven and painful, economic growth. Many countries are becoming modern industrialized states, and several are growing into great powers. The independent policy of most Third World states, which rests upon acquired national dignity, is increasingly affecting international affairs as a whole.

On the other hand, poverty, inhuman living conditions, illiteracy and ignorance, malnutrition and hunger, alarming child mortality, and epidemics remain common features of life for the two and a half billion people who inhabit these former colonies and semi-colonies. Such is the bitter truth. In the early eighties the per capita income in Third World countries was eleven times lower than that in the industrialized capitalist countries. This gap is widening rather than narrowing.

Nevertheless, the rich Western states continue to collect neo-colonialist "tribute." Over the past decade alone, the profits US corporations have siphoned off from the developing countries have quadrupled investments. Americans may call this profitable business.

We appraise the situation differently. But I'll go into that later.

The developing countries bear the burden of an enormous external debt. When combined with the volume of the profits taken out every year, the growing debt spells one thing—a bleak development outlook and the inevitable aggravation of social, economic and other problems that are already extremely serious.

I recall a conversation I had with President Mitterand. It boiled down to the following. Clearly, each capitalist enterprise strives for maximum profit. However, a capitalist or a company are forced, largely under worker pressure, to reckon with the fact that, if the enterprise is to function effectively, it is imperative that employees' incomes are guaranteed, and, despite their low level, are sufficient to enable them to restore their production capacities, maintain their health, upgrade their qualifications, and raise their children. The capitalist is forced to do this, realizing that in doing so he is ensuring himself profit today and tomorrow. But capitalism taken as a whole, represented by the Western countries, does not want to understand even this simple truth in its relations with its former colonies. Capitalism has brought economic relations with Asia, Africa and Latin America to a point where entire nations are doomed to economic stagnation, unable to meet their own essential needs, and bogged down in monstrous debts.

These countries will be unable, of course, to pay back the debts under the present conditions. If a fair solution is not found, anything could happen. The debt of the developing countries has turned into a time bomb of sorts. Detonation could have desperate results. A social explosion of tremendous destructive force is accumulating.

The developing countries' debt is one of the most serious problems in the world. It has been in existence for a long time. But it was either put off, overlooked or discussed in general terms. Western leaders underestimate the danger; they refuse to see the seriousness of the economic upheavals that may happen. That is why they propose half-baked measures and attempt to salvage the situation with palliatives. There is a patent reluctance to take real, substantial steps to normalize economic cooperation with the developing countries.

Extensive efforts are required if genuine changes are to be made and a new world economic order established. It will be a long and hard road, and one has to be prepared for any unexpected turn. The restructuring of international relations demands that the interests of all countries be considered, it requires a balancing of interests, but many do not want to give away anything of their own.

Regional Conflicts

The dire state of the developing countries is the real reason for many of the conflicts in Asia, Africa and Latin America. Discussing this with President Reagan at our meeting in Geneva, I told him that first of all one had to realize where regional conflicts come from.

The truth is that, although they are dissimilar in essence and in the nature of the opposing forces, they usually arise on local soil, as a consequence of internal or regional conflicts which are spawned by the colonial past, new social processes, or recurrences of predatory policy, or by all three.

Crises and conflicts are a seedbed for international terrorism. The Soviet Union rejects terrorism in principle and is prepared to cooperate energetically with other states in eradicating this evil. It is expedient to concentrate this work within the United Nations. It would be useful to establish under its aegis a tribunal for investigating acts of international terrorism. During a bilateral dialogue with the Western countries (in the past year there was a major exchange of views on this score between us and the USA, Britain, France, Federal Germany, Italy, Canada and Sweden) we came out for the elaboration of effective measures to combat terrorism. We are prepared to conclude special bilateral agreements. I hope that the front of the common struggle against international terrorism will broaden in the years to come. But one thing is indisputable: if terrorism is to be uprooted, it is imperative to eliminate the reasons that engender conflicts and terrorism.

I have often encountered leading Western politicians who regard the very existence of regional conflicts as the product of "Kremlin conspiratorial activity." How do things really stand?

In the Middle East, a conflict has been in existence between Israel and its neighbors for many years. Moscow is made out to be the culprit, as it invariably stands opposed to Israeli expansion and comes out in defense of the sovereign rights of the Arab peoples, including the Arab people of Palestine. Nonexistent anti-Israeli prejudices are ascribed to the Soviet Union, although our country was among the first to promote the formation of the state of Israel.

Important things have to be discussed seriously. The Middle East is a complicated knot in which the interests of many countries are intertwined. The situation there remains dangerous. We believe it to be important for the East and the West that we untie this knot; it is important for the entire world. But there is also the view that the Middle East issues are altogether impossible to resolve. It is difficult even to understand such a position, and it is impossible to agree with it for both political and moral considerations. Logically, the only conclusion that can be drawn is that the situation is bound to be further aggravated, and that there are bound to be new outbreaks of hostilities and more suffering for the peoples of the region. Wouldn't it be preferable to take an active stand and support the efforts of those who are looking for ways to end the Middle East deadlock by way of a just political settlement?

We understand that under the present circumstances it is difficult to reconcile the interests of the conflicting sides. Yet is is essential to try to reduce to a common denominator the interests of the Arabs, of Israel and of its neighbors and other states. However, we do not at all want the process of working towards a settlement, or the very goals of this process, in some way to infringe upon the interests of the United States and the West. We are not bent on elbowing the US out of the Middle East—this is simply unrealistic. But the United States should not commit itself to unrealistic goals either.

The main thing here is to take the interests of all sides into consideration. Specifically, this accounts for our long-standing initiative in respect to convening an international conference on the Middle East. I mentioned this in a conversation I had with Jimmy Carter. It took the Americans ten years to see from their own experience, although they could have drawn on the experience of their predecessors, that separate deals are not productive. Only now, having gone through a "retraining" course, does it look as though Washington is moving toward a more realistic assessment of the situation and returning to a broader discussion of these issues.

It is essential that the negotiations get off the ground. They should incorporate existing bilateral and multilateral contacts, and a more vigorous search for a just political settlement. If the conference does

174

not prove to be an umbrella for separate deals and steps, if it is aimed at a genuine Middle East settlement, with the interests of the Arab countries, including those of the Palestinians and Israel, being taken into due account, we are prepared to render all manner of assistance and to take part in all stages of the conference. And to do so constructively.

I want to stress in this connection that we do not bear any hostility toward Israel in principle. We recognize its legitimate right to existence. However, in the current situation and in the light of actions committed by Israel, we cannot agree to the establishment of diplomatic relations. If, however, the situation changes, if we see the possibility of normalization and settlement in the Middle East, this matter can be reconsidered. We have no complexes here. As for the contacts already existing between our countries, we will not abandon them.

Let us take another volatile area of the globe—Central America. What is the conflict all about here? The unpopular Somoza regime has been overthrown in Nicaragua, and the popular revolution has emerged victorious. Again, the Sandinista revolution was declared out of hand to be the "work of Moscow and Cuba." Such is the standard, hackneyed ideological substantiation for an undeclared war against a small country whose only "fault" is that it wants to live in its own way, without interference from the outside. Incidentally, what has happened in Nicaragua shows what can be expected in other countries. We find it preposterous when we hear allegations that Nicaragua "threatens" US security, and that Soviet military bases are going to be built there —bases which the Americans supposedly know about but which I, for one, have never heard of.

Margaret Thatcher and I had a lively debate on this point. I said that unbearable living conditions had forced the Nicaraguans to carry out the revolution. These conditions had been created by Britain's American friends, who have made all of Central America into their backyard, mercilessly scooping up its resources, and are now wondering why the people revolt. What has been happening in Nicaragua is the business of the Sandinistas and the Nicaraguan people. Our talk was a straightforward one. I asked Mrs Thatcher: "You accuse us of solidarity with Nicaragua, but do you consider it normal to render assistance to apartheid, or racists? Doesn't the way you look in the eyes of the world public opinion bother you? We sympathize with the liberation movements of peoples fighting for social justice, while you, as I see it, do not. Here our approaches differ."

Really, if the United States left Nicaragua in peace this would be better for the US itself, for the Latin Americans, and for the rest of the world.

Explosive problems cannot be shelved; they will not go away by themselves. The situation in Southern Africa has long been tempestuous. The South African population opposes both apartheid and the immoral oppressive regime whose international isolation is growing. But many in the West see a communist plot and Moscow influence behind that conflict situation, too, though there isn't a trace of a Soviet presence in South Africa, which can't be said of the US and its allies.

The same holds true of the situation in the Gulf region. The Soviet Union's evaluation of the situation and of the reasons for its exacerbation is known, it was expressed in official statements. The UN Security Council adopted a resolution demanding a ceasefire and a halt to all military activities as well as the withdrawal by Iran and Iraq of their troops to internationally recognized frontiers. The Soviet Union voted for the resolution. But the United States, acting contrary to the spirit of the Security Council resolution, is seeking a pretext to interfere in the Iran–Iraq conflict and is building up its presence in the Gulf region. It alleges that the Soviet Union threatens Western interests, which must be protected, and it furthermore promises to stay in the Gulf even after the conflict is over.

Such is the assessment of all regional conflicts as seen through the prism of Soviet–American confrontation. We have the impression that the United States needs regional conflicts so as to always have room to maneuvre by manipulating the level of confrontation and by using a policy of force and anti-Soviet propaganda. The Soviet Union, on the other hand, holds that these conflicts should not be used to engender confrontation between the two systems, especially when they involve the USSR and the USA.

As we took up the question of regional conflicts, the reader may wonder what I think of the Afghan issue. Probably, it is not universally known that Afghanistan was the first country with which the Soviet Union established diplomatic relations. We were always on friendly terms with that country, with its kings and tribal chiefs. Certainly,

Afghanistan has many problems owing to its extreme backwardness, which largely stemmed from the British rule. Therefore, it was quite natural that many Afghans wanted to help their people overcome medieval patterns, update state and public institutions, and speed up progress. But as soon as progressive changes were charted, imperialist quarters began to pressure Afghanistan from without. So, in keeping with the Soviet–Afghan treaty, its leaders asked the Soviet Union for help. They addressed us eleven times before we assented to introduce a limited military contingent into that country.

We want our soldiers home as soon as possible. The issue has been settled in the main. But it is connected with the need to settle the situation around Afghanistan politically. We support the present Afghan leadership's course of national reconciliation. The Soviet Union wants Afghanistan to be independent, sovereign and non-aligned as before. It is the sovereign right of the Afghan nation to decide which road to take, what government to have, and what development programs to implement. And the American interference delays the withdrawal of our troops and hampers the enactment of the policy of national reconciliation and, hence, the settlement of the whole Afghanistan issue. And the transfer of the Stingers to the counter-revolutionary bands, which use these missiles to down civilian aircraft, is simply immoral and totally unjustifiable.

Nations Have the Right to Choose their Own Way of Development

Every nation is entitled to choose its own way of development, to dispose of its fate, its territory, and its human and natural resources. International relations cannot be normalized if this is not understood in all countries. For ideological and social differences, and differences in political systems are the result of the choice made by the people. A national choice should not be used in international relations in such a way as to cause trends and events that can trigger conflicts and military confrontation.

It is high time Western leaders set aside the psychology and notions of colonial times. They will have to do this sooner or later. As long as the West continues to see the Third World as its sphere of influence and continues to exert its sway there, tensions will persist, and new hotbeds will appear as anti-imperialist resistance mounts.

Our Western opponents do not like it when we talk to them in this way. They lose their composure and grow indignant when we call a spade a spade. They interpret our evaluations as encroachment on traditional links between the United States and Western Europe, on the one hand, and developing countries on the other. They say we want living standards to fall in capitalist countries.

I have explained on many occasions that we do not pursue goals inimical to Western interests. We know how important the Middle East, Asia, Latin America, other Third World regions and also South Africa are for American and West European economies, in particular as raw material sources. To cut these links is the last thing we want to do, and we have no desire to provoke ruptures in historically formed, mutual economic interests.

But it is high time to recognize that the Third World nations have the right to be their own bosses. They have attained political independence after many years of hard struggle. They want to be economically independent as well. These countries' leaders (I have met many in person) enjoy the support of their people and want to do something for them. They want their countries to be genuinely independent and to be able to cooperate with others on equal terms. The desire of these nations to use their vast natural and human resources for national progress is understandable. They want to live no worse than people in developed countries. What they have now is undernourishment and disease. Their resources are exploited by developed states and incorporated into the latter's national incomes through the channels of a non-equivalent exchange. Developing countries won't put up with the situation for much longer.

Such is a contemporary reality which not all in the West wish to take into consideration, even though they are well aware of it. But it is something to be reckoned with, especially since dozens of countries are concerned.

The sooner this reality is brought home to everyone, in all continents, the sooner international relations will become normal. The global situation will thus improve. That's crucial. That's the key issue.

It is high time to consider the problem on a global scale, to seek a way to solve it on a basis of balanced interests and to find organizational forms for its solution in the framework of the world community. The United Nations is the best forum to discuss the issue. We are preparing our proposals on that score. I informed UN Secretary-General Perez de Cuellar about this during our meeting. He approved of the idea of bringing up the issue in the United Nations.

Most developing countries adhere to nonaligned policies. The nonaligned movement arose on that platform to unite over a hundred countries, which account for the bulk of the world's population. The movement has become a mighty force and a major factor in world affairs. It helps to form a new kind of international relations, whatever special features and nuances the movement has. The nonaligned movement personifies the desire of newly-free nations to cooperate with others on an equal basis, and to abolish dictat and hegemonistic attempts from international relations. The Soviet Union understands the goals of the movement and is in solidarity with it.

Quite recently, many nonaligned countries thought that disarmament and the elimination of nuclear arsenals were the prerogatives of superpowers, the United States and the Soviet Union, and were of little concern to developing countries. However, the movement displayed profound understanding of the interconnection between disarmament and development at the eighth conference of heads of state and government of the nonaligned countries in Harare. Its stand was officially voiced there: a well-grounded stand. If the arms race is stopped and disarmament effected, enough funds will be saved to settle the Third World's gravest problems.

I discussed the connection between disarmament and development with Mr Perez de Cuellar. We agreed that the issue deserves the United Nations' close attention. The Soviet Union tabled specific proposals at the UN Conference on the Relationship Between Disarmament and Development. It can only be regretted that the United States refused to take part in the conference.

Today, not just the socialist countries but even many capitalist states note the nonaligned movement as a major and positive factor in world politics. The Soviet Union welcomes this fact and takes it into consideration in its foreign policy.

179

The Asia–Pacific Knot

The East, specifically Asia and the Pacific region, is now the place where civilization is stepping up its pace. Our economy in its development is moving to Siberia and to the Far East. We are therefore genuinely interested in promoting Asia–Pacific cooperation.

The Soviet Union is an Asian, as well as European country, and it wants to see that the huge Asia–Pacific region, the area where world politics will most likely focus next century, has everything it needs to improve the situation in it, and that due account is taken of the interests of all the states and of a balance between them. We are against this region being somebody's domain. We want everybody to have genuine equality, cooperation, and security.

In Asia, the issues of peace are perhaps no less acute and painful, and in some parts even more so, than in the other areas of the world. Naturally, the Soviet Union, India and other states concerned about this have put forward various initiatives in different years. The best known among them is a proposal to turn the Indian Ocean into a zone of peace. It was supported by the UN General Assembly and the nonaligned movement. A pledge not to use nuclear weapons first, which was assumed by the USSR and the People's Republic of China, has become a key factor of peace in Asia, the Pacific and indeed in the whole world.

When, as General Secretary of the CPSU Central Committee, I first met with Rajiv Gandhi, Prime Minister of the Republic of India, in May 1985, I suggested that in the context of previous initiatives, and to some extent of European experience, it would be a good idea to ponder on a general and integrated approach to the issue of security in Asia and on the possibility of coordinated efforts by Asian countries in that direction. This idea was maturing as I met with leaders of European states and with other political figures. I involuntarily compared the situation in Asia with that in Europe. And this made me think that the Pacific region, because of mounting militarization, also needed some system of "safeguards," like those provided by the Helsinki process in Europe.

180

The political report by the Central Committee to the 27th CPSU Congress stressed the growing significance in Soviet foreign policy of the Asian and Pacific directions. We stated that local solutions should be sought without delay, beginning with the coordination and then the pooling of efforts to produce political settlements to sensitive problems, so as, in parallel and on that basis, to at least take the edge off military confrontation in various parts of Asia and to stabilize the situation there. I advanced the pertinent proposals in Vladivostok in July 1986. (They concerned erecting a barrier against the spread and build-up of nuclear weapons in Asia and the Pacific region; reducing Pacific Ocean naval activities; cutting down the armed forces and conventional armaments in Asia; confidence-building measures and the non-use of force in the region.)

While on a visit to that city, it seemed particularly appropriate to examine issues of world politics from an Asia–Pacific angle. The situation in the Far East as a whole, in Asia and in adjacent ocean expanses, where we have long been living and sailing, is of paramount national interest to us. Here, in the vast space covering almost half the globe, there are many major countries, including the USSR, the US, India, China, Japan, Vietnam, Mexico and Indonesia. It also contains states considered to be medium-sized, but rather large by European standards—Canada, the Philippines, Australia and New Zealand, and, alongside them, dozens of small and quite tiny ones.

Incidentally, what a clamor was raised over my speech in Vladivostok. How many insinuations were made regarding the Soviet Union's decision to "tackle" the Pacific and to establish Soviet hegemony there, and, of course, to infringe upon US interests in the first place. But we are already used to such a "caveman-like" response to our initiatives. All our attempts, however tentative, to establish good relations or simply diplomatic or commercial ones with this or that country in the region are immediately regarded as crafty designs.

But what were the facts? A year after my trip to the Soviet Far East I gave an interview to the Indonesian newspaper *Merdeka*. Its editor-in-chief, B. M. Diah, quite correctly assessed the purport of my speech there as an invitation to all countries in the region to tackle their common problems together. But in listing the countries, he omitted to mention the United States. I pointed this out to him and said that we hoped to cooperate with the United States, too.

Speculation that our activities and our interest in this region constitute a threat to the interests of others is absurd. What was said in Vladivostok is an expression of a thought-out policy. No one should be worried by it. We state that we are prepared to cooperate with the US in the same way as with Japan, the ASEAN countries, India and other nations. We invite everyone to act together for peace and for the benefit of all.

In replying to *Merdeka*'s editor, I backed up our intentions in this region with new concrete proposals, the most significant of which is one proposing the elimination of all medium-range missiles in the Asian part of the Soviet Union, naturally on the basis of a "global zero" with the United States.

Our approach to this enormous part of the world, where so many different countries and peoples are situated, is based on the recognition and understanding of the realities existing in it. Our concepts on ways to ensure international security and peaceful cooperation in Asia and the Pacific Ocean rest on these realities, and stem from our genuine desire to build up new and just relations in this region together.

A year later we were able to identify several positive trends—I mentioned them in my interview with *Merdeka*'s editor. But the complexities and contradictions had not diminished, and the confrontational trends are growing. This induced us to propose additional measures to ease tensions in Asia and the Pacific, measures elaborating on and specifying the Vladivostok initiatives.

We follow carefully the stands and initiatives of the states situated in that part of the world. Original and constructive ideas have appeared of late and are circulating in regional contacts. The specific features of the world outlook of the people living there, their historical and political experience and their cultural identity can be very helpful in resolving the region's problems, and may well produce ideas which are understandable and acceptable to all.

We are impressed by ASEAN's growing contribution to international affairs. We are ready to develop our relations with each of the ASEAN nations individually and with ASEAN as a whole, with due respect for the independent contribution which ASEAN countries make individually and collectively to improve the international situation.

Why do I speak of the importance of an independent line pursued by individual countries or a group of countries? It is not because by supporting such a line we would like to act to the detriment of the other party, but because new international relations can be built solely on the basis of an independent line. Up until now international relations have depended greatly on moves by certain countries or groups of countries. This did not improve the situation in the world. Such is the lesson of the past which should be learned by all serious-minded politicians. New relations in our complex world, and in such an intricate region as Asia and the Pacific, can be built only along the road of cooperation where the interests of all states are brought together. The type of relationship inherited from the past, with a metropolis being on one side and colonies on the other, has outlived itself. It must give way to a new type of relationship.

There was much comment when it was suggested that there be in the foreseeable future a Pacific conference attended by all countries gravitating towards the ocean. This idea was put forward as a kind of working hypothesis, or, to be more precise, as an invitation to discussion. The similarity to Helsinki is explained by the fact that the world community does not yet have any other experience of this kind. It does not mean, however, that the European "model" can be transplanted to Asia–Pacific soil. But in our time any international experiment has some general, global traits.

Among the questions put to me by the newspaper *Merdeka* was this one: "How do you visualize the role of the USSR in the development of regional economic cooperation?" In line with the concept of our country's accelerated social and economic growth, we pay special attention to the territories east of the Urals whose economic potential is several times that of the European part of the USSR. We believe that joint firms and ventures set up in collaboration with the business circles of Asia–Pacific countries could take part in tapping the wealth of these areas.

On Nuclear Disarmament in Asia

Heeding the opinion and concern of Asian countries, the Soviet Union has taken a major step forward by agreeing to a "global double-zero" with regard to medium- and shorter-range missiles. We have also expressed readiness not to increase the number of nuclear-capable aircraft in the Asian part of our country if the US agrees not to deploy in that area additional nuclear weapons that can reach Soviet territory. We expect that all this will give an impetus to the process of nuclear disarmament in Asia.

Despite the complexity and motley design of the Asian and Pacific tableau and the uneven distribution of bright and dark colors in it, the essentially anti-nuclear make-up of the general picture is obvious. And it is already possible to start moving toward the elimination of nuclear weapons in Asia. A major step in this direction could, for example, be the creation of nuclear-free zones. The Soviet Union is known to have signed the protocols to the Rarotonga Treaty to establish such a zone in the South Pacific. We also support other countries' proposals to set up nuclear-weapon-free zones in South-East Asia and on the Korean peninsula. An international conference on the Indian Ocean could further the purpose of nuclear disarmament by considering and deciding the question of declaring this area of the world a zone of peace.

Our methods on and our approach to nuclear disarmament in Asia, as in Europe, are identical. Disarmament must be implemented under strict international verification, including on-site inspections. We urge the United States to start talks about nuclear armaments in the Asia–Pacific region and to solve this problem on a reciprocal basis, strictly observing the security interests of all.

Such, in general, is our concept of the way the Asian nuclear knot should be untied. By taking up the issue, the states situated in the region could embark upon building up a regional security system. What is actually meant by normal relations and a favorable situation for a region populated by two and a half billion people? It could be compared to building a house, with each of us putting a brick or two into its walls to raise an edifice of cooperation and mutual understanding step by step, through common efforts. This is a great, challenging, but feasible target.

Efforts in this direction by countries of the two continents—Europe and Asia—could be pooled together to become a common Euro–Asian process which would give a powerful impulse to an all-embracing system of international security.

The latest developments increasingly convince us that it was correct and timely for us to bring up the issue of security for the Asia–Pacific region. A great interest has been shown recently in the search for ways leading to constructive cooperation on a regional and continental scale. Also our bilateral relations with some countries of the Asia–Pacific region have become more dynamic.

Soviet–Indian Relations

India, a southern neighbor of ours with a population of 800 million, is a great power. It enjoys major influence in the nonaligned movement and the entire world, and is a crucial factor for Asian and global peace.

Soviet–Indian relations have steadily developed over many years. I have met Rajiv Gandhi, the Indian Prime Minister, several times, both in Moscow and in Delhi. My visit to India in 1986 left an indelible impression on me. We adopted the now famous Delhi Declaration during that visit.

The global interest in the document is natural. The Delhi Declaration is unprecedented. It demonstrates an entirely new, philosophical–political approach to interstate relations. The recognition of the priority of universal human values in this space and nuclear age forms the philosophical and ethical foundation. Though the document was elaborated by two countries, its significance goes far beyond bilateral and regional boundaries.

The very appearance of the Delhi Declaration reflects the unique nature of Soviet–Indian relations. We have different social systems, but this doesn't prevent the kind of cooperation between us that spiritually enriches both sides and leads to a broad concurrence of views on the fundamental questions of the day. Each country has arrived at the outlooks we share in its own way, and has its own motives for those attitudes.

Soviet–Indian relations are exemplary in many respects: in their diverse political, economic, scientific, technical and cultural content, in the deep respect and the liking our nations have for each other, and in the general tone of our ties which reflects our mutual confidence and our heartfelt desire for friendship. How is it possible that India and the Soviet Union, two states with different social and political

185

systems, have managed to develop relations of such a high quality? Because both of them base their policies—not in word but in deed—on the principles of sovereignty, equality, non-interference in others' internal affairs, and cooperation. Both recognize every nation's right to choose its own political system and pattern of social development.

So we have every reason to say with rightful pride that the Soviet Union and India represent an example of good interstate relations, an example for others to emulate. In our relations, we see a budding world order in which peaceful coexistence and mutually beneficial cooperation based on goodwill will be universal norms.

At A Difficult Watershed

I have met many African political leaders in the last year and a half or so (some of them more than once), and have had thorough discussions with them. These were Robert Gabriel Mugabe, Mengistu Haile-Mariam, Marcelino dos Santos, Oliver Tambo, Moussa Traoré, Mathieu Kérékou and Chadli Bendjedid, to name but a few. All of them are influential, widely recognized national leaders. I got the impression from our talks that Africa is going through an active period in its development which requires responsibility. Africa is in ferment. Vital changes are under way there, and many acute problems face that part of the world.

We don't see Africa as a homogeneous continent where all processes evolve to one and the same pattern. Like any other country in the world, every African country possesses its own inimitable features and conducts policies all its own. African leaders also are different. Some have been at the helm for relatively long periods of time, so that the world knows them. Others have only lately appeared on the African and world scenes, and are gaining practical experience.

We fully appreciate the formidable tasks facing progressive regimes in Africa. The fact is that their countries have historically been linked with their former colonial mother countries, and some of them even continue to be dependent on them economically. And although imperialism is out to retain its positions by economic and financial means, even by resorting to arms, they are determined to pursue a course toward consolidating gains.

The Soviet Union supports these efforts and these policies, for only inviolable political sovereignty and economic independence can provide a sound basis for international relations in today's world. Every African nation is lawfully entitled to a free choice of a way of development, and we resolutely condemn all attempts to interfere in their domestic affairs. Our country has always acted, and will continue to act, in support of the national liberation struggle of African nations, including those in southern Africa, where one of the last bastions of racism is situated.

When I met Oliver Tambo, President of the African National Congress, I said to him: "We side with you in your struggle against the apartheid regime and its henchmen, for a democratic state and independent development, for equality of all races and ethnic groups. Significantly, more and more white South Africans are condemning apartheid, voicing support for the ANC's goals, and seeking contacts with it. That proves once again that there is no future in apartheid."

We have bonds of friendship with the frontline states in southern Africa. We support their just stances and strongly condemn South Africa's hostile actions against them.

The Soviet Union has no special interests in southern Africa. We want only one thing: nations and countries in the region must at last have the chance to settle their development issues, their home and foreign affairs independently, in peace and stability.

Latin America: A Time of Major Change

We also proceed from the same general principles in our relations with Latin American countries. That part of the world has unique traditions and vast potential. Its nations show a great striving for a better future. They want to make their hopes come true despite all the obstacles. The way to freedom is always a difficult one, but we are sure that the Latin American drive for progress will gain momentum.

US right-wing forces and propaganda portray our interest in Latin America as an intention to engineer a series of socialist revolutions there. Nonsense! The way we have behaved for decades proves that

187

we don't plan anything of the kind. Such schemes run counter to our theory, our principles, and our entire concept of foreign policy.

I said to President Reagan: "For decades you have looked upon Latin America as your doorstep, and behaved there accordingly. Nations have had enough of this. Whether they realize their aspirations by peaceful or military means is their own affair. It was you who planted a bomb in Latin America in the form of its mammoth foreign debt. You should really think about this."

Perhaps the US ruling circles do understand this but will not admit it, for they would then have to change their policy, and everybody would see that the "hand of Moscow" is a big lie.

We do sympathize with the Latin American countries in their efforts to consolidate their independence in every sphere and cast off all neo-colonialist fetters, and we have never made any secret of this. We much appreciate the energetic foreign policies of Mexico and Argentina, their responsible stances on disarmament and international security, and their contribution to the initiatives of the Six. We support the peace-making efforts of the Contadora Group, initiatives by Central American heads of state, and the Guatemala City accord. We welcome the democratic changes in many Latin American countries, and appreciate the growing consolidation of the countries of the continent which will help preserve and strengthen their national sovereignty.

At the same time, I'd like to emphasize once again that we do not seek any advantages in Latin America. We don't want either its raw materials, or its cheap labor. We are not going to exploit anti-US attitudes, let alone fuel them, nor do we intend to erode the traditional links between Latin America and the United States. That would be adventurism, not sound politics, and we are realists, not reckless adventurers.

But our sympathies always lie with nations fighting for freedom and independence. Let there be no misunderstanding on that score.

Cooperation, not Confrontation

It's my conviction that the human race has entered a stage where we are all dependent on each other. No country or nation should be regarded in total separation from another, let alone pitted against another. That's what our communist vocabulary calls internationalism and it means promoting universal human values.

The ruling circles of the West will eventually have to reckon with the interests of Third World nations. Once I asked Gary Hart: "Can't America offer a different policy to developing countries than the one it pursues today? The US can do much to build new interstate relations, and lose nothing economically in the process. On the contrary, America stands to gain from that. Why should the United States reject the opportunity as if it doesn't see on which side its bread is buttered?"

A great deal depends on the position of the United States and the West as a whole. Above all, it depends on them whether we shall be able to untie the knot of the modern world's problems and break the deadlock over the existing development opportunities. If we succeed in building new relations based on equality and due regard for everyone's interests, why should we need the existing military machine that was designed as an instrument of an expansionist foreign policy?

Understandably, that machine has been built up over the centuries, and it's not so easy to destroy it overnight. But we have approached the point where destroy it we must, since millions of Asians, Africans and Latin Americans want to live like human beings. I am convinced that the United States and the Soviet Union can contribute a lot to the search for ways to establish new global relations.

We call on the US Administration to join hands with us in searching for solutions to the Third World's problems. There are other ways besides compulsion to do it. What we propose is quite realistic. The United States should find a way to divert its might, its capital— everything that is now being squandered for military purposes—to meeting different needs, to solving the modern world's economic and social problems. I'm positive that this is quite possible. More than that, the United States could enlist the assistance of other Western countries. And may I repeat that all the while it would stand only to gain.

189

6

Europe in Soviet Foreign Policy

May I now make a personal comment. I made my first trip abroad as General Secretary of the CPSU Central Committee to France in October 1985. About a year earlier, in December 1984, I visited Britain at the head of a delegation of the USSR Supreme Soviet. Both those trips set me thinking about many things and, first of all, about the role and place of Europe in the world.

Francois Mitterrand expressed what seemed to me an important idea at that time. "Why not assume the possibility," he said, "of gradual advance to a broader European policy?" A year later, in Moscow, he said: "It is necessary that Europe should really become the main protagonist of its own history once again so that it can play in full measure its role of a factor for equilibrium and stability in international affairs." My thoughts went along the same track. Direct contacts with the leaders of two leading West European states, with parliamentarians and representatives of political parties and business interests, helped me make a better and more accurate appraisal of the European situation.

At the 27th Congress of the CPSU, the European direction in our foreign policy was characterized as a most important one. We would like the position of the Soviet leadership with respect to Western Europe to be correctly understood by everyone.

Both before and since the Congress I have met and talked with many prominent West European personalities belonging to different political camps. Those contacts have confirmed that the West European states are also interested in developing relations with the Soviet Union. Our country holds a prominent place in their foreign policies.

So, why such great attention to Europe?

Heritage of History

Some in the West are trying to "exclude" the Soviet Union from Europe. Now and then, as if inadvertently, they equate "Europe" with "Western Europe." Such ploys, however, cannot change the geographic and historical realities. Russia's trade, cultural and political links with other European nations and states have deep roots in history. We are Europeans. Old Russia was united with Europe by Christianity, and the millennium of its arrival in the land of our ancestors will be marked next year. The history of Russia is an organic part of the great European history. The Russians, Ukrainians, Byelorussians, Moldavians, Lithuanians, Letts, Estonians, Karels and other peoples of our country have all made a sizable contribution to the development of European civilization. So they rightly regard themselves as its lawful inheritors.

Our common European history is involved and instructive, great and tragic. It deserves to be studied and learned from.

Since long ago, wars have been major landmarks in Europe's history. In the twentieth century, the continent has been the seat of two world wars—the most destructive and bloody ever known by mankind. Our people laid the greatest sacrifices at the altar of the liberation struggle against Hitler's fascism. More than twenty million Soviet people died in that terrible war.

We are by no means recalling this here in order to belittle the role of the other European nations in the fight against fascism. The Soviet people respect the contribution made by all the states of the anti-Hitler coalition and by the Resistance fighters in the defeat of the fascist vermin. But we can never agree with the view that the Soviet Union joined in the fight against Nazi Germany "only" in 1941, whereas before that the others had to fight Hitler "single-handed."

When Mrs Thatcher told me something to that effect, I objected, reminding her that the Soviet Union had fought against fascism politically from 1933 and, from 1936, with arms too, by assisting the republican government in Spain. As for the non-aggression pact with Germany (whose meaning is constantly being distorted by our opponents), it could have been avoided, as could many other things, if the ruling circles of Britain and France had agreed to cooperate with the Soviet Union against the aggressor at that time.

And who handed over Czechoslovakia to the Nazis? On his return from Munich, Chamberlain said that he had brought peace to the British people, but in effect everything turned out otherwise: he had brought them war. That was mainly because the British rulers had only one thought on their minds: how to turn Hitler against the East, against the Soviet Union, and how to crush communism.

I don't want to simplify matters, for the East European nations also received a difficult legacy. Take, for example, relations between Russia and Poland. For centuries they were complicated by a struggle between the ruling circles of the two countries. Kings and tsars had set Poles to fight Russians and Russians to fight Poles. All those wars, violence and invasions poisoned the two peoples' souls and evoked mutual animosity.

Socialism marked a drastic turn in the centuries-old history of this part of the world. The defeat of fascism and the victory of socialist revolutions in the East European countries created a new situation on the continent. A powerful force emerged which set out to break the endless chain of armed conflicts. And now the people of Europe have entered a fifth decade without war.

At the same time, Europe remains an arena of sharp ideological, political and military confrontation. Some would trace the division of Europe to Yalta and Potsdam and question the historic agreements signed there. But that is to turn the facts upside down. Yalta and Potsdam laid the foundation for the postwar arrangement of Europe. They are vital in that they were essentially anti-fascist, democratic agreements. They provided for the elimination of Hitler's "new order" which had deprived entire nations and states of independence and even hope for freedom and sovereignty. The logic of the old political thinking led to the division of Europe into two mutually opposed military blocs. There is a version circulating in the West according to which Europe was split up by the communists. But what about the Fulton speech of Churchill? Or the Truman Doctrine? The political division of Europe was started by those who brought about the disintegration of the anti-Hitler coalition, launched the Cold War against the socialist countries and set up the NATO bloc as an instrument of military–political confrontation in Europe. It should be reiterated that the Warsaw Treaty was signed *after* the establishment of NATO.

Because of NATO, Europe once again found itself harnessed to a chariot of war, this time one loaded with nuclear explosives. And today the main blame for the continued division of Europe must be placed on those who have turned it into an arena of nuclear missile confrontation and are calling for a revision of the European borders, ignoring politico–territorial realities.

For a start, we have repeatedly suggested scrapping the military blocs, or at least the military wings of the two alliances. But since this proposition of ours has not been accepted, we must take this reality into account as well. Even so, we believe that, blocs or no blocs, we must still pave the way for a better world and for improved international relations that would at some stage lead to all military alliances being disbanded.

There have been quite a few dramatic situations and events in the postwar history of Europe, but anyway the European states, in accordance with the concrete conditions and opportunities, made their choice: some of them remained capitalist while others moved towards socialism. A truly European policy and a truly European process can only be promoted on the basis of recognition of and respect for that reality.

We resent the belief that Europe is doomed to confrontation between blocs and to a continual preparation for war against each other. That the socialist countries have not resigned themselves to that prospect is confirmed by the initiative, put forward by them, that led all Europe, the US and Canada to Helsinki. The Final Act adopted there showed real ways of attaining unity for the continent on a peaceful and equitable basis.

However, the impetus provided by the famous conference in the capital of Finland started waning under the pressure of the winds of a second "Cold War." Much has been said about the causes of this, but this is not what we are talking about now. By way of self-criticism I will mention just one such cause: the weakening in the economic positions of socialism which we allowed in the late seventies and early eighties. On the other hand, this proves yet again, contrariwise, as it were, that socialism is meant to play the decisive role in subduing the enemies of *détente* and in normalizing relations among all European states to make them those of good neighbors. Whenever socialism lets up, militarism, power politics and imperial ambitions surge.

Today, the Soviet Union and the socialist community have assumed the initiative once again. By fortifying socialism, we impart additional strength and vitality to the Helsinki process. It is high time everyone realized the simple truth that the existing barriers cannot be overcome by the West imposing its ways upon the East or vice versa. We must turn by joint efforts from confrontation and military rivalry towards peaceful coexistence and mutually beneficial cooperation. It is only via this understanding that our continent can be united.

Europe is Our Common Home

This metaphor came to my mind in one of my discussions. Although seemingly I voiced it in passing, in my mind I had been looking for such a formula for a long time. It did not come to me all of a sudden but after much thought and, notably, after meetings with many European leaders.

Having conditioned myself for a new political outlook, I could no longer accept in the old way the multi-colored, patchwork-quilt-like political map of Europe. The continent has known more than its share of wars and tears. It has had enough. Scanning the panorama of this long-suffering land and pondering on the common roots of such a multi-form but essentially common European civilization, I felt with growing acuteness the artificiality and temporariness of the bloc-to-bloc confrontation and the archaic nature of the "iron curtain." That was probably how the idea of a common European home came to my mind, and at the right moment this expression sprang from my tongue by itself.

Then it came to have a life of its own, so to speak, and appeared in the press. There were some reproaches, too; it was said to be abstract and meaningless. So I decided to spell out all my views on this matter. A suitable occasion presented itself during my visit to Czechoslovakia, which lies exactly at the geographical center of

Europe. That prompted the "European theme" in my public address in Prague.

Europe is indeed a common home where geography and history have closely interwoven the destinies of dozens of countries and nations. Of course, each of them has its own problems, and each wants to live its own life, to follow its own traditions. Therefore, developing the metaphor, one may say: the home is common, that is true, but each family has its own apartment, and there are different entrances, too. But it is only together, collectively, and by following the sensible norms of coexistence that the Europeans can save their home, protect it against a conflagration and other calamities, make it better and safer, and maintain it in proper order.

Some people may think this a beautiful fantasy. However, this isn't fantasy, but the outcome of a careful analysis of the situation on the continent. If the world needs new relations, Europe needs them above all. One may say that the nations of Europe have conceived them in suffering, and deserve them.

The concept of a "common European home" suggests above all a degree of integrity, even if its states belong to different social systems and opposing military–political alliances. It combines *necessity with opportunity*.

Necessity: Imperatives for Pan-European Policy

One can mention a number of objective circumstances which create the need for a pan-European policy:

1. Densely populated and highly urbanized, Europe bristles with weapons, both nuclear and conventional. It would not be enough to call it a "powder keg" today. The mightiest of military groups, equipped with up-to-the-minute hardware which is constantly updated, confront each other. Thousands of nuclear warheads are concentrated here, while just several dozen would be suffice to turn European soil into a Gehenna.

2. Even a conventional war, to say nothing of a nuclear one, would be disastrous for Europe today. This is not only because conventional weapons are many times more destructive than they were during the

195

Second World War, but also because there are nuclear power plants consisting of a total of some 200 reactor units and a large number of major chemical works. The destruction of those facilities in the course of conventional hostilities would make the continent uninhabitable.

3. Europe is one of the most industrialized regions of the world. Its industry and transport have developed to a point where their danger to the environment is close to being critical. This problem has crossed far beyond national borders, and is now shared by all of Europe.

4. Integrative processes are developing intensively in both parts of Europe. It is time to think what will come next. Will the split in Europe be further aggravated or can a blend be found to the benefit of both the Eastern and the Western parts in the interests of Europe and indeed the rest of the world? The requirements of economic development in both parts of Europe, as well as scientific and technological progress, prompt the need for a search for some form of mutually advantageous cooperation. What I mean is not some kind of "European autarky," but better use of the aggregate potential of Europe for the benefit of its peoples, and in relations with the rest of the world.

5. The two parts of Europe have a lot of their own problems of an East–West dimension, but they also have a common interest in solving the extremely acute North–South problem. This does not mean, of course, that the countries of Eastern Europe share the responsibility for the colonial past of West European powers. But that's not the point. If the destinies of nations in the developing countries are neglected, and the very acute problem of how to bridge the gap between the developing and industrialized states is ignored, this may have disastrous consequences for Europe and the rest of the world. (In this regard we share the spirit and thrust of the Brandt Commission's reports on the North–South issue and the report of the Socialist International, "A Global Challenge," prepared under the guidance of Willy Brandt and Michael Manley.) West European states, like the Soviet Union and other socialist countries, have broad ties with the Third World, and could pool their efforts to facilitate its development.

Such are, by and large, the imperatives of a pan-European policy determined by the interests and requirements of Europe as an integrated whole.

Europe's Opportunities

Now, about the opportunities the Europeans have and the prerequisites they need to be able to live as dwellers in a "common home."

1. The nations of Europe have the most painful and bitter experience of the two world wars. The awareness of the inadmissibility of a new war has left the deepest of imprints on their historical memory. It is no coincidence that Europe has the largest and the most authoritative antiwar movement, one which has engulfed all social strata.

2. European political tradition as regards the level of conduct in international affairs is the richest in the world. European states' notions of each other are more realistic than in any other region. Their political "acquaintance" is broader, longer, and hence closer.

3. No other continent taken as a whole has such a ramified system of bilateral and multilateral negotiations, consultations, treaties and contacts at virtually every level. It has to its credit such a unique accomplishment in the history of international relations as the Helsinki process. Hopeful results were produced by the Stockholm Conference. Then the torch was taken up by Vienna where, we hope, a new step in the development of the Helsinki process will be made. So, the blueprints for the construction of a common European home are all but ready.

4. The economic, scientific, and technical potential of Europe is tremendous. It is dispersed, and the force of repulsion between the East and the West of the continent is greater than that of attraction. However, the current state of affairs economically, both in the West and in the East, and their tangible prospects, are such as to enable some modus to be found for a combination of economic processes in both parts of Europe to the benefit of all.

Such is the only reasonable way for a further advance of European material civilization.

Europe "from the Atlantic to the Urals" is a cultural–historical entity united by the common heritage of the Renaissance and the Enlightenment, of the great philosophical and social teachings of the nineteenth and twentieth centuries. These are powerful magnets which help policy-makers in their search for ways to mutual understanding and cooperation at the level of interstate relations. A tremendous potential for a policy of peace and neighborliness is inherent in the European cultural heritage. Generally, in Europe the new, salutary outlook knows much more fertile soil than in any other region where the two social systems come into contact.

I frankly admit that we are glad that the idea of a "common European home" finds understanding among prominent political and public figures of not only Eastern, but also Western Europe, including those whose political views are far removed from ours. Thus, Foreign Minister Genscher of Federal Germany has declared a readiness to "accept the concept of a common European home and to work together with the Soviet Union so as to make it a really common home." Federal President Richard von Weizsaecker, Italian Foreign Minister Giulio Andreotti, and other leaders have spoken to me in the same vein. So, the awareness of the community of European culture, of the interconnection and interdependence of the destinies of all countires of the continent, and of the vital need for cooperation by them, has not yet been lost.

However, there are ideologists and politicians who continue to sow mistrust towards the Soviet Union. The majority of West European countries, following in the wake of the US, publish a great many hysterical articles, but, as always, the French right-wing press is the most zealous. It is simply horrified by the very prospect of a better situation in Europe. Take, for example, the French weekly *L'Express*. On 6 March 1987 it ascribed to us a desire to establish domination over Europe. An article published under the glaring title "Gorbachev and Europe" is patterned after Little Red Riding Hood and the Big Bad Wolf.

I thought: could European readers, European nations be so naïve as to believe such scribbling? We have faith in the common sense of the Europeans, and we realize that sooner or later they will know the truth from lies. Judging by the published results of public opinion polls, the majority of people in Western Europe seem to appreciate the Soviet Union's open European policy aimed at putting an end to the constant quarrels on that continent.

198

Two German States

Pondering the concept of a common European home, we cannot but express our attitude to the situation which was produced by the Second World War in the heart of Europe where the two German states —the German Democratic Republic and the Federal Republic of Germany—now exist. I've had a rather detailed talk on the matter with West Germany's Federal President Richard von Weizsaecker. He said that people in West Germany are lending an attentive ear to the slogan of a "common European home." "How do you understand this in West Germany?" I asked. And now let me reproduce here the short dialogue that followed:

Richard von Weizsaecker: It is a reference-point which helps us visualize the way things should be arranged in this common European home. Specifically, the extent to which the apartments in it will be accessible for reciprocal visits.

Mikhail Gorbachev: You are quite right. But not everyone may like receiving night-time visitors.

Richard von Weizsaecker: We also aren't especially pleased to have a deep trench passing through a common living-room.

He is referring to the fact that the FRG and the GDR are divided by an international border passing, in particular, through Berlin. Such is a historically shaped reality engendered by the agreement following the Second World War.

We can only guess how Germany would look today had it implemented the Potsdam Agreement in its entirety. There was no other basis for Potsdam unity. But not only did the then US, British and French leaders sabotage the accords with us; the West German supporters of power policy also opposed Potsdam. To them Potsdam was a nightmare. We all know the result.

We, naturally, are bound to be alerted by statements to the effect that the "German issue" remains open, that not everything is yet clear with the "lands in the East," and that Yalta and Potsdam are "illegitimate." Such statements are not infrequent in the Federal Republic of Germany. And let me say quite plainly that all these statements about the revival of "German unity" are far from being "Realpolitik," to use the German expression. It has given the FRG nothing in the past forty years. Fueling the illusions about a return to the "Germany of the borders of 1937" means undermining the trust in the FRG among its neighbors and other nations.

No matter what Ronald Reagan and other Western leaders say on that score, they cannot actually offer anything realistic to the FRG as regards the so-called German issue. What has formed historically here is best left to history. This also holds true for the issue of the German nation and of the forms of German statehood. What is important now is the political aspect. There are two German states with different social and political systems. Each of them has values of its own. Both of them have drawn lessons from history, and each of them can contribute to the affairs of Europe and the world. And what there will be in a hundred years is for history to decide. For the time being, one should proceed from the existing realities and not engage in incendiary speculations.

By way of a digression, may I cite a recollection which I shared with Weizsaecker. In 1975, when the thirtieth anniversary of the Victory over Nazism was being marked, I was in the FRG. Near Frankfurt, I talked to the owner of a gas station. He told me: "Stalin declared: 'Hitlers come and go but the German people remain' but then, at the end of the war, the Soviet Union divided the German people."

A debate followed. I reminded him of the plans to partition the German state worked out by Churchill and by the American politicians back in the war years. We opposed those plans and wanted the establishment of a single sovereign and democratic German state. I reminded him of the fact that the Western powers had supported the creation of a separate state in West Germany and that the German Democratic Republic had appeared later. And, also, after the Yalta and Potsdam conferences, we were for the establishment of an integral, sovereign and, above all, peaceful German state on the basis of denazification, democratization and demilitarization of Germany. But in the West there were forces which acted in a way that led to the present set-up. So, the Soviet Union is not to blame for the split of Germany; those who are to blame for it should be sought elsewhere. And today there exist two German states, a reality recognized by international treaties. Any realistically-minded politician can be guided only by this and this alone.

Such was our conversation.

Even after having gone through that terrible war, the Soviet Union took a principled stand. A sense of reality did not betray us. We did not confuse the German people with the Nazi regime. And we do not blame it for the woes which Hitler's aggression caused us.

In our relations with the Federal Republic of Germany, we take into account its potential and possibilities, its place in Europe and in the world and its political role. History compels us to treat each other properly. Europe's development is impossible without active cooperation by our two states. Solid relations between the FRG and the USSR would be of truly historic significance. While keeping their own identities, within their systems and their alliances, both states can play a major role in European and world development. The Soviet Union is interested in good security for the Federal Republic of Germany. If the FRG were unstable, there could be no hope of stability for Europe, and hence for the world. Conversely, stable relations between the FRG and the USSR would appreciably change the European situation for the better.

Europe and Disarmament

Everything discussed at Reykjavik has a direct bearing on Europe. In our contacts with the USA we never forget about Europe's interests.

After Reykjavik I met with the heads of government of a number of West European NATO countries, namely Poul Schluter of Denmark, Rudolph Lubbers of the Netherlands, Gro Harlem Brundtland of Norway, Steingrimur Hermannsson of Iceland, and with Amintore Fanfani and Giulio Andreotti, representatives of the Italian leadership. We had many discussions on the subject of "Europe and disarmament."

I heard many interesting comments from those with whom I had conversations. Afterwards we in the Soviet leadership seriously thought over their arguments and ideas and those of them we deemed right we took into account in our policy. This, specifically, concerns

Euromissiles. But there were also disputes, which with Margaret Thatcher and Jacques Chirac were particularly heated, about their concept and the general NATO notion of "nuclear deterrence." I expressed to them my surprise at the commotion which Reykjavik caused in some Western capitals. There were no reasons whatsoever to view its results as a threat to Western Europe's security. Such conclusions and assessments are the fruit of the obsolete thinking of the Cold War times.

In speaking with foreign leaders I sometimes ask directly: "Do you believe that the Soviet Union intends to attack your country and Western Europe in general?" Almost all of them answer: "No, we do not." But some of them immediately make a reservation, saying that the very fact of the USSR's immense military might creates a potential threat. One can understand such reasoning. But it is far less clear when national prestige and grandeur are linked with possession of nuclear arms, though it's known for a fact that if a nuclear war were to break out these weapons would only invite strikes and have no other real significance.

When we talk about disarmament as a vital unit which should be laid first in the construction of a common European home, we address, above all, the European nuclear powers—Britain and France. The Soviet Union showed immense trust in Western Europe by agreeing in the course of the current negotiations on disarmament, not to take their nuclear potential into account. The main motive behind this move is that we rule out, even in our thoughts, to say nothing of our strategic plans, the very possibility of a war with Britain or France, let alone with non-nuclear European states.

And when, in connection with our proposals, we encountered speculation as to whether Moscow was planning a trick and wanted to split NATO, to lull Western Europe's vigilance and then overrun it, when the idea of a nuclear-free Europe began to be attacked as harmful and dangerous, I said publicly to all these people: "What are you afraid of, gentlemen? Is it so difficult to rise to the level of real assessments for the truly historic processes which are taking place in the Soviet Union and the entire socialist world? Can you not understand the objective, unbreakable connection of these processes with genuinely good intentions in foreign policy?"

It is high time to put an end to the lies about the Soviet Union's

202

aggressiveness. Never, under any circumstances, will our country begin military operations against Western Europe unless we and our allies are attacked by NATO! I repeat, never!

Let Western Europe quickly get rid of the fears of the Soviet Union which have been imposed upon it. Let it give thought to the idea that elimination of nuclear weapons in Europe would create a new situation not only for the West but also for us. We cannot forget that incursions into our territory in the pre-nuclear era were made more than once from the West. And does not the fact that all NATO military exercises invariably include offensive scenarios speak for itself?

We regard as of great political importance the fact that Greece, the Netherlands, Spain, Italy, Sweden, Finland and many other European countries have raised their voice in favor of resolving the Euromissiles issue.

In the West they talk about inequalities and imbalances. That's right, there are imbalances and asymmetries in some kinds of armaments and armed forces on both sides in Europe, caused by historical, geographical and other factors. We stand for eliminating the inequality existing in some areas, but not through a build-up by those who lag behind but through a reduction by those who are ahead.

In this field there are many specific issues awaiting solutions: reduction and eventual elimination of the tactical nuclear weapons, to be coupled with a drastic reduction of the armed forces and conventional weapons; withdrawal of offensive weapons from direct contact in order to rule out the possibility of a surprise attack; and a change in the entire pattern of armed forces with a view to imparting an exclusively defensive character to them. I spoke about it specifically at a meeting in Prague. Proposals on that score are detailed in the Budapest program of the Warsaw Treaty Organization.

A major confidence-building measure in the spirit of new thinking concerning their military doctrine, which is strictly defensive in all its components, was announced by the Warsaw Treaty countries at a meeting of their Political Consultative Committee in Berlin in May 1987.

Measures such as the creation of nuclear-weapon-free zones and zones free from chemical weapons would also help strengthen European security. We support the offer by the governments of the German Democratic Republic and Czechoslovakia to the West

German government to create a nuclear-weapon-free corridor in Central Europe. The Social Democratic Party of Germany is known, also, to have contributed to forming the concept of such a corridor. We are prepared to guarantee and respect the non-nuclear status of such a zone. We think that Poland's compromise plan on the issue of arms reduction and confidence-building measures in Central Europe is timely and promising.

We believe that armaments should be reduced to the level of reasonable sufficiency, that is, a level necessary for strictly defensive purposes. It is time the two military alliances amended their strategic concepts to gear them more to the aims of defense. Every apartment in the "European home" has the right to protect itself against burglars, but it must do so without destroying its neighbors' property.

European Cooperation

The building of the "European home" requires a material foundation —constructive cooperation in many different areas. We, in the Soviet Union, are prepared for this, including the need to search for new forms of cooperation, such as the launching of joint ventures, the implementation of joint projects in third countries, etc. We are raising the question of broad scientific and technological cooperation not as beggars who have nothing to offer in return. Unfortunately, this is the area where most of the artificial barriers are being erected. Allegations have been made that this involves "sensitive technology" of strategic importance. "Sensitive technology" is used to refer first and foremost to electronics. However, electronics is now used in practically all industries which rely on advanced methods of production.

Western Europe will not get ahead technologically via the militarist Star Wars program. Nor does the militarization of space open the way to technological progress. This is sheer demagogy flavored with technological imperialism. Many opportunities and areas exist for peaceful scientific and technological cooperation. There is the experience of the joint project to study Halley's comet through the space probe Vega. This project found new construction materials and other discoveries were made in radio electronics, control systems, mathematics, optics, etc. Giulio Andreotti's idea of a "world laboratory" also seems promising. It represents a largely new international research project which looks like getting off the ground.

As to cooperation in utilizing thermonuclear energy, a scientific base has been created by scientists from a number of countries working on ideas suggested by their Soviet colleagues. American scientists could join in this research. There are also such possibilities as joint exploration and use of outer space and of planets of the solar system, and research in the field of superconductivity and biotechnology.

True, all this would increase the European states' mutual interdependence, but this would be to the advantage of everyone and would make for greater responsibility and self-restraint.

Acting in the spirit of cooperation, a great deal could be done in that vast area which is called "humanitarian." A major landmark on this road would be an international conference on cooperation in the humanitarian field which the Soviet Union proposes for Moscow. At such a conference the sides could discuss all aspects of problems which are of concern to both East and West, including the intricate issue of human rights. That would give a strong new impetus to the Helsinki process.

However, when we invited the Western countries seriously and constructively to discuss human rights and compare, in an atmosphere of mutual openness, how people really live in our country and in the capitalist countries, the latter appeared nervous, and are now trying to reduce things to individual cases and avoid discussing the rest. I have said, both in public and at meetings with foreign leaders and delegations, that we are prepared to discuss in a humane spirit individual cases, but we are also determined to openly and extensively discuss the entire range of these problems.

One might say that peaceful cooperation and competition between the East and West can and does benefit both sides. The small and medium-size countries of Europe have a great contribution to make to this cause. We have discussed this with former Prime Minister of Iceland Hermannsson, Dutch Prime Minister Lubbers, Swedish Prime Minister Carlsson and other leaders.

First Signs of the New Thinking in Europe

I think that recently, especially after Reykjavik, Western Europe has come to realize more keenly the need to contribute toward an improved situation continentally. And we appreciate the fact that Europeans are now doing a great deal to clear the political atmosphere in the world.

I don't think I will be making a major disclosure if I tell you a story recounted to me by prominent Italian statesman Amintore Fanfani. He once discussed the difficult international situation with Eduardo de Filippo, the internationally famous Italian film-maker. "What are we to do then?" de Filippo asked. "Put our trust in God," Fanfani said. "Then let us people not create obstacles for God," de Filippo replied.

This realization that we are all responsible for the world's future is especially important and valuable today. And some Western European politicians should be credited with recognizing the need for all Europeans to join forces and preserve the foundations laid at Reykjavik.

We can see the first signs of a new outlook on international affairs sprouting in Western Europe. Certain changes are also taking place among ruling circles. Many socialist and social democratic parties of Western Europe are working out new attitudes to defense policy and security. They are led by seasoned politicians with a broad vision of the world's problems.

Shortly before my visit to France in 1985, French journalists asked me to comment on our relations with the social democratic governments in Europe. I said that in the last few years we had been actively cooperating with the social democrats on matters related to war and peace. Meetings with delegations of socialist and social democratic parties account for a large part of my contacts with foreign leaders.

I have received the Consultative Council of the Socialist International led by Kalevi Sorsa, and have met Willy Brandt, Egon Bahr, Filipe Gonzalez and other social democratic leaders, and each time

206

we noted that our views on the crucial issues of international security and disarmament were close or identical. I am very sorry I never met Olof Palme whose tragic death was a great shock for us. The idea of "security for all," which was put forward by him and further elaborated by the International Palme Commission, has many points of similarity with our concept of comprehensive security.

The dialogue started between the communists and the social democrats by no means obliterates the ideological differences between them. At the same time, we cannot say that any of the participants in this dialogue has lost face or been placed under the thumb of the other side. Experience has shown that there is no risk of such an eventuality.

We have good relations and useful contacts with social democrats in the Federal Republic of Germany, Finland, Sweden and Denmark, with the British Labour Party, Spanish socialists, etc. We value the contacts a great deal. In general, we are open to cooperation with all forces that are interested in overcoming the dangerous tendencies in the development of the world situation. Nevertheless, I think that Europe's contribution to the cause of peace and security could be much bigger. Many West European leaders lack the political will and, perhaps, opportunities. And yet, life will force everyone to change to realistic assessments of what is taking place.

On Europe and the United States

It is regrettable that the governments of the NATO countries, including those who in words dissociate themselves from the dangerous extremes of American policy, eventually yield to pressure thereby assuming responsibility for the escalation in the arms race and in international tension.

Here is one example. In April 1986 American war planes bombed Tripoli, Benghazi and other facilities in Libyan territory. The pretext for that act of direct aggression is absolutely untenable by the standards of a civilized society. American war planes took off from bases in Britain and flew through the air space of Western Europe. And what about Western Europe? The governments of the NATO countries silently watched the developments and did not dare to oppose this US action. I told the Swedish Prime Minister, with whom I talked hours after the news of those air raids came in, that such a stand reminded me of the appeasement of aggressors on the eve of the Second World War. And what if the American military take a notion to punish one of the Warsaw Treaty countries by bombing it? What then? Act as if nothing happened? But this is war! The responsibility of all has immeasurably increased in our nuclear age.

There is an old Greek myth about the abduction of Europe. This fairy-tale subject has suddenly become very topical today. It goes without saying that Europe as a geographical notion will stay in place. Sometimes, however, one has the impression that the independent policies of West European nations have been abducted, that they are being carried off across the ocean; that national interests are farmed out under the pretext of protecting security.

A serious threat is hovering over European culture too. The threat emanates from an onslaught of "mass culture" from across the Atlantic. We understand pretty well the concern of West European intellectuals. Indeed, one can only wonder that a deep, profoundly intelligent and inherently humane European culture is retreating to the background before the primitive revelry of violence and pornography and the flood of cheap feelings and low thoughts.

When we point to the importance of Europe's independent stance, we are frequently accused of a desire to set Western Europe and the United States at loggerheads. We never had, and do not have now, any such intention whatsoever. We are far from ignoring or belittling the historic ties that exist between Western Europe and the United States. It is preposterous to interpret the Soviet Union's European line as some expression of "anti-Americanism." We do not intend to engage in diplomatic juggling and we have no wish to provoke chaos in international relations. That would be incompatible with the prime objective of our foreign policy—promoting a stable and lasting peace built on mutual trust and cooperation among nations. Our idea of a "common European home" certainly does not involve shutting its doors to anybody. True, we would not like to see anyone kick in the doors of the European home and take the head of the table at somebody else's apartment. But then, that is the concern of the owner of the apartment. In the past, the socialist countries responded positively to the participation of the United States and Canada in the Helsinki process.

Europe's Responsibility

Thus, without belittling the role and the importance of other continents and other peoples, we are talking about the unique role Europe has to play.

The success of the European process could enable it to make an even bigger contribution to the progress of the rest of the world. Europe must not shun participation in resolving such problems as hunger, debt and under-development and in eliminating armed conflicts.

There is no doubt that all European peoples without exception favor an atmosphere of neighborliness and trust, coexistence and cooperation on the continent. This would be a triumph for the new political thinking in the full sense of the word. Europe can set a worthy example. The world currently stands at a crossroads, and which direction it will pursue depends largely on Europe's political position.

No one can replace Europe with its vast possibilities and experience either in world politics or in world development. Europe can and must play a constructive, innovative and positive role.

7

Problems of Disarmament and USSR–USA Relations

While still a student at Moscow University, I took an interest in the history of the United States. I read several books by American authors and traced the history of our relations. There were abrupt ups and downs in these relations: from the wartime alliance to the Cold War of the forties and fifties; from the *détente* of the seventies to a drastic deterioration at the turn of the eighties.

The interval between the April 1985 Plenary Meeting, which was a turning point for us, and the publication of this book saw a great many events, including some directly connected with the development of Soviet–American relations. Now we keep up a dialogue with the US. The US President and I periodically write to each other. Our negotiators discuss really important problems.

There has been a slight thaw in such areas as scientific and cultural cooperation in the last year or two. Currently, the Soviet Union and the United States are discussing, at various levels, issues that were once subjects for mutual recrimination. Outlines of contact have begun to emerge, even in the field of information activity, which must be rid of the propaganda of violence and enmity, and of interference in each other's internal affairs.

Well, has the ice been broken, and is our relationship entering a quieter and more constructive phase? One would like this process to continue, but to claim that some notable headway has been made would be to sin against the truth. If we care about a real improvement in Soviet–American relations, we must appraise their state honestly. The change for the better, if any, has been extremely slow. Now and again the former inconsistent modes of approach prevail over the imperative need to revitalize Soviet–American relations.

The progress of high technology and informatics have now brought people closer together. These processes can be used to promote greater mutual understanding. They can also be used to divide people. There have been immense losses on that account already. But now the world has reached a point where we—I mean both US and the USSR—have to think of how we are going to continue. If we change nothing, it is difficult to foresee where we shall be ten, fifteen, twenty years from now. It seems to me that concern for our countries and for the future of all civilization is increasing. It is growing within the Soviet as well as within the American nation.

I will never accept the claim—whatever anyone might tell me— that the American people are aggressive toward the Soviet Union. I cannot believe that. There are, perhaps, some individuals who are pleased that there is tension, confrontation or intense rivalry between our countries. Perhaps some people do gain something from it. But such a state of things does not meet the larger interests of our peoples.

We are thinking, after all, of what must be done for our relations to improve. And they do need to. For not only have we failed to advance in this sense since the mid-seventies, but much of what was then created and done has been destroyed. We have not been moving forward, rather the other way round. We say that the Americans are to blame. The Americans say the Soviet Union is to blame. Perhaps, we should seek out the reasons behind what happened, because we must draw lessons from the past, including the past record of our relations. That is a science, a serious and responsible science, if one sticks to the truth, of course. And yet today what we must think of most is how we are going to live together in this world and how we are going to cooperate.

I have had a lot of meetings with American politicians and public figures. Sometimes it creates quite a crowded schedule for me, but on each occasion I try to find the time for such meetings. My mission is, as I see it, not only to get across an understanding of our policy and our vision of the world, but to understand and appreciate more fully the American frame of mind, to learn better what the American problems are, and, in particular, the specific political processes in the US. One cannot do otherwise. A scientific policy must be built on a strict assessment of reality. It is impossible to move toward more harmonious relations between the US and the USSR while being mesmerized by ideological myths.

We don't communicate enough with one another, we don't understand one another well enough, and we don't even respect one another enough. Certain forces have done a great deal to bring about such a state of affairs. Many misconceptions have built up to hamper co-operation and stand in the way of its development.

The history of Soviet–American relations in the postwar period is not the subject of this book. But recalling in one's mind's eye even the events of the recent past one can see the disservice done by prejudice and rejection of new ideas. When I met former US President Jimmy Carter early in the summer of 1987, I told him frankly that we did not by any means consider everything that occurred during his presidency to have been negative. There were some positive things, too. I refer, in particular, to the SALT-II Treaty which, even though never ratified, does play a useful part in spite of the present line of the US Administration. The spirit of this treaty is alive. But at the same time, one cannot fail to see that many opportunities have been missed. We believed, and still believe, that, as the eighties loomed up, major accords were just a stone's throw away for such areas as anti-satellite weapons, the arms trade, reductions in military activity in the Indian Ocean and the Middle Eastern settlement issues. Ten years ago! How much time and how many resources have been wasted on the arms race, and how many human lives have been lost!

What Do We Expect from the United States of America?

When I responded to *Time* magazine late in August 1985 I said: "Our countries simply cannot afford to allow matters to reach a confrontation. Herein lies the genuine interest of both the Soviet and American people. And this must be expressed in the language of practical politics. It is necessary to stop the arms race, to tackle disarmament, to normalize Soviet–American relations. Honestly, it is time to make these relations between the two great peoples worthy of their historic role. For the destiny of the world, the destiny of world civilization really depend on our relations. We are prepared to work in this direction."

We must learn to live in a real world, a world which takes into account the interests of the Soviet Union and the US, of Britain and France and the Federal Republic of Germany. But there are also the interests of China and India, Australia and Pakistan, Tanzania and Angola, Argentina and other nations; the interests of Poland, Vietnam, Cuba, and other socialist countries. Not to recognize them would be to deny those people the freedom of choice and the right to a social set-up that suits them. Even if they err in their choice, they must themselves find a way out. That is their right.

I have spoken about this with many Americans including Mr George Shultz, who was in Moscow in the spring of 1987. We had a wide-ranging conversation, but I kept bringing him round to the same idea: let us try and live in a real world, let us take the interests of both nations into account. And that is impossible without taking into account the interests of other members of the world community. We shall not have proper international relations if we proceed from the interests of the USSR and the US alone. There has to be a balance.

This matter takes on a new aspect at each stage of history. Interests change, so does the balance. That implies new modes of approach. I repeat it would be dangerous and damaging to build politics at the end of the twentieth century on the approach that inspired Churchill's Fulton speech and the Truman Doctrine. An earnest effort to reshape Soviet–American relations is long overdue. Once that is admitted, the habit to command will have to be dropped. Neither the Soviet Union, nor the United States, nor any other country can regard the world or any part of it as an object for exploitation, not even under a cloak of "national interest."

Attempts to build relations on dictatorial practices, violence and command hardly succeed even at this point. They soon won't succeed at all. The process of grasping the new realities is not a simple one. It requires everybody's time and effort. But once started, that process will go on. We must learn to listen to one another, and to understand one another. We are in favor I told Mr Shultz, of cooperating with the US, and I mean cooperating constructively, for nobody else will take on the responsibility that the USSR and the US have to bear.

I recall my conversation with the former President of the United States of America, Mr Richard Nixon. He quoted Winston Churchill's words, not prophetic, I hope, that the bright wings of science might bring the Stone Age back to Earth, and he stressed that I, as General Secretary, and President Reagan and his successors, would have to make the historic choice in favor of a peaceful future. I told Mr Nixon

213

then that I had once seen a film about a journey made by some American tourists down the Volga. There were shots of our citizens alongside Americans. And it was not easy to tell an American from a Russian. People were talking away and one felt they were talking like friends, understanding each other: that is just what politicians fail to do well enough.

It is good that it is not only politicians who speak to each other, but that grass-root representatives of the people do so also. That is very important. I would welcome that. Let Soviet people and Americans meet more often, and let them form their own impression of each other. Communication, direct communication of people is a great thing. Without it, without full-scale communication and mutual understanding between peoples, politics can do little.

I pointed out to Mr Nixon that the fact that it was our two countries that were in possession of a colossal military, including nuclear, arsenal was the most serious reality in today's world. I told him that if we built our policies with respect to each other and with respect to the rest of the world on erroneous premises, things could reach an extreme point of confrontation fraught with the most tragic consequences for the USSR, the US and the whole world.

And today I am ready to repeat what I said in that conversation: there is the firm intention in Soviet society, not only in the leadership, to look for ways toward normalizing Soviet–American relations, to find and enlarge the areas of common ground so as to arrive at a friendly relationship in the long run. Perhaps, this might seem too much to hope for at this juncture. Yet we are convinced that this is the choice to make, for otherwise it is impossible to imagine what we would arrive at.

For better or worse, there is no subjunctive mood in politics. History is made without rehearsals. It cannot be replayed. That makes it all the more important to perceive its course and its lessons.

The US: "Shining City Atop A Hill"

We have too often encountered distorted perceptions about our own country as well as widespread anti-Soviet stereotypes—and therefore we know only too well what evil can be produced by a conscious or unconscious falsehood—to view the US solely in black and white.

I know that American propaganda—yes, propaganda—presents America as a "shining city atop a hill." America has a great history. Who will question the importance of the American Revolution in mankind's social progress, or the scientific–technological genius of America and its achievements in literature, architecture and art? All this America has. But America today also has acute social and other problems, to which not only has American society not yet found an answer, but, even worse, it is looking for answers in places and in such a way that may lead to others having to pay.

The United States has a huge production potential and an enormous material wealth, but, at the same time, it has millions of unfortunate people. This is something to ponder. An almost missionary passion for preaching about human rights and liberties and a disregard for ensuring those same elementary rights in their own home. This also provokes thought. Endless talk about man's freedom and attempts to impose its way of life on others, wide-scale propaganda of the cult of force and violence. How are we to understand this? Arrogance of power, especially military power, constant growth in arms spending and gaps in the budget, an internal, and now also an external debt. For what? What motivates the US? We ask ourselves all these and many other questions, trying to grasp the American reality and to see the mainsprings behind US policy.

I admit frankly that what we know does not support the idea of the United States of America as a "shining city atop a hill." With equal definiteness I can say that neither do we consider the US an "evil empire." Like all countries America in reality casts both light and shadows. We see the US as it actually is—diverse in its opinions both in and about American society.

The Soviet leadership does not perceive the US in just one dimension, but clearly distinguishes all the facets of American society: the millions of working people going about their daily chores who are generally peacefully disposed; realistically minded politicians; influential conservatives, and alongside them, reactionary groups who have links with the military–industrial complex and who profit from arms manufacturing. We see a healthy, normal interest in us and also a fairly widespread, blinding anti-Sovietism and anti-communism.

We believe that the political system and social order of the United

States is the business of the American people themselves. They have to decide how to govern their country, and how to elect their leadership and their government. We respect this sovereign right. If we began to doubt the choice of the American people, what would come of it? Politics must be built on realities, on an understanding of the fact that each nation has a right to independently choose its way of life, and its own system of government.

The United States is a power with whom we shall have to live and build relations. This is a reality. For all the contradictory nature of our relationships it is obvious that we can do nothing in terms of securing peace without the US, and without us the US also will accomplish nothing. There is no getting away from each other. Contacts and a dialogue are needed; we must look for ways to improve our relationship.

We know very well and understand that the US has an administration—the White House—and Congress. And we want to cooperate with both the administration and Congress. We are currently expanding our perceptions of the American political process. We see, in particular, the difference between the views of the Defense Secretary, a civilian, and the US professional military. For the former, business and arms orders mean a great deal, whereas the realistic professionals are well aware of what they have in their hands and what this may bring to the world. Such an understanding attests to the display by the military of a sense of realism and responsibility. It is very important that the military should correctly understand the present situation.

Let me add that we do not intend to shape our relations according to the political situation inside the United States. Today the Republicans stand at the helm in the US, tomorrow it will be the Democrats or the Republicans once again. There is no particular difference. But there are the interests of the US as a state to consider. And we shall maintain relations with the administration that is in power. Let American affairs remain American, and our affairs ours. Such is our basic stand.

The "Enemy Image"

We certainly do not need an "enemy image" of America, neither for domestic nor for foreign-policy interests. An imaginary or real enemy is needed only if one is bent on maintaining tension, on confrontation with far-reaching and, I might add, unpredictable consequences. Ours is a different orientation.

For our part the Soviet Union has no propaganda of hatred toward Americans or disregard for America. In our country you won't find this anywhere, neither in politics nor in education. We criticize a policy we do not agree with. But that's a different matter. It does not mean that we show disrespect for the American people.

In the summer of 1987 I met with a group of Russian teachers from the US who had taken a two-month training course in Leningrad. It was a good conversation—frank and warm. I shall cite one brief excerpt from the verbatim report.

Mikhail Gorbachev: Have you encountered even one instance of a disrespectful attitude toward Americans during your stay?

D. Padula: No, though a man in the street once asked me, when would there be peace? I told him I hoped peace would come soon.

Mikhail Gorbachev: This is very interesting information. I am convinced, friends, that, wherever you may go in the Soviet Union, you will not encounter a disrespectful attitude toward Americans. Not anywhere. You can also read our press. You will find there criticism, analysis, judgment and assessments of government policy, of statements and actions by particular groups, but never any disrespectful mention of America or Americans. So that, if "the Reds are coming," they're coming together with you along the common road of mankind.

Yet some people in the United States, it turns out, "need" the Soviet Union as an enemy image. Otherwise it is hard to understand some films, the inflammatory American broadcasts from Munich, the spate of articles and programs full of insults and hatred toward the Soviet people. All this dates back to the forties, if not earlier.

I would not idealize each step in Soviet foreign policy over the past several decades. Mistakes also occurred. But very often they were the consequence of an improvident reaction to American actions, to a policy geared by its architects to "roll back communism."

We are sensitive and, frankly, cautious about the efforts to give the Soviet Union the image of an enemy, especially as they do not just involve ideological exercises along the lines of the usual fantastic stories about a "Soviet military threat," "the hand of Moscow" "the Kremlin's designs" and an absolutely negative portrayal of our internal affairs. I

217

do not even want to point out the absurdity of such assertions, but neither can we ignore the fact that everything in politics has its own aim. It is thus a question of a political practice with certain intentions and plans behind it. We must get rid of any presence of chauvinism in our countries, especially considering the power they both possess. Chauvinism can bring into politics elements that are inadmissible.

It is a sad, tragic fact that Soviet–American relations have been slipping downhill a long time. Short periods of improvement gave way to protracted spells of tension and a build-up in hostility. I am convinced that we have every opportunity to rectify the situation, and it appears that things are moving that way. We are prepared to do everything to bring about changes for the better.

Who Needs the Arms Race and Why?

Pondering the question of what stands in the way of good Soviet–American relations, one arrives at the conclusion that, for the most part, it is the arms race. I am not going to describe its history. Let me just note once again that at almost all its stages the Soviet Union has been the party catching up. By the beginning of the seventies we had reached approximate military–strategic parity, but on a level that is really frightening. Both the Soviet Union and the United States now have the capacity to destroy each other many times over.

It would seem logical, in the face of a strategic stalemate, to halt the arms race and get down to disarmament. But the reality is different. Armouries already overflowing continue to be filled with sophisticated new types of weapons, and new areas of military technology are being developed. The US sets the tone in this dangerous, if not fatal pursuit.

I shall not disclose any secret if I tell you that the Soviet Union is doing all that is necessary to maintain up-to-date and reliable defenses. This is our duty to our own people and our allies. At the same time I wish to say quite definitely that this is not our choice. It has been imposed upon us.

All kinds of doubts are being spread among Americans about Soviet intentions in the field of disarmament. But history shows that we can keep the word we gave and that we honor the obligations assumed.

Unfortunately, this cannot be said of the United States. The administration is conditioning public opinion, intimidating it with a Soviet threat, and does so with particular stubbornness when a new military budget has to be passed through Congress. We have to ask ourselves why all this is being done and what aim the US pursues.

It is crystal clear that in the world we live in, the world of nuclear weapons, any attempt to use them to solve Soviet—American problems would spell suicide. This is a fact. I do not think that US politicians are unaware of it. Moreover, a truly paradoxical situation has now developed. Even if one country engages in a steady arms build up while the other does nothing, the side that arms itself will all the same gain nothing. The weak side may simply explode all its nuclear charges, even on its own territory, and that would mean suicide for it and a slow death for the enemy. This is why any striving for military superiority means chasing one's own tail. It can't be used in real politics.

Nor is the US in any hurry to part with another illusion. I mean its immoral intention to bleed the Soviet Union white economically, to prevent us from carrying out our plans of construction by dragging us ever deeper into the quagmire of the arms race.

I ask the reader to take a look at the experience of postwar decades. The Soviet Union emerged from the Second World War in a very difficult condition. Yes, we had won the struggle against fascism, won together with the US and other anti-Hitler coalition participants. But whereas not a single enemy bomb was dropped and not a single enemy shot was heard on the US mainland, a large part of the territory of our country was an arena for the fiercest battles. Our losses—both human and material—were enormous. Nevertheless, we succeeded in restoring what had been destroyed, in building up our economic potential and in confidently tackling our defensive tasks. Is this not a lesson for the future?

It is inadmissible that states should base their policies on mistaken views. We know that there is an opinion current in the US and the West generally that the threat from the Soviet Union comes not because it possesses nuclear weapons. They reason as follows, as I have already mentioned in another connection: the Soviets well know that if they attack the US, they can't escape retaliation. The US is equally well aware that retaliation will follow an attack on the USSR. Therefore only a madman would unleash nuclear war. The real threat, according to these people, will arise if the Soviet Union accomplishes its plans of accelerating socio–economic development and shows its new economic and political potential. Hence the desire to exhaust the Soviet Union economically.

We sincerely advise Americans: try to get rid of such an approach to our country. Hopes of using any advantages in technology or advanced equipment so as to gain superiority over our country are futile. To act on the assumption that the Soviet Union is in a "hopeless position" and that it is necessary just to press it harder to squeeze out everything the US wants is to err profoundly. Nothing will come of these plans. In real politics there can be no wishful thinking. If the Soviet Union, when it was much weaker than now, was in a position to meet all the challenges that it faced, then indeed only a blind person would be unable to see that our capacity to maintain strong defenses and simultaneously resolve social and other tasks has enormously increased.

I shall repeat that as far as United States foreign policy is concerned, it is based on at least two delusions. The first is the belief that the economic system of the Soviet Union is about to crumble and that the USSR will not succeed in restructuring. The second is calculated on Western superiority in equipment and technology and, eventually, in the military field. These illusions nourish a policy geared toward exhausting socialism through the arms race, so as to dictate terms later. Such is the scheme; it is naïve.

Current Western policies aren't responsible enough, and lack the new mode of thinking. I am outspoken about this. If we don't stop now and start practical disarmament, we may all find ourselves on the edge of a precipice. Today, as never before, the Soviet Union and the United States need responsible policies. Both countries have their political, social and economic problems: a vast field for activities. Meanwhile, many brain trusts work at strategic plans and juggle millions of lives. Their recommendations boil down to this: the Soviet Union is the most horrible threat for the United States and the world. I repeat: it is high time this caveman mentality was given up. Of course, many political leaders and diplomats have engaged in just such policies based on just such a mentality for decades. But their time is past. A new outlook is necessary in a nuclear age. The United States and the Soviet Union need it most in their bilateral relations.

We are realists. So we take into consideration the fact that in a foreign policy all countries, even the smallest, have their own interests. It is high time great powers realized that they can no longer reshape the world according to their own patterns. That era has receded or, at least, is receding into the past.

More About Realities:
Removing the Ideological Edge from Interstate Relations

We should have long ago taken a sober view of the world around us and of our past. We should have fearlessly seen where we are. When one country sees another as evil incarnate, and itself as the embodiment of absolute good, relations between them have reached a stalemate. I am not thinking of anti-communist rhetoric here, however pernicious, but of the inability, or reluctance, to realize that we all represent one human race, that we share a common destiny and have to learn to be civilized neighbors on our planet. Today's generations inherited Soviet–American confrontation from the past. But are we doomed to carry enmity on?

On the whole, we have long lived in peace. But the current international situation can't be described as satisfactory. The arms race, especially the nuclear arms race, goes on. Regional conflicts are raging. The war danger grows. To make international relations more humane is the only way out—and that is a difficult thing to do. This is how we pose the question: it is essential to rise above ideological differences. Let everyone make his own choice, and let us all respect that choice. And for that a new mode of political thinking is necessary, one that proceeds from realization of the general interdependence and from the idea that civilization must survive. If we reach an understanding on the criteria of such new thinking, we shall arrive at valid decisions for global issues. If political leaders realize that point and implement it practically, it will be a major victory for reason.

When we speak about improving the global situation, we single out two criteria for a realistic foreign policy: consideration for one's own national interests and respect for other countries' interests. That stance is sound and reasonable; one to be defended persistently. We think so and act accordingly.

221

Alienation is Evil

We often hear that the Soviet Union and the United States can well do without each other. To tell the truth, I sometimes say it too. Well, it's true from the economic viewpoint, considering our negligible economic contacts today. Contacts or no contacts, we live on, and learn the lessons Americans teach us.

Our fodder grain imports were a sensitive issue. Now we have secured our position by making import contracts with many countries and introducing intensive agricultural technologies to boost grain yields at home. Our present task is to start exporting grain in the near future.

The West has set up COCOM. The United States is on guard lest its limitations are violated and sees to it that the lists of goods not open for sale to the Soviet Union are enlarged. America doesn't hesitate to interfere in the domestic affairs of the participants in the prohibitive program.

The Soviet Union reacted promptly by elaborating the corresponding program, named Program 100 because it dealt with one hundred materials. We put it through in less than three years. Some ninety percent of the materials we use are home-made. So we can say that we have coped with the task in the main.

We said right out that it was time to get over our inferiority complex. Ours is a vast country with immense resources and a tremendous scientific potential. Our capitalist partners abroad are not always reliable and sometimes use trade for political blackmail and intimidation. The measures we have taken are already bearing fruit. Pioneering developments have been made in computer and supercomputer technologies, superconductivity and other fields. The United States hopes it will always lead the world: a futile hope, as many American scientists realize.

Our countries have been alienated from each other for years, and both the Soviet and the American economies have lost many brilliant opportunities. We have failed to do many good things together because of suspicion and lack of confidence. Alienation is an evil. Besides, economic contacts provide the material basis for political *rapprochement*.

Economic contacts create mutual interests helpful in politics. If we boost our trade and economic relations and continue the cultural process currently going on, even if it is slower than we would like, we shall be able to build confidence between our countries. But the United States has created many obstacles in the economic field.

We do still import grain—but rather to keep up trade. It may die otherwise. But we may soon need no grain imports at all, as I have said. And Soviet–American trade in other goods is practically nonexistent. As soon as some Soviet goods penetrated the American market, the United States anxiously started to take measures to prohibit or at least limit trade. There are legal acts galore in America which prevent trade with the Soviet Union from developing.

America manages without the Soviet Union and we, too, manage without America as far as trade goes. But as soon as we come to think of how much the world depends on our two countries and on understanding between them, we realize that our mutual understanding must develop. So, our trade must develop too. That would be only normal, even exciting.

Certain groups in the United States are not especially forthcoming and show no desire to reciprocate. They lack the capacity to be open. "If something can be obtained from the Soviet Union, America's here. But when it comes to mutual profit, forget it."

Something depends on the Soviet Union, too: much, in fact. We may be bad traders. Or we may fail to make the necessary effort because we manage without it. Both sides must work to remove the obstacles.

That's the right approach to the confidence issue. Incantations don't work here. Confidence comes as the result of practical action, including common efforts to develop trade, economic, scientific, technological, cultural and other ties. Both sides must work to stop the arms race and go over to disarmament. If we work together to settle regional conflicts, our mutual confidence will gain too.

When I hear that we must first take care of confidence and the basic problems will be solved later, I can't comprehend it. It sounds more like a lame excuse. Is confidence a divine gift? Or will it arise of itself if the Soviet Union and the United States both repeat that they support confidence? Nothing of the kind. Arousing confidence is a long process. Its degree always depends on practical relations, on cooperation in many fields.

We must get to know each other better if we are to avoid incidents pregnant with disaster. I repeat once again: not only economic factors prompt us to cooperate. Political goals are more important here than economic ones. We must always bear in mind our main goal of normalizing Soviet–American relations. We must remember it, however far off it may seem, and however our path toward it may be obscured by domestic and international factors.

Realistically minded people in America and elsewhere want co-operation, not confrontation. Information and personal contacts show this to be the case. Such people welcome realism in Soviet policy, and attach great hopes to it. I meet many businessmen, and I see they think in terms of the overall picture, though they never forget about business. It's always a pleasure to meet Dr Armand Hammer. He does much to promote understanding and friendly contacts between our two countries. I recently heard of Mr Bronfman, one of America's richest citizens, suggesting a toast to Gorbachev's health and telling his companion: "I've got everything I could get from this life materially. But now it is the future of mankind that matters. If the Soviet Union continues to develop, it will be able to preserve the balance of forces and, consequently, there will be a market and peace."

Undoubtedly, the Soviet Union and the United States are two powerful states with vast interests. Each has its allies and friends. We have our foreign policy priorities, but this does not necessarily mean that we are doomed to confrontation. A different conclusion would be more logical—the Soviet Union and the United States are especially responsible for the future of the world.

The bulk of nuclear weapons is concentrated in the Soviet Union and the United States. Meanwhile, ten percent or even one percent of their potential is enough to inflict irreparable damage on our planet and all human civilization.

This point of view implies, too, that we and the Americans bear the greatest responsibility toward the world's nations. Our two countries and peoples and their politicians bear a special, unique responsibility to all human civilization. The American people were strong enough to make America what it now is. And the Soviet Union proved strong enough to make a once backward country an advanced power. And today, in spite of all the hardships we have experienced in our difficult history, the Soviet Union is a mighty developed state and a well-educated nation with a vast intellectual potential. So I think we and the Americans, with our historic achievements, will have the wisdom, ability, responsibility and respect for each other that is necessary to get to grips with reality and avert catastrophe.

We are keenly aware of the mountains of problems that have accumulated between our two countries. It is impossible to quickly discuss and settle problems that have accumulated over years. It would be an illusion, an empty dream to think otherwise. The most important thing in Soviet–American relations is not to chase myths but to see things the way they are. We look at the world, the United States included, from a position of realistic politics. And we proceed from the fundamental fact that neither the American people nor the Soviet people want self-destruction. Convinced of this, we have embarked upon a path dedicated to bettering relations with the United States, and we expect reciprocity.

On the Road to Geneva

In the course of a major "stocktaking" of our domestic affairs and the international situation after the April 1985 Plenary Meeting of the Soviet Communist Party Central Committee, the Soviet leadership came to the conclusion that the situation in the world was too dangerous to allow us to miss even the slightest chance for improvement and for more durable peace. We decided to try by persuasion, setting an example and demonstrating common sense, so as to reverse the dangerous course of events. The gravity of the situation convinced us that a one-to-one meeting with the US President was necessary, if only for a deeper exchange of views and for better understanding of each other's positions.

Several months before the meeting we began to pave the way by creating a more favorable climate. In the summer of 1985 the Soviet Union introduced a unilateral moratorium on all nuclear explosions and expressed its readiness immediately to resume the negotiations for a comprehensive test ban treaty. We also reaffirmed our unilateral moratorium on the testing of anti-satellite weapons and advanced a radical proposal for reduction in nuclear arsenals. We backed up our strong conviction that the arms race must not spread into space with a proposal for broad international cooperation in the peaceful exploration and use of space.

On the eve of the Geneva meeting, the Warsaw Pact countries declared at a meeting of their Political Consultative Committee in Sofia that they were determined to continue working toward peace, *détente*, against the arms race and confrontation, and for an improvement in the international situation in the interests of all countries of the world.

Geneva

All the details of the Geneva meeting are fresh in my memory. During the two busy days I had several one-on-one discussions with President Reagan. There were five such meetings to be exact, not counting when we met for a couple of minutes to bid each other goodbye.

As I have already said, our discussions were frank, long, sharp, and, at times very sharp. We saw that we had what I think is a spring board for working toward better Soviet–American relations. This was the realization that a nuclear war cannot be won and must never be fought.

That view was repeatedly expressed by the Soviet side and by the Americans as well. This means that the central issue in relations between our two countries today is security. I told the President that we must think of ways to improve bilateral relations in the interest of the Soviet and American peoples and then try to make those relations friendly, taking into account that our countries are not only different but also interrelated. For the alternative is universal destruction.

It was from this point of view that we talked about the need for measures to prevent an arms race in space and to halt it on Earth, and the importance of maintaining strategic parity and lowering its level. From this position we also discussed the outside world, which is a many-faceted community of nations, each with its own interests, aspirations, policies, traditions and dreams. We talked about the natural wish of every nation to exercise its sovereign rights in the political sphere and in the economic and social spheres as well. Each country has the right to choose a way of development, a system and friends. If we do not recognize this, we shall never be able to arrange normal international relations.

There were moments when the President concurred, but on many things we could not reach agreement. Our substantial differences on matters of principle remained. In Geneva we failed to find a solution to the fundamental problem of halting the arms race and strengthening peace.

However, even then, in the autumn of 1985, I believed, as I still believe, that the meeting was necessary and useful. In the most difficult periods of history moments of truth are needed like air. The arms race has made the international situation too disquieting and too much nonsense has been said on this score. The time has come to disperse this fog and check words by deeds. Nothing can do this better than direct discussion, and this is what summit meetings are for. In direct debate you can't hide from the truth.

In Geneva we got to know each other better, clearly saw the nature of our differences, and started dialogue. We signed an agreement on cultural exchanges which is already working to our mutual advantage. We realized that we still had a long way to go in order to achieve a satisfactory mutual understanding and that we had to work really hard to bring about a change for the better in Soviet—American relations and in the world in general.

After Geneva

What happened after Geneva? We always knew that nothing would change by itself and that it required a good deal of initiative to continue what had been achieved. The binding agreements signed in Geneva, in which both sides pledged that a nuclear war must never be fought, that neither side would seek to achieve military superiority and that the Geneva negotiations should be accelerated, had to be translated into practical moves. And we made such moves.

Moratorium

On 1 January 1986, the term of our unilateral moratorium on nuclear explosions expired, but the Soviet Union extended it. It was a very serious decision which involved some risks for us because advances in space technology continued and new types of nuclear weapons, such as nuclear-pumped lasers, were being developed. Yet we had the courage to do what we did and invite the United States to follow suit in the interest of world peace.

A nuclear test ban is a touchstone. If you sincerely wish to eliminate nuclear weapons, you will agree to ban tests because such a ban will lead to a reduction of the existing arsenals and an end to their modernization. If you do not want this to happen, you will do everything to ensure that testing continues.

A nuclear test ban is a measure that would immediately introduce a new, encouraging element in Soviet–American relations and the international situation as a whole. There was a good basis for carrying out this measure. The Soviet Union and the United States are both signatories to the treaty banning nuclear tests in three environments. We had worked out an agreement on the limitation of underground nuclear explosions and had some experience in negotiating their total prohibition.

Earlier the stumbling block was the verification problem. To remove it we declared that we were prepared to accept verification in any form and use to this end both national technical facilities and international facilities involving third countries.

Being an action rather than just a proposal, the Soviet moratorium on nuclear explosions bore out the seriousness and sincerity of our nuclear disarmament program and our appeals for a new policy—a policy of realism, peace and cooperation.

People of good will acclaimed our decision for a moratorium on nuclear explosions. We heard words of approval and support from all over the globe. Politicians and parliamentarians, public figures and organizations viewed this action as an example of a correct approach to present-day problems and as a hope for deliverance from the fear of nuclear catastrophe. The Soviet moratorium was endorsed by the UN General Assembly, the most representative body of states in the world. We were supported, also, by outstanding physicists and physicians, who realize perhaps better than anyone else the dangers of the atom. The Soviet moratorium inspired members of the scientific community in many countries to vigorous actions.

However, all these obvious and encouraging manifestations of the new thinking are being countered by militarism and the political attitudes linked with it, which have so dangerously lagged behind the sweeping changes taking place internationally. The US Administration reacted un-equivocally to the extension of the Soviet moratorium—it went on with a series of nuclear tests. Its spokesmen officially declared that it is Moscow's business whether to test nuclear charges or not. As far as the United States was concerned, the tests would continue without any let-up.

Silence reigned at Soviet test sites. Of course, we weighed the dangers involved in Washington's actions and saw how demonstra-tively and impudently the American Administration was pushing its line in total disregard for the appeals to put an end to all nuclear explosions. Nevertheless, having examined the problems from all angles, and guided by a sense of responsibility for the fate of the world, the Politburo of the CPSU Central Committee and the Soviet government resolved in August 1986 to extend the unilateral mora-torium on nuclear tests until 1 January 1987. The United States, however, elected not to follow the Soviet example.

I do not think our moratorium was unproductive. World public opinion learned that nuclear tests could be ended and it learned who was opposed to this. It's true that a historic chance to halt the arms race was missed then, but the political lessons of all this have not been wasted. Now that an agreement has been reached to start full-scale, stage-by-stage negotiations on nuclear testing by 1 December, we can congratu-late ourselves and everyone for having got the matter off the ground.

The Nuclear Disarmament Program

On 15 January 1986 we advanced a fifteen-year program providing for the stage-by-stage elimination of nuclear weapons by the end of the twentieth century. We carefully worked out this program, seeking to ensure a mutually acceptable balance of interests at each stage so that no one's security would be undermined at any point. Any other approach would be simply unrealistic. On the basis of this program our representatives tabled major compromise proposals at the Geneva talks. They touched upon medium-range missiles, strategic offensive weapons, and non-militarization of outer space.

The Statement of 15 January was of a policy-making nature. We wanted to single out the main threat to civilization related to nuclear weapons and nuclear explosions, without overlooking the questions pertaining to the prohibition and elimination of chemical weapons and a drastic reduction in conventional armaments. This was a set of measures in general outline. The overriding principle in operation at all stages was the maintenance of a balance. No political games or ruses are needed, but political responsibility and a clear understanding that no one is out to deceive anyone else when the issue at stake is as sensitive as a state's security.

Such a step as the one we took on 15 January 1986 required not only an understanding of our responsibility, but also political resolve. We proceeded from the need for new approaches to security issues in the nuclear space age. This was the will of our entire people. In taking this step, the last thing we contemplated was a propaganda dividend to outdo the other side. The move was dictated by a sense of responsibility about preventing nuclear war and preserving peace. Our stance here accorded with world public opinion; among other things, it was a response to the appeal of the Group of Six (India, Argentina, Sweden, Greece, Mexico, Tanzania).

We are profoundly devoted to the idea of a nuclear-free world. Enriched by the Indian political tradition and the specifics of Indian philosophy and culture, this idea was developed in the Delhi Declaration on Principles for a Nuclear-Weapon-Free and Non-Violent World. For us this is not some slogan that was invented to stagger the imagination. Security is a political issue, not a function of military confrontation. Failure to understand this can only result in war with all its catastrophic consequences. If the huge stockpiles of nuclear, chemical and other weapons that have been accumulated are unleashed, nothing will remain of the world. What we are talking about is the survival of humanity. For us the idea of a nuclear-free world is a conviction which we arrived at through a great deal of suffering. We regard security as an all-embracing concept which incorporates not only military–political aspects, but economic, ecological and humanitarian ones as well.

230

At the 27th Congress of the CPSU we substantiated from all angles the concept of building an all-embracing system of international security. We presented it to the entire world, to the governments, parties, public organizations and movements which are genuinely concerned about peace on Earth.[1]

We are not reneging on any of the proposals in our Congress

[1] We see the Fundamental Principles of this system as follows:

1. *In the miltary sphere*
   i renunciation by the nuclear powers of war—both nuclear and conventional—against each other or against third countries;
   ii prevention of an arms race in outer space, cessation of all nuclear weapons tests and the total destruction of such weapons, a ban on the destruction of chemical weapons, and renunciation of the development of other means of mass annihilation;
   iii a strictly controlled lowering of the levels of military capabilities of countries to limits of reasonable sufficiency;
   iv disbandment of military alliances, and, as a stage toward this, renunciation of their enlargement and of the formation of new ones;
   v balanced and proportionate reduction of military budgets.
2. *In the political sphere*
   i strict respect in international practice for the right of each people to choose the ways and forms of its development independently;
   ii a just political settlement of international crises and regional conflicts;
   iii elaboration of a set of measures aimed at building confidence between states and the creation of effective guarantees against attack from without and for inviolability of their frontiers;
   iv elaboration of effective methods of preventing international terrorism, including those ensuring the safety of international land, air and sea communications.
3. *In the economic sphere*
   i exclusion of all forms of discrimination from international practice; renunciation of the policy of economic blockades and sanctions if this is not directly envisaged in the recommendations of the world community;
   ii joint quests for ways of a just settlement of the problem of debts;
   iii establishment of a new world economic order guaranteeing equal economic security to all countries;
   iv elaboration of principles for utilizing part of the funds released as a result of a reduction of military budgets for the good of the world community, of developing nations in the first place;
   v the pooling of efforts in exploring and making peaceful use of outer space and in resolving global problems on which the destinies of civilization depend.
4. *In the humanitarian sphere*
   i cooperation in the dissemination of the ideas of peace, disarmament, and international security; greater flow of general objective information and broader contact between peoples for the purpose of learning about one another; reinforcement of the spirit of mutual understanding and concord in relations between them;
   ii extirpation of genocide, apartheid, advocacy of fascism and every other form of racial, national or religious exclusiveness, and also of discrimination against people on this basis;
   iii extension—while respecting the laws of each country—of international cooperation in the implementation of the political, social and personal rights of people;
   iv solution in a humane and positive spirit to questions related to the reuniting of families, marriage, and the promotion of contacts between people and between organizations;
   v strengthening of and the quests for new forms of cooperation in culture, art, science, education, and medicine.

program; we are prepared to consider in a most careful manner any ideas that could promote peaceful coexistence as the loftiest, universal principle of interstate relations.

We also spoke at the Congress about Soviet–American relations. I want to call to mind our statement on this score: "It is the firm intention of the Soviet Union to justify the hopes of the peoples of our two countries and of the whole world who are expecting from the leaders of the USSR and the US concrete steps, practical actions, and tangible agreements on how to curb the arms race." The entire essence of Congress's stand on Soviet–American relations can be expressed in a few words—we live on the same planet, and we won't be able to preserve peace without the United States.

The US Since Geneva

How has the US Administration behaved since Geneva? A strident campaign aimed at instigating anti-Soviet passions was started for the umpteenth time. Attempts were made again and again to portray the Soviet Union as some kind of bugbear, to increase fears in order to get the latest military budget through Congress. The "evil empire" epithet has been trotted out. The President has again confirmed that he is not going to scrap this term.

All this could be put down to rhetoric, but, as I have already said, hostile rhetoric also ruins relations. It has a snowballing effect. Things are now far more serious. There has been, for instance, a demand for the Soviet Union to cut its diplomatic staff in the US by forty percent; American warships crossed Soviet territorial waters near the Crimean coast; a military attack was launched against sovereign Libya. We assessed such actions by the American Administration in the post-Geneva situation as a challenge, not only to the Soviet Union but to the whole world, including the American people.

It was then that the US stated its intention to pull out of the SALT-II Treaty. This document was declared "dead." Instead of proceeding to new major agreements to end the arms race, the Administration preferred to dismantle the existing agreements. A campaign was begun to brainwash the American and world public in order to destroy the unlimited Anti-Ballistic Missile Treaty.

The post-Geneva period has shown that whereas in the past we could only surmise, today we have at our disposal facts which attest to the US Administration's reluctance to comply with the Geneva accords. However, while continuing to act in the old way, it wanted to "calm" the public. We again began asking ourselves whether Washington really thinks it is dealing with weak-willed people, that it can go on acting like a gambler, that the Soviet Union shudders at the sight of ever new militarist postures?

At that time I was to speak in the city of Togliatti. I was to explain to the working class of this city, and to all Soviet people, what had happened since Geneva.

We accomplished a great deal, and we fulfilled our commitments to the world, taking a highly responsible attitude to our commitments at Geneva.

But what about the United States? I cited the facts, and again the question arose as to what the United States really wants if one is to judge by its real policies rather than its statements. Not only did the Administration abandon *détente*, it seemed scared by any manifestations of a thaw. I had to tell the Soviet people honestly whose interests such policies were expected to promote. Indeed, it was not the American people that wanted the military threat to increase—was it? The US military–industrial complex had to be spoken about which, like the ancient Moloch, not only devours the immense resources of the Americans and other peoples, but also devours the fruits of the efforts to eliminate the threat of nuclear war.

Of course, our people are alarmed by the Strategic Defense Initiative. We have said this more than once. But maybe they are merely trying to intimidate us again? Perhaps it is better to stop fearing SDI?

Indifference was certainly inadmissible. We saw that although millions of Americans, including prominent political and public leaders, ordinary people, scientists, religious leaders, and school and university students, were against SDI and nuclear tests, some quarters in the United States had gone crazy over the Star War program. This was all the more dangerous because it ensued directly from a rapid militarization of political thought. And yet it was necessary to get rid of the impression about us for which we were not responsible. They

233

think that if the USSR is afraid of SDI, it should be intimidated with SDI morally, economically, politically and militarily. This explains the great stress on SDI, the aim being to exhaust us. So, we have decided to say: yes, we are against SDI, because we are for complete elimination of nuclear weapons and because SDI makes the world ever more unstable. But for us the issue involves responsibility rather than fear, because the consequences would be unpredictable. Instead of promoting security, SDI destroys the remnants of what might still serve security.

Speaking in Togliatti, I decided to say once again that our response to SDI would be effective. The United States hopes that we will develop similar systems, so it can get ahead of us technologically and take advantage of its technological superiority. But we, the Soviet leadership, know that there is nothing which the US could achieve that our scientists and engineers could not. A tenth of the US investments would be enough to create a counter-system to frustrate SDI.

Thus we have resolved to debunk entirely the demagogical statements that we are faltering in the face of SDI.

In my address, I repeated the formula of the Party Congress—we do not want more security, but we will not settle for less.

Summing up the results of the post-Geneva months, we wanted to tell the West, the United States and NATO that there was no way we would abandon our policy of peace, though we took into account the true Western policies. We would not beg for peace. We had more than once responded to challenges and would do so again.

It seemed that the United States should have responded to our initiatives and moves since the Geneva summit by meeting us halfway and reacting to the aspirations of the people. But that was not the case. The ruling group placed selfish interests above those of mankind and its own people. What was also significant was that it did it so bluntly and defiantly, totally ignoring world public opinion.

Such attitudes indicate that the feeling of responsibility has been ousted again by the habitual mentality that one can get away with anything.

The hopes that arose after the Geneva summit, everywhere, including in American society, soon gave way to disillusionment, because everything in US real politics remained as it had been.

234

The Lesson of Chernobyl

April 1986 taught us a grave lesson in what an atom out of control is capable of doing, even an atom used for peaceful purposes. I refer to the tragedy of Chernobyl. The entire truth has been revealed as to how it happened, and why, and as to its consequences. Those to blame for the catastrophe have already been brought to trial. The world knows what was done in our country to reduce the extent of that misfortune.

We many times discussed the incident at the Central Committee's Politburo. Soon after the first few reports had reached us we realized that the situation was serious and that we were responsible both for the evaluation of the accident and for the right conclusions. Our work is open to the whole nation and the whole world. To think that we can settle for half-measures and dodge an issue is inadmissible. There must be full and unbiased information about what happened. A cowardly position means an unacceptable policy. There are no vested interests that would compel us to conceal the truth.

The Soviet leadership was directly involved in the efforts to cope with the aftermath of the accident. We regarded it as our duty to the people and as our international responsibility. The best scientists, physicians and technical personnel were summoned to eliminate the consequences of the accident. We got help—which we very much appreciated—from scientists, industrial firms and physicians, including from America. And, finally, we made some cruicial conclusions concerning the further development of the nuclear power industry.

Thanks to the selfless efforts of tens of thousands of people and nationwide support, including donations, we succeeded in containing the consequences of the accident. But we do not regard this as a reason for remaining silent. We are not inclined to oversimplify the situation, either for ourselves or for others. The work goes on. It will take years, though the situation, I repeat, is under control.

And that was an accident involving just one reactor. Chernobyl mercilessly reminded us what all of us would suffer if a nuclear thunderstorm was unleashed.

I won't recall all the lies concocted about Chernobyl. May I just say that we appreciated the understanding and help of all those who felt for us in our misfortune, but we also witnessed again how much malice and malevolence there was in the world.

Reykjavik

We realized that the militarist group in the United States (I mean neither the Republican or Democratic Party, but those firmly linked to the arms business) stood in awe of the slightest hint at a thaw in relations between our countries. That group had been doing everything possible and impossible to forget all about the Geneva summit, to erase the spirit of Geneva, remove any and all obstacles in its way and continue the arms race without hindrance, including in the new direction—toward outer space.

But we were also well aware that the militarist group was far from the only entity on the US political scene. American politcians who had taken realistic positions and bore no illusions about the world situation advocated continuing negotiations with the USSR in search of ways to normalize Soviet–American relations, knowing that the arms race would result in serious negative consequences for the United States itself. But the interests of the militarist group always triumphed in one way or another, as had, in fact, often happened before.

Chances for a full-dress, fruitful Soviet–American summit were rapidly waning. Going to a new summit just to shake hands and maintain friendly relations would have been frivolous and senseless. And yet we could not accept the American "no" to our consistent efforts to achieve a *rapprochement* of positions and hammer out a reasonable compromise. We knew that we needed a breakthrough and that time was working against the interests of mankind. Then came the idea of holding an interim Soviet–American summit in order to give a really powerful impetus to the cause of nuclear disarmament, to overcome the dangerous tendencies and to swing events in the right direction. The US President accepted our initiative, which seemed quite inspiring. That was how the way was paved for the Reykjavik summit in October 1986.

In the course of our first discussion at Reykjavik I told the President that in the wake of the Geneva summit we had succeeded in activating the intricate and vast mechanism of the Soviet–American dialogue. But that mechanism had more than once faltered: there was no progress on the major issues both sides were concerned about—how to defuse the nuclear threat, how to put the impulse provided by the Geneva summit to advantage, and how to achieve specific accords. That troubled us much. I also told the President that the Geneva negotiations were choking on the endless discussions of dead issues. There were some fifty to a hundred alternatives in the air, but none which would pave the way toward progress.

We planned thoroughly for the Reykjavik summit and did a lot of preparatory work. We pursued a clear-cut and firm line—to agree in the long run on the complete elimination of nuclear weapons with equal security for the United States and the Soviet Union at all stages of progress toward that goal. A different approach would have been vague, unrealistic and invalid. The Reykjavik meeting, we were convinced, was to pave the way for signing agreements on fundamental arms control issues at our next meeting.

We brought with us to Reykjavik a set of drastic measures in draft form. Had these been accepted, mankind would have stood on the threshold of a new era, a nuclear-free era. The point at issue was not reductions in nuclear weapons, as it was in the SALT-I and SALT-II agreements, but rather the speedy elimination of these weapons.

The *first* proposal was on strategic offensive weapons. I declared our readiness to have these cut by fifty percent in the course of the forthcoming five years.

What I heard in response were all kind of things about levels, sublevels and mind-boggling estimates, something the delegations to the Geneva negotiations had chewed over and squashed for months before they found themselves in a blind alley. I began to argue but soon saw that the discussion was leading nowhere. To get out of the quagmire of stalemate—which had been created at the Geneva negotiations far from accidentally but with a deliberate intention to discredit the talks and make the whole thing look a farce—I offered a simple and clear solution. There was the triad of strategic weaponry

237

—ballistic land-based missiles, sea-launched missiles and aircraft. Both the USSR and the US had them, though the strategic offensive weapons of each side had their own historical differences. Let all three components or types of weapons, i.e. each of the three parts of the triad, be halved, fairly and equally.

To make an accord easier we made a significant compromise, removing our earlier demand that the strategic equation include American medium-range missiles that could reach our territory and American forward-based systems. We were also ready to take into account US concern over our heavy missiles.

The President agreed to this approach. Moreover, he advanced the idea of complete elimination of strategic offensive weapons over the forthcoming five years, something that I firmly supported.

Our *second* proposal concerned medium-range missiles. I suggested to the President that Soviet and American weapons of this class in Europe be completely eliminated. In that area, too, we were making big concessions. We ignored the British and French nuclear forces spearheaded against us. We agreed to have missiles with a range of less than a thousand kilometres frozen and immediately to begin negotiations on their future, certainly thinking toward Europe being ultimately rid of that type of missiles. Finally, we accepted the American proposal to sharply limit the number of medium-range missiles deployed in the Asian part of the Soviet Union, leaving a hundred warheads on such missiles to the east of the Urals in the USSR and a hundred warheads on the American medium-range missiles on US territory. As a result, there appeared a chance we would be able to instruct our foreign ministers to start working on a draft accord in medium-range missiles.

The *third* question which I put to the President in our first discussion and which we saw as part and parcel of our package was to strengthen the regime of the Anti-Ballistic Missile Treaty and achieve a nuclear test ban.

I tried to convince the President that, as we sought to reduce nuclear weapons, we ought to be sure that none of us would do anything to put the security of the other side in jeopardy. Hence the key meaning of the strengthening of the ABM Treaty. We also duly took into account the President's deep commitment to the idea of SDI. We proposed that it be recorded that laboratory research for SDI is permissable and then that the issue of the non-use of the right to abandon the ABM Treaty for ten years be resolved. The non-use of the right to abandon the ABM Treaty for ten years was indispensable to make us confident that, in dealing with arms control, we would safeguard mutual security and prevent attempts to gain unilateral advantages through deployment of space-based systems.

Politically, practically and technically, such limitations posed no threats to anyone. I will raise the point again later, but for the time being I would like to recall that in Reykjavik we proposed to the President that it be agreed that our representatives start negotiations on a nuclear test ban as soon as the meeting in the capital of Iceland was concluded. We adopted a flexible approach to that problem, too, having stated that we saw a fully-fledged treaty on the complete and final prohibition of nuclear testing as a process implying step-by-step progress. In this context, priority issues could include the "threshold capacity" of nuclear tests, the yearly number of such tests, and the future of the 1974 and 1976 treaties. We were quite close to finding appropriate formulas for that question, too.

I still think the way to a moratorium has not been hopelessly blocked. The fact that we had to resume testing is certainly not an indication that the United States alone can write the scenario. It's hard to say when realism will prevail in our evaluations of each other. But it will come one day, perhaps quite unexpectedly, because life makes us wiser. History is rich in examples showing how abruptly the situation may change.

And so the Reykjavik summit resulted in a chance that our foreign ministers would be directed to prepare three draft accords to be signed at the next Soviet–American summit. But the opportunity, so clear and palpable, to achieve a breakthrough on the way toward a truly historic compromise between the USSR and the USA, ultimately fell apart, though it had been within easy reach.

The stumbling block proved to be the American stance on the ABM Treaty. After Reykjavik I asked myself time and again why the United States had avoided an agreement on strengthening the regime of this treaty of unlimited duration. And each time the conclusion I came to was one and the same: the United States is not ready to part with its hope of winning nuclear superiority and this time wants to get ahead of the Soviet Union by speeding up SDI research.

In this context I would like to reiterate once more: if the United States succeeds in having its way with SDI, which we doubt very much, a Soviet answer will be forthcoming. If the United States does not give up SDI, we are not going to make life easier for the US. Our reply will be effective, credible and not too costly. We have a tentative scheme on how to puncture SDI without spending the fabulous sums the US will need to establish it. Let the Americans consider once again if it is worthwhile wearing themselves down with SDI. It would not offer dependable protection anyway.

But SDI means moving weapons to a new medium which would greatly destabilize the strategic situation. On the other hand, adherence to SDI speaks of political intentions and political aims: to place the Soviet Union at a disadvantage by hook or by crook. It was these political intentions, these illusory designs—to dominate the USSR through the Strategic Defense Initiative—that prevented Reykjavik from being crowned with decisions of historic significance.

Ronald Reagan and myself talked a good deal about it, and our discussions were rather heated. I was sincere when I told the President that our meeting could not produce one winner: we would both either win or lose.

And still Reykjavik marked a turning-point in world history. It tangibly demonstrated that the world situation could be improved. A quantitatively new situation emerged. Now no one can act in the way he acted before. At Reykjavik we became convinced that our course was correct and that a new and constructive way of political thinking was essential.

The meeting, as it were, raised to a new level the Soviet–American dialogue, as indeed it did the whole East–West dialogue. This dialogue has now broken free of the confusion of technicalities, of data comparisons and of political arithmetic, and has acquired new parameters. Reykjavik has become a vantage point for spotting prospects of solving difficult issues—I speak of security, nuclear disarmament and the need to stop new dimensions in the arms race. Reykjavik mapped out a route by which humankind can regain the immortality it lost when nuclear arms incinerated Hiroshima and Nagasaki.

We feel the meeting in Iceland was a landmark. It signified completion of one stage in the disarmament effort and the beginning of another. We broke down the old pattern of talks and brought the

Soviet–American dialogue out of what, I would say, was political fog and demagogy. During the years of negotiations numerous proposals by both sides had turned disarmament topics into absolute Greek even to political leaders, not to mention the public at large. Our latest nuclear disarmament program is simple and understandable to everyone. It boils down to four points expressed in a page and a half (as described on page 231). The broad public can understand it. This was our deliberate aim, to make the world public a kind of party to our talks.

After Reykjavik

The dialectics of Reykjavik are such: the objective is nearer and more palpable, while the situation has grown more complex and contradictory. One can clearly see that, on the one hand, agreement, unprecedented in scope, is within reach and, on the other hand, there are enormous barriers in its way. Generally speaking, we have never come so close to accord before.

And indeed, it turned out that on the first and second points of our platform—strategic weapons and medium-range missiles—we achieved understanding, difficult though it was. This alone added greatly to our experience. We appreciated the President's difficulties and knew that he was not free to decide. We did not overdramatize the fact that the ABM problem prevented Reykjavik from becoming a total success. We decided: let the President think over everything that has taken place, let him consult Congress. One more attempt might be necessary to step over what divides us. We can wait. So we did not withdraw the proposals we brought to Reykjavik.

Reykjavik gave us an important insight into where we stand. Some clear-cut thinking is needed here and the approach must not be primitive. I would not on any account call Reykjavik a failure. It was a stage in a long and difficult dialogue, in the quest for solutions which must be large-scale. Only then is agreement possible. From Reykjavik we drew the conclusion that the need for dialogue had increased. This is why after Reykjavik I am an even greater optimist.

The text of this book was already on the publisher's desk when

241

Eduard Shevardnadze and George Shultz agreed in Washington that an agreement on medium- and shorter-range missiles would be drafted shortly and signed before the end of the year. This will be the first, major step toward disarmament. And this will also be a practical result of the Reykjavik meeting, proof that it was a historic meeting, a turning-point. And thus we have the answer to a question which was often asked then: has the world become a safer place since Reykjavik?

Some people tried to explain the Reykjavik drama (the situation was really dramatic) as though the whole matter hinged on one word and crumbled because of that word. No, it was a matter of principle. We made great strides to meet the other side, but we could not make a concession that would jeopardize the security of our state. Back in Moscow I twice spoke on the Reykjavik results, and not only to restore the truth, which was being distorted. My aim was first of all to determine what to do next. I said at the time and I am still convinced that the non-success of Reykjavik was due to two strategic misconceptions typical of certain Western circles.

First, that the Russians are afraid of SDI and would therefore make any concessions. And *second*, that we have a greater interest in disarmament than the United States. These sentiments had their impact on the course of the Reykjavik talks. We soon felt what was expected of us: the American delegation had arrived without a definite program and wanted only to put pickings in its basket.

The American partners stubbornly pushed us toward what had been fruitlessly discussed by our delegations at the Geneva talks. We, for our part, wanted to put what had been in principle agreed at the Geneva summit into practical and real terms. In other words, we wanted to give an impulse to the process of the elimination of nuclear weapons.

Indeed, all the previous talk had been about the limitation of nuclear weapons. Now it was about their reduction and elimination. That being so, it was necessary to seal all openings for outflanking maneuvres that could guarantee superiority. That is why the key point proved to be observance of the ABM Treaty. The US stand in Reykjavik on this issue clearly showed that the American side had not lowered its sights on supremacy. But it was found lacking both in responsibility and in the political determination to cross that threshold, because that would mean shaking off the influence of the military–industrial complex.

Nevertheless, we are not giving the matter up as lost. We proceed from the belief that Reykjavik has opened up new chances for all—Europeans, Americans and us—to see what is happening. One thing is clear to us, however: since the Americans want to get rid of the ABM Treaty and pursue SDI—which is an instrument for ensuring domination—than there is need for a package where everything is interconnected. And we wish to be fair: in advancing that package, we wanted to show to the world that SDI is the main obstacle to an agreement on nuclear disarmament.

The time that has passed since Reykjavik has been highly instructive. The militarist circles got a real scare. They tried, and still are trying, to pile up most absurd obstacles in the way of the process begun in Reykjavik, to make it somehow peter out. All kinds of stories were served up on what was discussed in Reykjavik and every effort was made to conceal the fact that the American side had come empty-handed to Reykjavik, prepared only to pick up Soviet concessions.

All sorts of things have happened in the days, weeks, months and now almost a year since Reykjavik. I choose to call a spade a spade: the US Administration has in fact set a course toward nullifying the Reykjavik results. None of its actions leave any doubt as to that. We saw the US begin to mix things up with regard to what actually took place in Reykjavik, and Western Europe stricken with near-panic feelings.

But the main thing is the activities of the United States. I mean the United States actually exceeding the limits of the SALT-II Treaty by deploying the 131st strategic bomber equipped with cruise missiles. Furthermore, I mean the ostentatiously loud debates in the Administration in favor of the so-called broad interpretation of the ABM Treaty. And in the first months of 1987 we heard from Washington that it was time for the US to start deploying the first SDI components in space.

The Geneva talks, too, were proceeding at a slack pace. Attempts were made to drag us back, and all those levels and sublevels were again thrown out on to the table. For propaganda purposes all that was garnished with talk about Soviet toughness and obstinacy; it was claimed that the USSR was setting out its proposals as a package and was preventing solutions where they were already possible.

What were we supposed to do? React in a similar fashion? But no good ever comes of such an attitude.

We did not follow the US "example" but said that we would continue to honor our commitments arising from the SALT-II Treaty. A bomber more or a bomber less means little in the context of the present strategic balance between the USSR and the USA. Washington's violation of the SALT-II Treaty was more of a political than a military nature. It was a sort of "invitation" to the Soviet Union to return to the pre-Reykjavik times.

We kept our cool when US right-wing groupings talked about stepping up SDI and immediately testing and even deploying space-based ABM systems.

As for the talk about the Soviet package, I still believe that, had the United States agreed to accept that package with possible specifications and certain modification, tremendous progress would have been made. Still earlier the package contained provisions for limiting and eliminating strategic offensive weapons and preventing the militarization of space. These issues are organically tied. This is strategic coordination. If there are no tough restrictions to prevent the arms race in space, there will be no reduction in the strategic offensive weapons. This must be perfectly clear to everyone.

In Reykjavik, we included into the package the question of medium-range missiles because we wanted to curtail the arms race in all the key directions simultaneously. At the same time, I repeat, we wanted to pinpoint SDI so that the whole world could see that it is the chief obstacle in the way of nuclear disarmament. Many Western politicians criticized and condemned us because we reintroduced medium-range missiles to the package. I know that various public quarters also disagreed with us. I think, however, that we made the right decision.

The Moscow Forum and Medium-Range Missiles

The Moscow forum "For the Nuclear-Free World and the Survival of Humanity" made a very deep impression on myself and other Soviet leaders. We became acutely aware of the sentiments of the world

244

public, its anxiety and concern about the fate of Reykjavik, about the fact that shortly after Reykjavik the Soviet Union had to suspend its unilateral moratorium on nuclear testing, that the United States undermined the SALT-II Treaty and that the ABM Treaty was in jeopardy. We in the Soviet Union gave it much thought and decided to take another step to invigorate the Geneva talks and achieve a positive shift in disarmament. What I have in mind is the singling out of the medium-range missile issue from the package.

And what happened?

Just like after Reykjavik, the NATO camp sounded an alarm. In response to our new step toward the West and before everyone's eyes, the NATO ruling circles began backing out of positions they had upheld for a long time, rejecting their own zero option or fencing it in with various conditions. They went so far as to suggest a build up of nuclear arsenals in Europe by deploying American shorter-range missiles, instead of a reduction of such arsenals.

We also hear the following statements: the West will give credence to the proposals of the Soviet Union on arms reduction if the USSR changes its political system, if it accepts Western society as a model. This is simply ridiculous.

After Reykjavik and especially after our proposal to conclude a separate agreement on medium-range missiles, the NATO circles raised a ballyhoo about the impossibility of securing peace in Europe without nuclear weapons.

I had a sharp debate on this issue with Mrs Thatcher. She claimed that for Britain nuclear weapons are the sole means of ensuring its security in the event of a conventional war in Europe. This is a philosophy of doom. I told the British Prime Minister: "When you are vowing that nuclear weapons are a blessing and that the US and the USSR may reduce their levels whereas Britain will keep aloof, it becomes only to obvious that we see in front of us an ardent supporter of nuclear weapons. Let us assume that we begin the process of disarmament, remove medium-range missiles from Europe and re-duce strategic offensive weapons by fifty percent or by another per-centage, while you continue building up your nuclear forces. Have you ever thought what you will look like in the eyes of world public opinion?"

I thought it was my duty to recall that Britain had been a participant

245

in the trilateral negotiations on the general and complete prohibition of nuclear tests and then it lost all interest in those negotiations. We observed a moratorium on nuclear testing for eighteen months, whereas Britain did not.

The existence of nuclear weapons is fraught with a permanent risk of unpredictability. If we follow the logic that nuclear weapons are a blessing and a reliable guarantee of security, then off with the nuclear non-proliferation treaty too. Especially as dozens of states now have the scientific, technological and material capability to build their own bomb. What moral right do the current nuclear powers have to reject the same to, say, Pakistan, Israel, Japan, South Africa, Brazil or any other country? But what then would become of the world, of international relations?

Evaluating the situation, the Politburo of the CPSU Central Committee confirmed the Soviet leadership's resolute disapproval of the stand which claims that the conducting of international affairs and national security are realizable only through reliance on nuclear weapons.

Now back to the issue of the medium-range missiles. Strictly speaking, it was President Reagan who proposed the zero option for Europe. Helmut Schmidt, too, claims an exclusive right to this idea. Indeed, Schmidt was the first to advance this proposal when he was the Chancellor of the Federal Republic of Germany. In Reykjavik the President and I found a solution and practically brought it to the stage of agreement. Now it can be realized. A West German newspaper wrote that there are people in Federal Germany who insist that Gorbachev be taken at his word. But having agreed to the zero option, Gorbachev took them at their word. Well, let them now prove, the newspaper goes on, that it was no mere jabbering when they offered their zero, counting that the Russians would reject it all the same. I chuckled at reading that. But then I thought: well, maybe the paper is right after all.

The problem of shorter-range missiles could also be resolved. We are for the elimination of these missiles. Now let us see what has happened. In April 1987 George Shultz arrived in Moscow and tried to convince us that the United States must have the right to build up its arsenal by having a number of missiles of this class deployed until the Soviet Union completely eliminates its missiles. It is a strange logic; a reversed logic. We are willing to eliminate the shorter-range missiles that are being withdrawn from the German Democratic Republic and Czechoslovakia and we are ready then to eliminate the remainder. But when we made this proposal, they in NATO again began fidgeting around it like a cat around a bowl of steaming food. History repeating itself.

This, however, did not discourage us. Having scrutinized the situation that emerged at the Geneva talks in the spring and early summer and heeding the voice of the European and Asian public, we took another major step.

On 22 July 1987, I announced on behalf of the Soviet leadership that the USSR is ready to eliminate *all* its medium-range missiles in the Asian part of its territory, too. This would remove the issue of retaining the one hundred warheads on medium-range missiles about which we agreed with the US President in Reykjavik and which was later discussed by our representatives in Geneva. Naturally, this is on condition that the United States does the same. Shorter-range missiles will also be eliminated. In a word, the Soviet Union is ready to implement the global double-zero option.

With a clear conscience we can say: the Soviet Union has done everything it could to give life to the first ever major agreement on the elimination of two, rather than just one, classes of nuclear weapons.

But how many barriers have been set up and are being placed in the way of agreement! What a hurdle has to be cleared for reason and common sense to prevail over nuclear mania!

Judge for yourselves what we felt when, having agreed to "double zero," we were told that seventy-two Pershing-1A missiles would remain on the territory of the Federal Republic of Germany and that a respective number of American nuclear warheads for these missiles must remain. So it comes out that everything—the non-nuclear status of the FRG, and the Treaty on the Non-Proliferation of Nuclear Weapons, and the principle of equality of the parties concerned—must go by the wayside. But what if, with things in this kind of shape, the German Democratic Republic, Czechoslovakia or Poland should ask us to give them something to counterbalance the US–West German nuclear missile complex? What then—should we accept the situation where the arms race, having been barred along one avenue, starts up along a new one?

I told the US Secretary of State: "Do you really think that we are so weak as to be ready and willing to woo your Administration endlessly? Or maybe you think that we are more interested in the development of Soviet–American relations and the American side, consequently, has nothing to do for its part? If you do, that is an illusion, an extremely dangerous illusion. I say this directly without any diplomatic wrappings."

The world is sick and tired of tension. People have been waiting impatiently for a chance to improve the situation and reduce the war danger. The Soviet Union made unprecedented concessions to enable such a chance to emerge. If this chance is missed, an imprint will be left on all world politics.

Why, properly speaking, should we, the Soviet Union, be so much in a hurry in such matters, one might wonder? For, indeed, we would have to scrap more medium-range missiles than the West and do just about the same thing with shorter-range missiles. Who is spurring us on? There is only one thing that makes us hurry—this is our clear understanding of the need to do something, to take some real steps so that the process of disarmament might actually start, even if slowly, even if it is dependent on particular circumstances, but at least start.

Solutions to dramatic problems must be sought at all discussions and forums, and above all at the Geneva talks. We are giving tremendous attention to them. I think the readers now know what we have done for progress to be made over there.

And we do not want simply to conduct negotiations. I must state openly that the simple fact that negotiations are going on suits some people in America. But it does not suit us. It's good that the talks are going on. But it is essential to move toward something so as to make progress, to arrive at agreements and let the Soviet and American people and the whole world get, through the Geneva accords, the solution to the outstanding problems that will remove the nuclear threat and pave the way to disarmament.

That is what we are striving for. If the talks are used as a screen for continuing all military programs and escalating defense budgets, then we are against them, resolutely against them. That is an unacceptable approach.

Of course, it is not easy to change the approaches on which East–

West relations have been built for fifty years. But the new is literally knocking at every door and window. We, the present generation of political leaders, must pay heed to that. Unfortunately, many politicians are still mesmerized by old complexes and stereotypes.

The time has come to make a choice. We all have to stand the test of goodwill, political courage and common sense. It is clear that a successful solution to the problems connected with medium- and shorter-range missiles will have great significance and important consequences for the entire process of disarmament. It would be a factor for the confidence that is so badly needed.

Naturally, we will continue negotiations on strategic arms and their reduction. There is rough equality and parity between the US and the USSR in terms of the power and the potential of the strategic forces. I have more than once heard the American side say that the US regards our ICBMS (Inter-Continential Ballistic Missiles) as a particular threat. We see the American SLBMs (Submarine-Launched Ballistic Missiles) as a great threat because they are less vulnerable, also tipped with independently targetable warheads, and have great homing accuracy. We see another threat coming from the numerous military bases ringing the USSR. Nevertheless, there is a strategic parity between us. Therefore, since a strategic parity is assured today within the present structure and with the present strategic offensive arms holdings, the balance would be maintained after a fifty percent reduction, but at a lower level. And that would change the situation. This is what I suggested to President Reagan in Reykjavik—cutting down the entire triad and each of its parts by fifty percent. That would have been a major achievement.

Of course, the ABM Treaty must be abided by faithfully. As far as SDI is concerned, we do not object to research within the limits of laboratories, institutes, factories and test ranges. Our proposal, as a matter of fact, takes into account the five to eight points the United States stands by within the framework of its approach to SDI. So let the specialists sit down together, sort it all out and see which of the components may be put out into space and which may not. Our compromise ideas provide a good opportunity for solution.

The Soviet Union has taken many steps to create a new situation and new opportunities for improving Soviet–American relations and making them more dynamic. None of the previous administrations in

249

the last few decades has had such chances to do something to improve relations with the USSR. Well then? There is nothing to boast about! We have not moved an inch forward so far.

And time is running out. We were convinced that either we would reach accords, or that there would be nothing left for us to do except throw brushwood into a smouldering fire of Soviet–American relations to keep it from going out altogether.

We have taken the steps necessary to rid our policy of idealological prejudice. That is what the West must do, too. It must, first of all, get rid of the delusion that the Soviet Union needs disarmament more than the West and that just a little pressure could make us renounce the principle of equality. We will never do that.

Look: all the Soviet proposals, no matter how thoroughly they are studied, envisage equality and a balance at all stages. This concerns nuclear arms, conventional weapons and chemical weapons, and concerns any goegraphical area—East, West, Europe and America. We prepare our proposals thoroughly, proceeding from the idea that no country would agree to act to the detriment of its security.

When we submit our proposals at the negotiations, for instance at the Geneva talks or elsewhere, we proceed from the idea that if we take into account only the interests of the Soviet Union and ignore the partner's interests, no agreement will be reached. We call on the American side to do the same—to treat us in the same way because we will never tolerate the superiority of the other side or any infringements on our security. And we do not want to prejudice the USA's security. If both sides display such an approach, the most resolute headway in all fields of Soviet–American cooperation will be possible.

Of course, we can wait till another Administration comes to power but we would prefer to come to terms with the present one. We have made a certain start; there are personal contacts and a certain measure of understanding. We deem it most important to create a normal atmosphere in which it would be possible to make a step at long last toward an accord. But the American side stumbles time and again. Still worse, each time we take a step to meet Washington, the counteraction forces strive to complicate the whole matter and to stop the movement forward by intensifying their activity.

One of the latest illustrations of this is the case of eavesdropping in the embassies. I proposed to George Shultz a "new concept": that he and Shevardnadze are the main spies. And our ambassadors in Moscow and Washington are spies, too. They hold their posts precisely to inform their country of the state of affairs and the intentions of the other country. And all this fuss of spy mania in the embassies is senseless. We know all the main things about the US and the US knows everything about us. This time the spy craze was engineered because it has become a rule: when definite contours become visible, when it becomes possible to resolve something in our relations, they immediately use a trick or ploy to torpedo it.

I know that various false conjectures have been made about the attitude of the Soviet leadership to President Ronald Reagan. I have personal impressions of the President. We have met twice and talked for many hours. In my opinion, a serious dialogue is being held between the President and myself, despite all the difficulties. Sometimes we say unpleasant things to each other and even say them in public and in rather sharp words. For my part, I say that we will continue our efforts. We will seek cooperation and productive talks with any President, with any administration the American people elect. To elect the President—a Democrat or a Republican—is the Americans' own affair. I repeat that we will cooperate with the administration which is entrusted by the American people to govern their country. I think one should act in this way in all cases. Let the Americans live in their country as they like and we will live in the Soviet Union as we desire. And let us never divide the list of politicians into favorites and non-favorites, into respected and not respected. There are realities, and they should be considered. Otherwise politics would turn into improvization, into moves from one extreme to another, into unpredictability. It would be wrong to act in such a way in politics, particularly in relations between such states as the United States and the Soviet Union. It is a very serious matter.

It is very important that both the Soviet Union and the United States should proceed from the conviction that we must come to terms, that we are duty-bound to learn to live in peace.

Great work of historic importance lies in store both for the Soviet Union and the United States. Neither of our countries alone will be able to do this work. I mean the issue of concerns of our days— staving off the threat of humanity's destruction in a nuclear war. If this work is performed successfully, there are grounds to foresee a bloom in Soviet–American relations, a "golden age" which would benefit the USSR and the USA, all countries, and the whole world community.

Conclusion

And now it's time to round off. Just a few words in conclusion.

I'm deeply convinced that the book is not yet finished, nor can it be finished. It should be completed with deeds, with practical action designed to reach the goals which I have tried to describe frankly on these pages.

The restructuring doesn't come easily for us. We critically assess each step we are making, test ourselves by practical results, and keenly realize that what looks acceptable and sufficient today may be obsolete tomorrow.

The past two and a half years have given us a great deal. The coming years, and maybe even months, will see fresh unconventional moves. In the course of the restructuring we are expanding and clarifying our notions about the yesterday, today, and tomorrow of socialism. We are discovering ourselves anew. This was and is being done, as I've said already, not to catch the imagination, nor to "gain affections," nor to win applause. We are motivated by the ideas of the 1917 October Revolution, the ideas of Lenin, the interests of the Soviet people.

We believe that the fruits of the restructuring will benefit international relations, too, including Soviet–American relations. New political thinking is an imperative of the times.

Great are the dangers facing mankind. There are enough elements of confrontation, but the forces wishing and capable of stopping and overcoming that confrontation are growing in strength and scope before our very eyes.

Moving from suspicion and hostility to confidence, from a "balance of fear" to a balance of reason and goodwill, from narrow nationalist egoism to cooperation—this is what we are urging. This is the goal of our peace intiatives, and for this we shall continue, tirelessly to work.

There is a great thirst for mutual understanding and mutual communication in the world. It is felt among politicians, it is gaining

253

momentum among the intelligentsia, representatives of culture, and the public at large. And if the Russian word "perestroika" has easily entered the international lexicon, this is due to more than just interest in what is going on in the Soviet Union. Now the whole world needs restructuring, i.e. progressive development, a fundamental change.

People feel this and understand this. They have to find their bearings, to understand the problems besetting mankind, to realize how they should live in the future. The restructuring is a must for a world overflowing with nuclear weapons; for a world ridden with serious economic and ecological problems; for a world laden with poverty, backwardness and disease; for a human race now facing the urgent need of ensuring its own survival.

We are all students, and our teacher is life and time. I believe that more and more people will come to realize that through RESTRUCTURING in the broad sense of the word, the integrity of the world will be enhanced. Having earned good marks from our main teacher—life—we shall enter the twenty-first century well prepared and sure that there will be further progress.

We want freedom to reign supreme in the coming century everywhere in the world. We want peaceful competition between different social systems to develop unimpeded, to encourage mutually advantageous cooperation rather than confrontation and an arms race. We want people of every country to enjoy prosperity, welfare and happiness. The road to this lies through proceeding to a nuclear-free, non-violent world. We have embarked on this road, and call on other countries and nations to follow suit.

Mikhail Sergeyevich Gorbachev was born on 2 March 1931 in the village of Privolnoe in the Stavropol Territory (Southern Russia). Since March 1985 he has been General Secretary of the CPSU (Communist Party of the Soviet Union) Central Committee, Chairman of the USSR Council of Defense and Member of the Presidium of the USSR Supreme Soviet (the Soviet Parliament), having joined the Communist Party in 1952.

He graduated from the Law Department of Moscow State University in 1955 and from the Stavropol Agricultural Institute in 1967.

At the age of fifteen he began work as a harvester operator. In the mid-fifties he was a leader of the Stavropol Komsomol, being Secretary of the City Komsomol Committee and later Secretary to the Territory Komsomol Committee. In 1966 he became Secretary of the Stavropol City Committee of the CPSU and later First Secretary of the Stavropol Territory Committee of the CPSU.

In 1970 he was elected to the Supreme Soviet of the USSR. In 1971 he was elected a Member of the CPSU Central Committee at the 24th Congress of the CPSU, and in 1978 he was elected Secretary of the CPSU Central Committee at the Plenary Meeting of the CPSU Central Committee. He moved to Moscow at this time.

He became an Alternate Member of the Politburo in 1979, and has been a Member of the Politburo of the CPSU Central Committee since 1980.